WI

DRAWN

WITHDRAW

At the Turn of a Civilization

At the Turn of a Civilization

David Jones and Modern Poetics

Kathleen Henderson Staudt

Ann Arbor

THE UNIVERSITY OF MICHIGAN PRESS

Copyright © by the University of Michigan 1994
All rights reserved
Published in the United States of America by
The University of Michigan Press
Manufactured in the United States of America

1997   1996   1995   1994   4   3   2   1

Library of Congress Cataloging-in-Publication Data

Staudt, Kathleen Henderson, 1953–
    At the turn of a civilization : David Jones and modern poetics /
Kathleen Henderson Staudt.
        p.   cm.
    Includes bibliographical references and index.
    ISBN 0-472-10468-3 (alk. paper)
    1. Jones, David Michael, 1895–1974—Criticism and interpretation.
    2. Modernism (Literature)—Great Britain. 3. Poetics.   I. Title.
PR6019.053Z89   1993
821'.912—dc20   93-33881
                                                                CIP

A CIP catalogue record for this book is available from the British Library.

Grateful acknowledgment is made to the following for permission to use
copyrighted materials: Faber and Faber, Ltd., for quotations from *In Parenthesis,
The Anathemata,* and *The Sleeping Lord* by David Jones; Harcourt Brace & Company
for the excerpt from "East Coker" in *Four Quartets,* by T. S. Eliot, copyright © 1943
by T. S. Eliot and renewed 1971 by Esme Valerie Eliot, reprinted by permission of
Harcourt Brace & Company; Seamus Heaney for quotations from his poem
"North"; New Directions Press for quotations from *The Cantos* by Ezra Pound; the
Trustees of the David Jones Estate for quotations from *Epoch and Artist* and *The
Dying Gaul,* from the letters of David Jones, and from unpublished material by
David Jones; Viking Penguin for an excerpt from *Finnegans Wake* by James Joyce,
copyright © 1939 by James Joyce, copyright renewed © 1967 by Giorgio Joyce and
Lucia Joyce, used by permission of Viking Penguin, a division of Penguin Books
USA Inc.

*To my parents
and their parents*

Preface

I am very grateful to the institutions and individuals who have supported my work on this book over the many years that have gone into its writing. The initial research for this study was funded by faculty grants from Drexel University and by a research grant from the National Endowment for the Humanities, which also enabled me to travel to England, Wales, and Canada to examine unpublished manuscript materials.

I did most of the writing in a world somewhat removed from academic life, and I am grateful to those colleagues and friends who have sustained me throughout this process by correspondence, conversation, and collegial goodwill, especially those who have read and critiqued the manuscript at various stages. I thank Thomas Whitaker, who introduced me to David Jones's work, directed my earliest explorations of some of the questions addressed in this book, and encouraged my subsequent research. I also thank William Blissett, Peter Hawkins, Thomas Dilworth, and Vincent Sherry for the care they devoted to reading and commenting on the manuscript at various stages. Special thanks to Philip Davies, Daniel Huws, and Huw Jones of the National Library of Wales, Aberystwyth, and to Mary Cronin, director of libraries at Boston College.

I could not have finished this book without a network of people whose indispensable friendship, advice, and moral and practical support have made my continued work on this writing possible. Following the example David Jones sets in the preface to *The Anathemata*, I list their names here as they occur to me, trusting that each knows how he or she has helped. Special thanks to Roger and Mary Allen, John Scott, Chris Carter-Husk, Libby Flanagan, Carole Calder, Fran Yuan, Rich Vogel, Mike and Sue Mossing, Amy Mangold, Nancy Yanapoulos, Sara Rosen, Cindy Strong, Sharon Reiss-Baker, Liz Burrows, Tricia Emlet, Debra Oleshansky, Irene Stone, Kathleen Jump, Jane Behrens, Cynthia McKee, Denise Fields, Jackie Ogg, Chris Bragg, Kit Carlson, Annie Scheiner, and John Mulligan—my thanks, for everything.

Finally, and most important, I want to thank my family—my husband, Lou, for all his love and encouragement, and my children, David and Sarah (both born during the gestation of this book), for all the joy that they have brought to my life.

Contents

Prologue: "At the Turn of a Civilisation"

The title of this study is taken from "A, a, a, DOMINE DEUS," the opening poem of David Jones's *The Sleeping Lord and Other Fragments* (1974). The poet is searching among the artifacts of the technological world for materials that might embody a religious vision for his time. Reflecting on this frustrated search, he writes:

> I have been on my guard
> not to condemn the unfamiliar.
> For it is easy to miss Him
> at the turn of a civilisation.
>
> (*SL*, 9)

These lines, and the poem as a whole, serve as a touchstone for the following reading of Jones's work. They demonstrate his awareness of himself as a man of the twentieth century who finds his cultural surroundings radically "unfamiliar." In contrast to the prevailing outlook, this artist still regards the search for sacred presence—the "Him" of these lines—as a valid activity. In keeping with this commitment, the poet's problem is to find objects and images among the artifacts of his time that will enable him to re-present a sacred order for his generation.

Jones's view of himself as a poet working in unsympathetic surroundings "at the turn of a civilisation" connects him to other poets of the generation that lived through the two world wars and the technological and social changes of this historical period. T. S. Eliot notes in his preface to Jones's *In Parenthesis* that "the lives of all of us were altered by the [Great] War, but David Jones is the only one to have fought in it" (*IP*, viii). Partly as a consequence of his service with the Royal Welsh Fusiliers, Jones's work in the verbal and visual arts depicts with unusual vividness the discontinuities between what the modernists perceived as a more unified prewar culture and the cultural fragmentation of the decades following the First World War. Like his better known contemporaries Eliot and Pound, Jones tried to devise poetic techniques and a poetic language that would somehow come to terms with what he called "The Break" between the contemporary world and a more unified past culture (*A*, 15). In the years before the Second World War, he was attracted to a conservative, even protofascist traditionalism that appealed to a number of British Catholics of his circle, including Eliot. This attraction is reflected in Jones's appreciation for Oswald Spengler's historical paradigm and in his interest in past cultures, which he viewed as more sympathetic to the artist's vocation. Finally, however, his work defies easy ideological characterization, promoting a quietly subversive vision of the poet's relation to the modern world.

Other aspects of his education and heritage contribute to Jones's sense of alienation from his time. Born in Brockley, Kent, of Welsh and English parentage, he developed early in life a love for Welsh culture and history. Though he lived in Wales for only a few months at a time during a few years of his life, and though he never mastered the Welsh language, the things of Wales emerge in Jones's work as important symbols of a beloved heritage from which the twentieth-century artist feels severed. His training as a visual artist—at the Camberwell Art Academy before the war, at Westminster School of Art afterward, and at Eric Gill's community of craftsmen at Ditchling in the 1920s—led to a profound appreciation for the particular and the concrete and to a veneration for the artist's craft as tantamount to a religious vocation in the modern world. A convert to Roman Catholicism in 1921, Jones consistently describes the artist's activity as a sacramental enterprise, necessarily engaged with the material and temporal order, even when that order seems most alien to the poet's vocation, as it does in Jones's moment of history.

In 1933–34, a period during which he was working with great intensity on his painting and on *In Parenthesis*, Jones suffered his first attack of the crippling neurotic condition that plagued him throughout his creative life. René Hague, with whom he was staying at the time, recalls, "The form it took was an increasing quietness, a brooding, outward signs (in language and behavior) of an exasperated bafflement" (Jones, *DGC*, 55). Acutely depressed and unable to work, Jones followed the advice of doctors who prescribed travel, and he embarked on the most significant journey of his life. With his friend Tom Burns, he traveled to the Middle

East, where he stayed with his friends Manya and Ralph Harari (*DGC*, 55–56). The images of British-occupied Jerusalem that Jones brought back from that trip figured importantly in parts of *The Anathemata* and shaped the underlying myth of the poems in *The Sleeping Lord*. He later wrote to Saunders Lewis that most of his work from *The Anathemata* on derived from the trip to Jerusalem in 1934 (Cookson 1973–74, 24–25).

Much of *The Anathemata*, Jones's most important poetic work, was composed in London during the early 1940s. Letters from that period record Jones reading Oswald Spengler's *Decline of the West* against a background of preparations for blackouts and reports of damage from the German bombs. After the war, but before the completion of *The Anathemata*, he suffered another severe attack of his neurasthenia. He spent most of 1946–47 at Bowden House, a private nursing home at Harrow-on-the-Hill, where he was treated by Dr. William Stevenson. Stevenson convinced him of the value of Freudian psychotherapy, which helped Jones as no previous treatment had to return to his painting and his poetic work (*DGC*, 131–41). In a footnote to the preface to *The Anathemata*, he thanks "those doctors, necessarily unnamed, and nurses who, by the practice of their arts, aided me to re-continue the practice of mine" (*A*, 39).

Jones spent the next two decades living in Harrow, first at Northwick Lodge (1946–64), and later at Monksdene Hotel. In March 1970, he suffered a mild stroke and a serious fall that forced him to move to Calvary Nursing Home in Harrow. During this period, Jones wrote many of the essays collected in *Epoch and Artist* (1959) and *The Dying Gaul* (published posthumously in 1978). He also revised and reworked the material from the *Book of Balaam's Ass* and other earlier manuscripts to produce some of his finest poems, published in 1974, the year of the poet's death, as *The Sleeping Lord and Other Fragments*.

Jones's work as a poet—the primary concern of this study—falls into two main stages. *In Parenthesis*, published in 1937, has been regarded by many as the last and most sensitive of modernist poetic responses to the First World War and to the wider modern sense of the separation between our time and a more coherent past cultural order. Between the publication of *In Parenthesis* and the beginning of his work on *The Anathemata*, Jones worked for a time on a manuscript he called "The Book of Balaam's Ass." Although he abandoned this project in the early 1940s, portions of the work composed during this period ultimately became part of *The Sleeping Lord*. The manuscripts published by René Hague and Harman Grisewood in *The Roman Quarry* (1981) reveal the extent to which the work of this period helped to shape *The Anathemata* and *The Sleeping Lord*. The larger enterprise reflected in Jones's work from "The Book of Balaam's Ass" through *The Anathemata* and *The Sleeping Lord* is the primary focus of the following study. This body of work, especially *The Anathemata*, reflects Jones's most important contribution to the canon of modern poetry and to poetic issues that have preoccupied modernist and postmodernist poets.

Like Gerard Manley Hopkins, William Blake, Christopher Smart, and James Joyce—all writers whom he admired—David Jones is likely to remain a poet who cannot easily be classified with a major movement or historical period. He is neither typically modernist nor entirely postmodernist, though aspects of his work intersect with the concerns of both poetic movements. His materials are obscure, and his style is often apparently impenetrable on a first, or even a second, reading. Nonetheless, David Jones is a poet whose work richly rewards careful reading and prolonged acquaintance, and whose poetic theories, both implicit and explicit, respond with powerful originality to the artistic predicament of poets working in the later part of the twentieth century.

Part 1

"Tradition," "Paideuma,"
"Order of Signs"

That was a way of putting it—not very satisfactory:
A periphrastic study in a worn-out poetical fashion,
Leaving one still with the intolerable wrestle
With words and meanings. The poetry does not matter.

—T. S. Eliot

I have tried to write Paradise

Do not move
    Let the wind speak
        that is paradise.

Let the Gods forgive what I
    have made
Let those I love try to forgive
    what I have made.

—Ezra Pound

I have watched the wheels go round in case I might see the living creatures like
the appearance of lamps, in case I might see the Living God projected from the
Machine. I have said to the perfected steel, be my sister and for the glassy towers I
thought I felt some beginnings of His creature, but *A, a, a, Domine Deus,* my
hands found the glazed work unrefined and the terrible crystal a stage-paste . . .
Eia, Domine Deus.

—David Jones

Chapter 1

Past and Present:
Jones and the Modernists

Readers both sympathetic and unsympathetic have noted affinities between the style and concerns of David Jones and those of other modernists. John Holloway wrote that without *In Parenthesis,* there would be a major gap in the literary history of this century (1964, 113), and T. S. Eliot praised the same work as "a work of genius" (Jones, *IP,* vii). Elsewhere, Eliot includes Jones with himself and Pound as a typically modernist writer, praising his poetic language and vision of the common modern experience (1955, 23). W. H. Auden called Jones's *Anathemata* "one of the most important poems of our time" (1954, 67), and William Carlos Williams, a judge when the National Institute of Arts and Letters awarded the Loines Award to *The Anathemata* in 1954, wrote to Ezra Pound recommending the poem (1957, 324–25). Many readers of Jones's work have discerned a Poundian influence, particularly in *The Anathemata,* though Jones claims not to have read *The Cantos* until well after most of his major published poetic work was completed (see *DGC,* 160; Corcoran 1982, 28). Others point to similarities between Jones and James Joyce, whose technique Jones greatly admired (Bonnerot 1974; Blamires 1972, 194; Rosenberg 1964, 115).

Some critics have attacked Jones's poetry for defects that he might be said to share with the work of his contemporaries—for his obscurity or for what some have seen as his advocacy of a reactionary primitivism. Sympathetic readers, however, stress the catholicity and humanity of Jones's poetic vision and praise the rich texture of his allusive language. He has been classified, for good or ill, according to the thematic materials of his poetry, grouped with modern Catholic poets because of his use of Catholic theology and imagery or with important Anglo-Welsh poets because of his use of Welsh mythology and legend. Though there is truth in many of these passing observations and classifications, Jones's relationship to the mainstream of Anglo-American modernism still awaits a thorough assessment.

Jones himself suggests the direction such an inquiry might take in a letter of 12 August 1957, where he complains to Harman Grisewood about recent reviewers' preoccupations with "influence." "They would be serving a much more useful purpose," he writes, "if they examined the nature of the problem facing *all* artists in *such and such a phase or set-up*, trying to discover how the different artists solved, or did not attempt to solve, the problems presented" (*DGC*, 174; Jones's italics). The "problem facing all artists" in Jones's time has much in common with what other critics have called the problem of modernity that haunts the poetry and poetics of the twentieth century, especially the work of Anglo-American poets writing during and between the two world wars. Critics as distinct in their methodologies as Robert Langbaum and Paul de Man seem to agree that to be modern in this century means by definition to be radically cut off from the past (see Langbaum 1957, 9; de Man 1971, 166–67). This sense of a break between his time and a past that was morally and aesthetically more ordered pervades Jones's poetry, as it does that of other modernist writers.

The effort to make order in a historical era that seems to deny all ordering principles takes different forms in the work of the major modern poets, but most of them, including Eliot, Pound, H. D., Joyce, Yeats, and Auden, reach into the past for materials out of which to construct a new vision of aesthetic and moral wholeness. Stephen Spender explains the modern's sense of alienation well when he suggests that most modernist writing displays in some form a "past consciousness living in the present."

> The modern is acutely conscious of the contemporary scene, but he does not accept its values. To the modern, it seems that a world of unprecedented phenomena has today cut us off from the life of the past, and in doing so from traditional consciousness. At the same time it is of no use trying to get back into the past by ignoring the present. If we consider ourselves as belonging not just to our own particular moment in time but also to the past, then we must also be fully aware of our predicament which is that of past consciousness living in the present. (1963, 78)

Spender shows how the moderns sought to use language as a means of connecting a past and present irrevocably severed by historical events.

To this end, they constructed their specialized, often dense and allusive poetic languages, incorporating material from past mythic, religious, and historical sources into the idiom of the twentieth century. It was an effort to create new modes of order out of what they perceived as a pervasive cultural fragmentation.

For Spender, the most successful of modernist poetic languages—from the focused allusiveness of *The Waste Land* to the notoriously obscure play of meanings and etymologies in *Finnegans Wake*—express an ironic awareness of the present moment's sterility, even absurdity, and at the same time imply a possibility of redemption or renewal through tenuous connections with a more coherent body of cultural awareness inherited from the past. Echoes of this more unified culture often seem embodied in the very form of modernist poetry, especially in the mythical method of *Ulysses* and *The Waste Land*, the multilingual punning in *Finnegans Wake*, and the dense allusiveness of Pound's *Cantos*. Indeed, one challenge of reading modernist literature, for those of us who take pleasure in such an activity, lies in deciphering allusions and finding that they open up possible patterns of coherence, even in extended works like the *Cantos*, where poetic structure and meaning are deliberately fragmented and open.

What Spender calls the modern predicament of "past consciousness living in the present" is reflected in various ways in the poetry and critical writing of Eliot and Pound, and it is reformulated with striking originality and urgency in the writing of David Jones. Eliot's sense of tradition typifies the conservative tendencies of modernism. Even in the early phase of his writing, represented by "Tradition and the Individual Talent" (1919), the poet-critic views "conformity between the old and the new" as both desirable and possible, and his concept of tradition emerges as a way of accommodating "novelty" in the new era without giving up the "ideal order" of the past (1950, 5).

In his later writing, Eliot's commitment to the past becomes more normative, extending beyond the literary to the political and social world of his time. In his essays of the 1930s, he advocates more explicitly a return to the moral and social order that the medieval Christian West comes to represent for him. His 1931 essay "Thoughts After Lambeth" insists on the need to "redeem the time," "so that the Faith may be preserved alive through the dark ages before us; to renew and rebuild civilisation and save the World from suicide" (1950, 42). Elsewhere in his writing of the 1930s, Eliot calls more explicitly for a new classicism, requiring discipline and conformity to standards from the past, and he stresses the poet-critic's moral role in society. In "Religion and Literature" (1935), he portrays the literary critic not only as a preserver but as an enforcer of Christian values: "It is our business, as readers of literature, to know what we like. It is our business as Christians, *as well as* readers of literature, to know what we ought to like; and it is our business as honest Christians not to assume that we do like what we ought to like" (1950, 353).

In passages like this, Eliot seems to view with increasing seriousness his public role as the promoter of a moral order based on the authority of the Christian tradition. This sense of the poet's mission to save civilization by preserving links to a better past pervades modernist thinking. We find it in Eliot's Christian conservatism, in Pound's avowed fascist allegiances, and in Yeats's neoromanticism, but it takes distinct forms in the writings of these different poets. A much more dynamic model of the past than Eliot's emerges in Ezra Pound's call for poets to construct a "new *paideuma*" for the contemporary age (1952, 57–62).

Pound's *Guide to Kulchur* praises the argument of Eliot's "Thoughts After Lambeth," and his contempt for the contemporary world order is even more bitter than Eliot's. Pound's appreciation of "Thoughts After Lambeth" is based not on sympathy for Eliot's advocacy of a return to "The Faith" but on a shared dismay at what he calls the *foetor* of modern intellectual and cultural life. *A Guide to Kulchur* proposes a more active way in which the poet and critic, as a public figure, can "redeem the time." The book presents a program for the reeducation of an elite of "cultured" men, working for a transformation of contemporary culture through the imposition of values derived from the past and shaped to the present— the development of a "new *paideuma*" (Pound 1952, 57–62). Pound takes the word *paideuma* from the German anthropologist Frobenius, defining it as "the tangle or complex of the inrooted ideas of any period" (57). Perhaps the most striking feature of Pound's *paideuma,* in contrast to Eliot's "tradition," is that it is seen as "ideas going into action" (34) rather than as Eliot's more static "ideal order" of monuments from the past. Hugh Kenner stresses this active dimension of *paideuma* in Pound's sense when he defines it as "a people's whole congeries of patterned energies, from their 'ideas' down to the things they know in their bones, not a *Zeitgeist* before which minds are passive" (1971, 507).

Like Eliot, Pound expects that what he sees as the vague, undisciplined liberal humanism of his day will lead nowhere. But rather than await its inevitable demise, Pound advocates the poet-critic's active involvement in its overthrow. In what he unabashedly calls a "totalitarian treatise" (1952,

27), Pound proposes to educate an elite of cultured men in a canon of classics from the past. The role of these poets and men of letters will be to put ideas into action in the political and economic orders, to establish against public ignorance a new cultural order for the twentieth century. Pound's desire to impose a new culture was consistent with his anti-Semitism and with his support of Mussolini and Italian fascism. The concept of *paideuma* as "ideas going into action" suggests the association for Pound between his definition of culture and a totalitarianism that would translate these concepts into political and economic structures to be imposed on a passively stupid public.

Though he appreciates Eliot's advocacy of the Western Christian tradition as an invigorating return to roots, Pound's model for a desirable cultural order is not medieval but simultaneously Confucian and classical, relying on nature and right reason as sources of renewal amid intellectual and aesthetic corruption. Some of the most memorable among the early cantos lash out angrily at the mental corruption and rot of the contemporary West, especially of British culture. Some of the most beautiful moments of the *Cantos* turn on the principles of order that Pound finds contained in Confucian thought and in Chinese written characters (see Kenner 1952, 76–102). The dynamic quality of the idea of reason and order put into action and set against public stupidity is embodied in Ezra Pound's Western heroes, especially John Adams, whose negotiations for a good treaty on fisheries and for a middle way in the settlement of political conflict marked for Pound the best moment in American political history. He looked on Mussolini as the potential leader of a political and economic order founded on a new *paideuma* that would embrace the poetic, the political, and the economic orders (Pound 1952, 195–96).

Despite his fascist political allegiances, Ezra Pound's call to "make it new" (1975, canto 53, 265), to use past culture as a way of transforming the present, has continued to appeal to poets, perhaps because of its implication that the poet's activity is necessary and in some way redemptive, even in a world that neither appreciates nor responds to it. The tone of the "Pisan Cantos," written when the failure of Mussolini's Italy and the totalitarian enterprise was no longer in doubt—and while the poet was being held prisoner in Pisa for treason—reflects a more inward effort to "redeem the time." Here Pound's rage against public stupidity and cultural bankruptcy persists, only tempered by gestures toward sources of order and permanence in the fragments of memory and tradition that the poet preserves. The bitterness of Pound's speaker shows in his portrayal of himself as the sole survivor, the "lone ant" from "the wreckage of Europe" (canto 76), a phrase that summarizes well Pound's sense, during this period, of his isolation as a "past consciousness living in the present." In subsequent cantos, the speaker increasingly emerges as a superior but unheard voice, oppressed by the folly of lesser men who rule the world and determine the culture.

Like Eliot and Pound, David Jones believes that the culture of his generation is fundamentally contrary to the poet's impulse, and like them, he seeks to maintain some fragile connection to the past. But his critique displays neither the contempt that pervades Pound's writings nor the lofty passivity implicit in Eliot's call to await the inevitable demise of the current order. In his prose writings, Jones consistently portrays the artist as the maker and rememberer who must continue to contrive works, regardless of their utility or of his contemporaries' indifference to them. In his essay "Past and Present" (1953), Jones insists "that the poet is a 'rememberer' and that it is a part of his business to keep open the lines of communication" between past and present (*EA,* 141). Jones wrote this essay in response to a review that criticized his *Anathemata* for its failure to respond to its time. He stresses the need for the artist to persist in his work, despite the evident disharmony between his vocation and the "present civilisational phase."

What I have suggested is that man-the artist, finds himself, willy-nilly, un-integrated with the present civilizational phase. I regard this as a regrettable matter of fact. I also say that there have been civilizational phases when this was less marked and that there have been true culture-phases when this was not marked at all, when man-the-artist was as integral to the pattern as is man-the-mechanic or managerial man to our pattern today.

But this does not in any sense mean that the activity called, somewhat redundantly, "making poetry" is irrelevant to our society. Still less that it cannot flourish in it and still less again that the maker is not conditioned by it. The works of Joyce, Picasso, Eliot and Britten, to take four names known to everybody, are quite sufficient to indicate what the Muses have managed to accomplish during the last few decades. . . .

So that, in one sense, we have no complaints. Not only can the artist function in peculiar situations but certain works could not be but for those situations. Rather as the poetry of *Super flumina Babylonis* resulted from the remembrance of a deportation. By a coincidence that famous psalm of exile also provides a clue: "If I forget thee, O Jerusalem: let my right hand forget her cunning." That is to say our making is dependent on a remembering of some sort. It may be only the remembering of a personal emotion of last Monday-week in the tranquility of next Friday fortnight. But a "deed" has entered history, in this case our private history, and is therefore valid as matter for our poetry. For poetry is the song of deeds. (*EA*, 139–40)

This passage reflects some of the detachment of Eliot's resolve to "redeem the time," but the subsequent argument that the poet, like the psalmist, must go on singing even in his exile evokes the isolation expressed by the speaker of Pound's "Pisan Cantos." Jones's emphasis on the role of poets and artists—representatives of "man"[1] as "rememberer" and maker of signs—displays none of the doctrinaire, polemical traditionalism found in Eliot's literary and cultural essays of the 1930s and 1940s, despite the poets' shared religious faith and their common apprehension of the Break between past and present.

Pound's "broken ant-hill" (canto 76) laments the loss of the tradition to which the poet belongs and which might have understood him. The community of European culture is desolated, and hence the poet's solitude is absolute. Pound's sense of finality is strikingly absent from Jones, even though he shares some of the disillusionment that pervades the "Pisan Cantos." Though he would agree that "what thou lovest well remains," Jones would not add that "the rest is dross" (canto 81). His idea of poetic redemption is a broad and catholic one. In one essay, he quotes the artist Stanley Spencer's remark that in a work of art, "all must be safely gathered in," and he connects the artist's ingathering to the prayer of Jesus in 17 John: "Of these thou hast given me have I lost none" (*EA*, 243). In *The Anathemata* and in his later writings about poetics, he extends the theological concept of sacrament to cover all forms of human making, hoping that the natural course of history will usher in a time when the activities of "man-the-artist" are once again valued. Meanwhile, his way of redeeming the time is to persist in making signs, in remembering the past anew, even though these activities may appear absurd in the contemporary world.

But Jones does not adopt an easy optimism. His life was plagued with long periods of incapacitating depression.[2] His letters during those periods reflect incomprehension and dismay at the state of his contemporary world in the political sphere, in the arts, and even in the Church. His later work dwells increasingly on the anachronistic position of the poet and the apparent futility of his work in an era that views his activities as superfluous. The preface to *In Parenthesis* represents one of his earliest attempts to sketch the main outlines of this problem. Here, as in the poem, Jones uses his experience as a soldier in the First World War to epitomize the modern dilemma.

> It is not easy in considering a trench-mortar barrage to give praise for the action proper to chemicals. We feel a rubicon has been crossed between striking with a hand weapon as men used to do and loosing poison from the sky as we do ourselves. We doubt the decency of our own inventions, and are certainly in terror of their possibilities. . . .
> Some of us ask ourselves if Mr. X adjusting his box-respirator can be equated with what the poet envisaged, in
> "I saw young Harry with his beaver on."
> We are in no doubt at all but what Bardolph's marching kiss for Pistol's 'quondam Quickly' is an experience substantially the same as you and I suffered on Victoria platform. For the old authors there appears to have been no such dilemma—for them the embrace of battle seemed one with the embrace of lovers. For us it is different.
> (xiv)

Jones's allusion to a rubicon crossed between the heroic combat of the past and the technological warfare of the present reveals an ironic perception of modern warfare that Paul Fussell has identified as a topos of literature dating from the First World War (1975, 18–35). Like the poem, this prefatory passage struggles to find a connection between what has been irrevocably lost—the apparently innocent heroism of Shakespeare's "young Harry with his beaver on" (*I Henry IV* 4.1)—and the technological impersonality of "Mr. X adjusting his box-respirator." The parallel between Bardolph's marching kiss for Mistress Quickly and the soldiers' farewells in Victoria Station suggests a continuity of some sort in the fundamental needs and emotions of the men who serve in battle, but modern warfare makes nonsense of the unity that an older culture saw between the embrace of lovers and the embrace of battle. Thus a male soldier's function at this particular moment in history is alien to his basic humanity. As another passage from the preface puts it:

> We stroke cats, pluck flowers, tie ribands, assist at the manual acts of religion, make some kind of love, write poems, paint pictures, are generally at one with that creaturely world inherited from our remote beginnings. . . . Yet we must do gas-drill, are attuned to many newfangled technicalities, respond to increasingly exacting mechanical devices; some fascinating and compelling, others sinister in the extreme; all requiring a new and strange direction of the mind, a new sensitivity certainly, but at a considerable cost. (xv)

For Jones, the "new and strange direction of the mind" demanded by contemporary culture parallels the historical and political fate of his father's native Wales. Jones's relation to Wales typifies for him the relation of all moderns to the past. In "Wales and Visual Form," a posthumously published essay drafted in 1944, he laments that the true Welsh culture was lost with the death of Llewelyn in 1282 (*DG*, 77). Though admitting the reality of this loss, Jones also insists that the nostalgia felt by those few who remember the things of Wales is shared by all moderns of the West, whom he identifies in this regard with Jews of the diaspora: "We all are as uprooted as the nation of the Jews and that is why we weep when we remember Sion—the old local Sions with their variants of the form-creating human cultures. We are all of the diaspora now" (*DG*, 88). The chief danger for his time, Jones suggests prophetically, is that artists, cut off from a historically rooted material culture, will create an increasingly disembodied art, out of touch with the bodily and the actual needs of humanity.

Wales was an important part of Jones's personal cultural heritage. His upbringing in suburban London was English and Anglican, but his father, James Jones, was Welsh, and Jones shared his father's attachment to the things of Wales from an early age. A memoir written late in the poet's life recalls his first visit to his father's country as a formative influence on both his visual and his aural imagination.

> From about the age of six, I felt I belonged to my father's people and their land, though brought up in an entirely English atmosphere. So it was natural that when, sometime in the first decade of the

twentieth century, I was taken to Gwenydd Wen, with the taut sea-horizon on the right and to the left the *bryniau* and west, and further off, the misted *mynyddoell* of Arfon, I felt a Rubicon had been crossed, and that this was the land of which my father had spoken with affection and suppressed pride—for James Jones was not given to voicing his deeper feelings. (*DG,* 23)

Beyond childhood visits like this one, Jones spent little time in Wales during his life. He never lived there, except for a few extended visits to the Gills at Capel y Ffyn in the 1920s and 1930s (*DGC,* 30–33; *EA,* 30). But his love for the sound of Welsh words and the shapes of the Welsh landscape is evident not only in his autobiographical passages but also in his poetry and visual art. Throughout his life, Jones steeped himself in the history, legends, and culture of Wales, and these materials emerge in various ways in his work.

Other modern poets have dealt with this sense of exile by creating or describing alternate worlds ruled by the poetic imagination. The most memorable of these, perhaps, is Yeats's Byzantium. But Byzantium is a world of pure imagination—"out of nature," divorced by definition from "the fury and the mire of human veins." Jones's Wales, in contrast, is tied both to the poet's own heritage as the son of a Welshman and to historical actuality. Throughout his work, Wales appears as the historic and particular home-place of the poet, where making and remembering are pursued and upheld as defining human activities.

Letters to his close friends Harman Grisewood and René Hague reveal that the fate of Welsh culture under English rule—what one essay calls "the *Gleichschaltung* of the Tudors of Mon" (*DG,* 85)—became a veritable obsession for Jones in the later years of his life. The longest of these letters, addressed to Harman Grisewood and dated 16 February 1966, comprises some thirty-one thickly covered pages, including multicolored inscriptions and a drawn map of Wales, and analyzes the death of Llewelyn as a crucial moment in the history of the Welsh people. This long letter closes with the exhausted exclamation, "Poor Powys, poor Wales, poor West. That is how I feel tonight." In other private letters, he compares the fate of Wales to the fate of various native peoples who have suffered at the hands of the empires of the West—notably the Algerians in revolt against France, the "red Indians" of North America, and the Arabs in Palestine.

The suppression of Welsh native language and culture takes on added significance for Jones in the 1960s and 1970s. He sees a clear analogy between the decline of Welsh language and culture and the Roman Catholic church's dismantling of the Latin Mass and many of its ritual accompaniments in the mid-1960s, under the Second Vatican Council. In a letter written in 1964, the year before that council abolished the Latin Mass, he writes to Grisewood:

> It's a terrible thought that the language of the West, of the Western liturgy, and inevitably the Roman chant, might become virtually extinct.
>   . . . At root, I don't believe it's a "religious" matter at all. I believe it's only part of the Decline of the West. . . . The *kind* of arguments used I find highly unsatisfactory, and they have just that same tang that distresses me so over the language of my father's *patria*. They prove by statistics that the Welsh language is dying and that it has no practical value anyhow. Damn such bloody arguments. (*DGC,* 209)

This and similarly forceful passages from the correspondence reveal that Jones's attachment to Wales and to the Latin liturgy goes beyond a mere sentimentality or nostalgia for what is lost. He regards the languages of the Mass and of Wales as substantial embodiments of the roots of Western culture. To lose touch with these roots, for him, is to be cut off entirely from the sources that have conditioned human experience in the West.

But Jones also discerns a curious durability in the things of Wales and in the sacramental tradition of the Western church. "It is the continuing fate of Celtdom," he writes in his essay "The Dying Gaul," "to be betrayed by the gods of the newer culture-phase" (*DG,* 52–53). According to Jones, with the Tudor Act of Union in 1603, "the Dying Gaul really did die" (57). Yet the essay concludes that "in other ways and diverse manners the Dying Gaul is not dead yet" (58). One irony of Welsh history, for Jones, is that though Wales was originally Catholic, along with the rest of Britain, the survival of Welsh nationalism and of the Welsh language is largely due to the influence of Calvinist Protestantism in Wales. The strength of Welsh Protestantism lies in the same anti-English feeling that Jones shares so strongly—the resentment at the Tudor Anglicization of Wales and the desire to preserve a unique identity.

The curious persistence of Celtic culture despite civilizational change is evident for Jones in the "essential Celticity" of James Joyce's work (*DG,*

58). The description of Joyce's work that closes "The Dying Gaul" applies in important ways to the place of Wales in all Jones's poetry from *In Parenthesis* through *The Sleeping Lord*.

> An art forged in exile by a man of our placeless cosmopolis, yet an art wholly determined by place, *a* place, an exact site, an art which, for its *materia poetica*, employs stuff from all the strata and the flux, from before and before again, to weave a word-web, a sound-web, round the "Town of the Ford of Hurdles" as Dublin was called by the Goidels.
>
> It is impossible in recalling the Dying Gaul not to recall James Joyce. And impossible in that recalling not to recall the words from the Dublin street-ballad: "Bedad he revives! See how he raises!" (58)

Jones's insistence, against all external evidence, on the survival of the Dying Gaul and of the poetic impulse that Wales represents, has led to one of the most common misreadings of his work. For a number of influential critics, Jones's evocation of a primitive, heroic past in opposition to the technological present rests on a naively conservative nostalgia that also implies a reactionary political ideology. Perhaps the best-known example of this misreading is Paul Fussell's critique of *In Parenthesis* as an attempt to glorify the Great War by equating it with the wars of medieval heroic literature. Referring to the passage from the preface to *In Parenthesis* where Jones juxtaposes "Mr. X adjusting his box-respirator" and "young Harry with his beaver on" (xiv), Fussell appears to mistake the pointed irony of Jones's comparison for a serious analogy.

> Actually, young Harry is not at all like Mr. X, but it is the ambition of *In Parenthesis* to obscure the distinction. The poem is a deeply conservative work which uses the (past not, as it often pretends to do, to shame the present, but really to ennoble it. The effect of the poem, for all its horrors, is to rationalize and even to validate the war by implying that it somehow recovers many of the motifs and values of medieval chivalric romance. (1975, 147)

Fussell insists on preserving a radical distinction between the young Harry of traditional heroic literature and the dehumanized and depersonalized Mr. X of modern warfare. This is consistent with his larger argument that the First World War marked a radical break from previous wars and brought with it a permanent change in modern attitudes toward the past. Jones's appreciation for this discontinuity is evident in his reflections on the differences between "striking with a hand weapon" and "loosing poisons from the sky" (*IP*, xiv). But the relationship between past and present experiences of war is more complex for Jones than Fussell's reading allows. The allusions to wars of the past that recur throughout *In Parenthesis* most often connect the battle of the Somme to the lost causes of military history. The whole poem turns on a typological identity between the Somme battle and the battle of Camlann, the first of a long series of defeats in the history of Wales. The Camlann allusion, as Thomas Dilworth puts it, "dominates all allusions to past warfare, and turns even historic victories—at Crécy, for example—into losses (1988, 79)."[3]

In this context, Jones's effort to connect young Harry and Mr. X points to a deeper continuity between the soldiers of the past and those of *In Parenthesis*. Whether the protective gear they wear is directed against hand weapons or chemical weapons, young Harry and Mr. X. share a common humanity, which they assert against a background of impersonal and dehumanizing political and technological forces. One of Jones's chief purposes in this poem is to reveal the basic continuity in the character, desires, memory, and impulses of individual men who find themselves in an impossible situation. In a reading that Jones in 1962 called "the only decent analysis of *In Parenthesis* that's ever appeared" (*DGC*, 188), John H. Johnston argues that the poem joins the heroic sensibility of the past with the inhumanity and mechanism of modern warfare to reveal a radical change. In older literature, allusions to a heroic tradition affirmed continuity between past and present experiences of war. Jones's poem, however, uses them to point out a contrast between the continuity of the soldiers' memories and the unprecedented character of the war in which they find themselves. Moreover, the war is not simply war, but a manifestation, for Jones, of a civilizational crisis that threatens the nature of "man"—a creature who remembers the past, who engages in gratuitous activities like "stroking cats and tying ribands" (*IP*, xv), and who makes signs in response to his experience of the world. Far from rationalizing or validating the present war, as Fussell suggests, the heroic allusions in *In Parenthesis* emphasize the contrast between the new and strange mechanisms at work on the battlefield and the soldiers on the field, who are much as they have always been.

What Jones refers to as "remembering" and "keeping open the lines of communication" (*EA,* 141) between past and present should be distinguished from modernist "nostalgia," which seeks a return to the past, and from "traditionalism" as a political or social perspective that seeks to reimpose the past onto the present—two tendencies of which critics have accused Jones's work.[4] Stephen Spender reflects that some moderns seem to be motivated by an intense hatred for the present.

> The peculiar modern disease is for certain individuals to feel that their genius, which belongs to another historic period, receives no nourishment from the present. They imagine themselves in fifth-century B.C. Athens or Renaissance Florence, and this becomes a fantasy which is then the most intense reality of their being. (1963, 214)

For Spender, the political implications of this kind of hatred of the present are ominous, and he is implicitly indicting Pound when he writes, "The sirens of nostalgia sang the speeches of Mussolini" (219). One version of this "nostalgic fallacy," as Spender calls it, is neo-traditionalism, which makes the imposition of works and traditions from the past a matter of critical dogma—here his criticisms are directed particularly at F. R. Leavis and "great tradition" critics.

Although Spender does not classify David Jones as either a modern nostalgic or a neotraditionalist, Elizabeth Ward adopts his term *modern nostalgic* to characterize Jones's poetic method (1983, 205). For her, *In Parenthesis* is simply the first example of what she criticizes in Jones as a persistently dualistic and antitechnological myth that exalts a primitive past over modern technological society.[5] The disturbingly reactionary political views that both Fussell and Ward discern, in different ways, in Jones's work need further examination, because as Ward rightly points out, the question has too often been sidestepped or minimized by Jones's readers and admirers. Ward goes so far as to suggest that Jones's views amount to a protofascism, in accord with the rightist political views of a number of British Catholics of the 1930s, among them some of Jones's closest friends. She describes in useful detail Jones's association with the "Chelsea group," which included his friends Harman Grisewood, Bernard Wall, Tom Burns, Christopher Dawson, and others. Ward points to two journals of the 1930s with which this group was associated, *Order* and *Coloseum,* to demonstrate their tendency to sympathize with the emerging fascist dictatorships of Italy and Germany rather than with British democracy, whose dedication to "progress" they rejected as a betrayal of fundamental Christian values (42–53).

Though her account of the ideological climate of this period is quite valuable and provocative, Ward's identification of Jones's aesthetic ideas with what she sees as the protofascist political ideology of his contemporaries is not convincing, larely because she tends to portray all forms of Catholic conservatism as based on ideas that are "if not flagrantly illiberal," then "anti-democratic" (51). These ideologically loaded terms condemn Jones, along with his associates, for an unwillingness to embrace wholeheartedly the technological progress and the democratic institutions of the time. By adopting this ideological stance, Ward dismisses as simplistic Jones's quite serious, if idiosyncratic, commitment to the solitary vocation of the artist as the perpetuator of culture in all epochs, regardless of political allegiances or public events.

The dualism implicit in Ward's method is clearest when she criticizes Jones's *The Sleeping Lord* for the obvious dialectical opposition it establishes between the Roman world of military and technological empire and a simpler order that this volume associates with rural and medieval Welsh culture and legend. In a striking line from "The Tutelar of the Place," one of Jones's Celtic speakers prays to be defended "in all times of *Gleichschaltung*, in the days of the central economies" (*SL*, 63). Ward finds disturbing political implications in Jones's failure here to distinguish morally between fascist and Marxist forms of centralized control— between Nazi Germany's *Gleichschaltung* and Soviet Russia's central economy. At the same time, she condemns the primitivism of Celtic culture, which embodies Jones's redemptive vision in this poem, pointing out that the defense of such primitivism is a fundamental precept of the fascist ideology that the poem seems to condemn (190). This criticism exemplifies the way in which rigid ideological categories can lead to misunderstanding and misrepresentation of Jones's poetic intentions. Jones's work insists repeatedly that the activities of artists and sign-makers assert human creative freedom in the face of all totalitarian impositions of value, whether conservative, liberal, political, religious, or aesthetic. In her eagerness to establish Jones's sympathy with antidemocratic ideologies, Ward appears to miss the more complex ideological implications of his suspicion of all institutionalized forms of what he calls "the utile" (*EA*, 180–85), including, later in his life, his distress at liturgical reforms in his own, Roman Catholic church.

Jones's political leanings in general were fundamentally conservative. He, like Eliot, was a royalist. He admired Neville Chamberlain and sent him a copy of *In Parenthesis* at the time of the Munich crisis. Yet his political views, as far as we know them from bits of his essays and from letters to friends, do not appear to reflect consistent adherence to the orthodoxies of right or left. His early association with Eric Gill's Community of St. Joseph and St. Dominic, at Ditchling Common in Sussex, exemplifies how difficult it is to categorize Jones's ideological commitments. Gill was the leader of a craftsmen's community at Ditchling that lasted from 1917 to 1924, and in 1921 he founded the "Guild of St. Joseph and St. Dominic, a religious guild for men who worked with their hands" (Speaight 1966, 110). He wrote extensively on the need for continuity between daily life, religious practice, and making as a solution to what he viewed as a fundamental and dehumanizing alienation between the worker and his craft brought about by technological society.[6] In its commitment to a medievalist model of a craftsman's community, Ditchling was in harmony with Christopher Dawson's later call for a return to more primitive values, though Gill's political loyalties tended more toward socialism than toward Dawson's more conservative vision of a return to a European Christendom.[7]

Jones lived at Ditchling from 1919 to 1923 and was received into the Roman Catholic church there in 1921. He formed many of his most important friendships at Ditchling, especially with Father Desmond Chute and with René Hague, one of Jones's most sympathetic readers and commentators. At Ditchling, Jones was first exposed to the ideas of Jacques Maritain and Maurice de la Taille, which had a profound effect on his poetic theory. Yet though Ditchling was indisputably a formative influence on his thought and life, Jones was by no means an orthodox disciple of Eric Gill. He never joined the Guild of St. Joseph and St. Dominic, and he dissociated himself from the bitter ideological disputes and personality conflicts that finally led to the dissolution of the community in 1924.[8]

The fundamental differences between the views of Jones and Gill concerning the artist in the contemporary world can be discerned in the gentle critique that Jones offers in his essay "Eric Gill as Sculptor." He writes of Gill, "He sought to work as though a culture of some sort existed or, at all events, he worked as though one should, and could *make* a culture exist" (*EA*, 288). By contrast, Jones seems to have been impatient with traditionalist programs that sought to restore or impose an older order— to "*make* a culture exist." He believes that poets must preserve, however tenuously, some connection with the moral and aesthetic impulses that governed past historical epochs, but that they can do this only by pursuing their craft, regardless of the historical phase in which they find themselves. This position can hardly be dismissed as escapism, because it rests, more than Gill's or Dawson's political reformism, on an awareness of the distance between the artist's vocation and the priorities of the artist's time. In a real sense it is a more subversive position[9] than that taken by other Catholic contemporaries, because it insists on the persistence of a mode of being, experiencing, and making that cannot be suppressed and that will ultimately triumph in some form because it is essential to human nature.

Yet Jones shared many of his contemporaries' gross errors in judgement regarding the direction and implications of the Nazis' rise to power. Like many other intellectuals of the 1930s, he read Hitler's *Mein Kampf* with a certain hesitant excitement that seems bewildering and repellent in light of subsequent history. A recently discovered typescript essay entitled "Hitler," written in 1939 but never published, illuminates the rather complex appeal that the fascist program held for Catholic conservative circles of the period. Jones's early sympathy with certain of Hitler's arguments reflects his distress at widespread economic and moral decadence.[10]

> In reading *Mein Kampf,* I was often reminded of the problems I used to hear discussed continuously by various groups of Catholic people concerning the recovery of social justice: how to break the "chain store," how to live uncorrupted by the "banking system," how to free men from the many and great evils of "capitalist exploitation," how to effect some real and just relation between the price of things and the labor expended. . . .
>
> That there is something radically wrong, seems by now obvious to us all. The cure, not so obvious. Now the writer of *Mein Kampf* shared this conviction with so many of our friends, he even names the same supposed evils. ("H," quoted in Dilworth 1989, 148)

Jones's desire to give the Germans a fair hearing was consistent with the poet's natural sympathy for vanquished peoples—a sympathy reflected in his devotion to Wales and to the tradition of the Dying Gaul. Harman Grisewood makes this point eloquently when he writes:

The Welsh of our own day were his brethren through their historic derivations rather than through their contemporary characteristics. The Germans in *Mein Kampf* were also a vanquished people, and oppressed by exultant and tyrannous conquerors. David's affinities, you remember, are with Hector and Priam rather than Achilles and Agamemnon. (Dilworth 1989, 154)

The Hitler essay also reveals, indisputably, the extent of Jones's blindness to the full threat of Nazism and to the appalling seriousness informing what he mistook for mere propagandistic rhetoric. The essay begins as an appeal to reason, an effort to emphasize "the complexity of international issues, which the press too often attempts to resolve into some simple right and wrong." Here Jones makes his appeal both as a Catholic and as a veteran of the First World War, and this combined perspective distinguishes his position from the rather simplistic ideological nostalgia of which Ward accuses him.

Those of us who fought in the last war are by this time very conscious that our heads were filled with a good deal of nonsense as to the nature and need of that struggle. That war may have been politically "unavoidable"—that makes the exploitation of our youthful innocence even more a matter for anger. . . . It is, then, especially for us ex-service men, a matter for concern that in any future call upon the heroic qualities of men in this country, the false cries should be silenced so that what is strictly the end to which this heroism proceeds is defined and clear. ("H," 2)

Jones's effort to establish the terms of the debate about an imminent war is difficult to appreciate from the vantage point of subsequent events, but when he wrote this essay, Jones was still unconvinced that the warnings about Hitler stood on firmer factual ground than the propaganda of the First World War. This led him to declare with uncharacteristic firmness:

There is no "necessity" now but one—and that is the avoidance of the suicide of Europe by the inception of a major war. I would say "at whatever cost"—because I have yet to be convinced that "the things more precious than peace" are other than hypothetically threatened. . . . Even admitting that an attempt to "dominate the world by force" (somebody else's force, of course) was imminent, and must "be resisted come what may"—even so, it would be important to examine what is indicated in "come what may." . . . It would still be important to know, beyond any shadow of doubt, that this feared domination was absolutely certain and absolutely the worst fate, otherwise the argument is invalid—we shall destroy ourselves and our supposed enemies owing to a misunderstanding.

Obviously, Jones was wrong about Hitler's intentions and policies. His chilling call for avoidance of war "at whatever cost" must be dismaying to the poet's admirers, even if it is granted that he is writing out of disgust at the shallowness of British propaganda in the immediate prewar period. It does not follow, however, that Jones derived his myth or ideology from the Nazis or that the kind of reverence for a mythic European past that his poetry displays inevitably leads to fascism. His flirtation with fascist ideology in the late 1930s marks him as a man of his time and condition, and there seems to be no reason to discredit his decision to withhold this essay from publication once the full outrage of the Third Reich became clear. Grisewood and Blissett recall his deep anguish as the news of Nazi death camps and the horror of Hitler's program became official public knowledge (Dilworth 1989, 158–59; Blissett 1981, 12).

Because of what the unpublished Jones essay now reveals, it is clear that Elizabeth Ward oversimplifies what she insists on calling Jones's fascist leanings when she quotes selectively from an important letter he wrote to Harman Grisewood in the mid-1930s recording his responses to *Mein Kampf*. The portions that Ward quotes from the letter demonstrate Jones's initial sympathy with certain of Hitler's ideas. But Ward's discussion leaves out passages from the same letter that express Jones's characteristic reservations about what he reads. The complete text of this letter reads as follows, with the material that Ward excludes printed in italics:

It is amazingly interesting in all kinds of ways—but pretty terrifying, too. God, he's *nearly* right.—but this *hate* thing mars his whole thing, I feel. *I mean it just misses getting over the frontier into the saint thing—he won't stand any nonsense or illusions or talk—but, having got so far, the conception of the world in terms of race struggle (that's what it boils down to) will hardly do. But I do like a lot of what he says—only I must admit he sees the world as just going on* for ever *in this steel grip.* Compared to his opponents he is grand, but compared to the saints he is bloody. *And I think I mean also by saints—lovers, and all kinds of unifying makers.*

Anyway, I back him still against all this currish, leftish money thing, even though I'm a miserable specimen and dependent upon it. (*DGC*, 92–93; cf. Dilworth 1989, 158)

Ward concedes that Jones's judgement, as she presents it, represents "ignorance rather than informed sympathy for Nazi goals" (55), but she fails to emphasize adequately Jones's recognition of the hatred and violence that Hitler preaches, and she omits from her quotation Jones's explicit rejection of the racism and totalitarianism advocated by Nazism.

By omitting these qualifications, Ward implies that David Jones sympathized with Nazi ideas more than he actually did, so she is able to contend that

David Jones remains profoundly implicated in the political extremism represented by the Chelsea group as a whole not only by virtue of his public association with its leading members, but in that the philosophical and historical assumptions on which their rejection of contemporary Western democracy was based were identical to those which underlay his aesthetic theories and helped to determine the form and direction taken by his art. (55)

Even if this claim were substantiated by Jones's work, it would constitute questionable grounds for dismissing the whole corpus of his poetry. Ward's argument that Jones should remain unread because of his ideology shares in a more widespread error of late twentieth-century writers on modernism—our tendency to be unforgiving toward those who embraced and later abandoned elements of the fascist program, while we judge much less harshly those who similarly flirted with Stalinism during the 1930s. The error may seem justified in light of the horrors of the Holocaust, but it tends to suppress honest efforts to understand and to learn from the perceptions and misapprehensions of the people who lived in those times. In any case, there seems to be no basis for Ward's discernment of protofascism in Jones's poetry.[11]

Although the themes in his poetry have clear political implications, especially in the anti-imperialism of the later work, Jones is not concerned with returning to a particular social and cultural order—the kind of return advocated implicitly by Eliot in his account of the current order as a temporary deviation from Western Christendom. Nor is his work primarily an apologia for the Western Christian tradition, although some of his most sympathetic critics have tended to present it in this way. In the introduction to his monumental study of the "shape of meaning" in Jones's work, Thomas Dilworth writes that

no other writer in the English language has tested traditional values as he has in the face of political totalitarianism, technological pragmatism, and modern mechanized warfare. . . . David Jones places what he sees as the crisis of modern civilization in the context of a coherent cultural analysis involving an original combination of aesthetics, metaphysics and political morality. (1988, 36)

Though Dilworth's work as a whole is extremely helpful to Jones's readers in its tracing of allusions and its detailed analysis of the poetry, his implicit and explicit depiction of Jones as a cultural analyst and an apologist for traditional values can be misleading. This is especially obvious when Dilworth describes *The Anathemata* as

an anatomy of western culture from its prehistoric beginnings to the present. The tendencies distinctive of this genre are to catalogue, to enumerate, to digress and to illuminate through encyclopedic erudition. The initial indications of the poem's genre are the presence of notes on the pages of primary text and the quantitative near-equivalence of notes to text. (1988, 152)

Dilworth here follows Northrop Frye in using the term "anatomy" as the equivalent of the Menippean satire, a genre whose best example before Swift, Frye believes, is Burton's *Anatomy of Melancholy*. "The creative treatment of exhaustive erudition" is one organizing principle of this work, which also includes the "dissection and analysis" characteristic of anatomy (Frye 1957, 311).

The piling up of erudition, the lists, footnotes, and scholarly asides in the anatomies that Frye discusses suggest affinities to the forms we see in David Jones, and in this sense Dilworth's reading responds to the initial impression the reader has on seeing a page of Jones's poetry, particularly *The Anathemata*. However, I argue that the motivating intention of Jones's poetry is almost never "to illuminate through encyclopedic erudition" or to offer the systematic "cultural analysis" and testing of "traditional values" that Dilworth sees as central issues in his work. The same impulse to find in Jones a highly original analyst and apologist for traditional cultural values leads Dilworth to read Dai Greatcoat's boast in *In Parenthesis* as an examination of the issue of the morality of war (1988, 112–16) and to discover in the fragmented and open arrangement of the poems of *The Sleeping Lord* a Christian synthesis that suggests, dialectically, a way out of the dialogical struggle between imperialism and culture that orders this sequence (287).

Although my reading of Jones shares more with Dilworth's appreciation for the poet's craft and cultural insight than with Ward's ideological critique, I caution against the impression conveyed by Dilworth's work—and by many of the most sympathetic readings of Jones—that Jones writes primarily as an apologist for Christianity, for Welsh culture, or for any of the other cultural, political, and anthropological visions that he draws on so freely as what he calls his *materia poetica.* Jones's poetics rests not on cultural analysis but on his belief that sign-making is a fundamental human impulse, and that this basic quality of human nature is expressed in the works of poets and artists. Thus he looks to the past not so much for the enunciation of values but for evidence of continuity in the activities and concerns of humanity, summarized in his use of "man-the-artist" as the paradigm of human experience in all eras. Jones's use of the past contributes to modernist thought, less in its implicit political content than in the poetic logic of his typological vision. By allowing mythic and historical events to interpret one another, this typological vision implies the continuing presence of sources of order and intelligibility that enable poets to continue their work in any era, past, present, or future.

If any concept in Jones's work corresponds to Eliot's concept of tradition or Pound's *paideuma* as an ordering principle drawn from the past and applicable to the present, it is his view of Western culture and history as an "order of signs," a phrase derived from the writings of the Jesuit theologian Maurice de la Taille. Like the concept of tradition discussed in Eliot's later essays, Jones's order of signs is tied ultimately to a Christian transcendental order and is defined in terms taken from the Catholic Christian tradition. Yet the order of signs is less specifically literary than Eliot's tradition, encompassing as it does ancient and modern history, pagan myth, and Christian ritual. And like Pound's *paideuma*, it depends on human action, both historical and artistic, for its perpetuation.

Jones is fond of quoting a phrase from Maurice de la Taille where the theologian, describing the actions of Jesus at the Last Supper, writes, "He placed Himself in the order of signs." This phrase appears as the epigraph to Jones's essay collection *Epoch and Artist* and is quoted in the conclusion to his important essay "Art and Sacrament." Its context in de la Taille's writing suggests that it also provided a primary theme of *The Anathemata*. The phrase occurs at a climactic turn in de la Taille's discussion. Beginning his argument with the Catholic doctrine that the Real Presence of Christ's body is signified by the bread in the Eucharist, de la Taille adds that that Body is a sign of the unity of all Christian souls in Christ. The entire passage reads, "He placed Himself in the order of signs, in the order of symbols, to have the joy of symbolizing and, by symbolizing it, of building up the mystical Body of which we are the members" (1930, 212). In this account, the "joy of symbolizing," which for Jones identifies humanity as a sign-making species, is shared by the Incarnate God. De la Taille suggests that in offering the bread as a sign of his body, Jesus was demonstrating the fullness of his humanity. At the same time, he was insuring the continuity of his "mystical Body," the church, for as long as such sign making persists.

Jones finds even more resonance in the idea of an order of signs than de la Taille's theology implies. For the poet, the sign-stream that constitutes the Western tradition is made intelligible by hidden correspondences among myths, rituals, and actual events in history. Jones stresses repeatedly that neither the Incarnation nor the Mass would make sense if humankind were not already a sign-making species and if certain signs already central to Western culture were not fulfilled and completed in the Passion story. As he puts it in "Art and Sacrament" (1955):

> What was accomplished on the Tree of the Cross presupposes the sign-world and looks back to foreshadowing rites and arts of mediation and conjugation stretching for tens of thousands of years in actual pre-history. Or, to speak in theological terms, the Tree of the Cross presupposes the other Tree, and stretches far back to the "truly necessary sin of Adam" and the "happy fault" so that St. Thomas in the Good Friday hymn could write *Ars ut artem falleret*.[12]
> (*EA*, 168)

This passage evokes the patristic tradition of typological or figural interpretation of Scripture, in which events in the Old Testament are seen as figures or foreshadowings of events in the New Testament.[13]

Jones expands the scope of this tradition to include history, geology, myth, legend, and ritual from all parts of the Western European tradition. Thus he is able to connect the activities of Jesus as Redeemer and as human sign-maker to other redemptive actions in human history and to the poet's vocation in the present. The nature of this typological connection is most clearly explained in his "Introduction to the *Rime of the Ancient Mariner*," published as a separate essay in Jones's posthumous volume *The Dying Gaul.*

The essay on Coleridge's poem originated as an extended preface to the 1964 reissue of Douglas Cleverdon's Golden Cockerel Press edition of *The Rime of the Ancient Mariner.* Jones's engravings for the original edition, which appeared in 1928, represent some of his finest work as an artist. His essay reads Coleridge's Mariner as a type of Christ. For example, the beneficent rain that comes after seven days and nights of waiting is for Jones a response to "the Crux-cry, 'I thirst'" (*DG,* 198). Expanding the medieval tradition that regarded Ulysses as a type of Christ, Jones insists that such Celtic figures as St. Brendan, Bran, Medduin, and Arthur also illuminate Coleridge's tale (191). The latter part of Jones's long essay carries the medieval tradition forward to include *The Dream of the Rood,* the Chester and Townley plays of the Flood and Noë (217), Chaucer's *Shipman's Tale* (127–29), and Milton. This fascinating, if unorthodox, reading concludes that "all these various images of whatever provenance have a bearing on Coleridge's poem, because . . . the poem cannot escape evoking the whole argosy of man" (223).

Jones justifies his free use of both Christian and classical sources to illuminate Coleridge's poem by recalling the remarks of Minucius, an early Christian layman with whom Jones appears to identify in some ways. One passage from the Ancient Mariner essay demonstrates how Minucius's typological vision appeals to Jones's love of particularity and detail.

> I have it here somewhere among my books but can't find it. But I remember that Minucius is with two friends, one of the old religion of the Roman state, the other, I think, a practising lawyer and a fellow convert. The three are strolling on the seafront on a bank-holiday at Ostia sometime in the first half of the second century. I seem to recollect that they played, or noticed boys playing, that innocent game with pebbles which we call "ducks and drakes," and that Minucius at some point observes, or makes his lawyer friend observe, that the masts and sail-yards of the square-rigged Roman vessels were an abiding, visible image of the Cross. (*DG,* 214–15)

The use of contemporary details here—the bank holiday, the children playing at ducks and drakes—already demonstrates the way in which

Jones's typological imagination connects past and present historical moments. Only in the last line of this typically digressive passage does Jones get to the point he is making about Minucius. Yet the passage as a whole shows that Jones appreciates Minucius, not only for his insight, but also because he was a fairly ordinary early Christian ("nothing is known of this educated layman," Jones notes, "except that he was a member of the Church in Rome long before his class") who saw things typologically.

The point of the story is not only to join Minucius in pointing out a similarity between the square-rigged vessels and the cross—an analogy central to the section of *The Anathemata* entitled "Keel, Ram and Stauros"—but to show that the typological mode of perception—seeing reality both as concrete and as significant of something other—can be a natural way of seeing the world. Much of Jones's visual art, especially of his later period, shows his tendency to see types and figures of Christ's passion in the world around him. His highly symbolic painting of a tree outside his window, entitled *Vexilla Regis* (1947), is perhaps the fullest development of this kind of typological vision in Jones's art (see Hills 1989; *DGC*, 149–52).

His essay on Coleridge's poem goes on to show the more specifically literary and poetic potential that Jones finds in the typological vision. Recalling the Greek and Roman fathers of the Church who originated the typological method and applied it to the classical voyage tales of Homer and Virgil, Jones writes:

> They saw that the ship, the mast, the voyagings, the odysseys and argosies, the perils and ordeals that were part and parcel of classical tradition, could and should be taken as typic of the Church's voyaging. They had a perception of the vessel of the *ecclesia,* her heavy scend in the troughs of the world-waters, drenched with inboard seas, to starboard Scylla, to larb'rd Charybdis, lured by persistent Siren calls, but secure because to the transomed stauros of the mast was made fast the Incarnate Word.
>
> All this: the barque, the tall mast, the hoisted yard, the ordeals of the voyage, has in various ways filtered down through the centuries. It could not very well be otherwise for, after all, there is but one voyager's yarn to tell. (*DG,* 215)

The typical "voyager's yarn" described in this essay becomes one of the most important ordering schemes in parts 2–6 of *The Anathemata,* which most Jones readers now refer to as the "voyage sequence" of the poem. Beginning in the middle of part 2, "Middle-Sea and Lear-Sea," the poem presents a series of voyage narratives describing various historically tagged sea captains who travel from the Mediterranean to the British Isles, bringing Roman civilization to "our" Germanic and Celtic forbears. Although the skippers of these voyages belong to distinct historical periods and even emerge as separate personalities, they tend to blend together into a single archetypal mariner or voyager figure whom Jones identifies once more with the shifting persona of Christ and priest, referred to in the poem simply as "he." In these central sections of the poem, the voyage yarn emerges as a figure of Christ's passion, which one important note to the poem calls "the Argosy of the Redeemer" (*A*, 106 n. 2).

In *The Anathemata*, typology functions as an ordering principle analogous to the "mythical method" that Eliot discerned in Joyce's *Ulysses*. Eliot hailed Joyce's use of myth as a new principle of order, able to replace traditional narrative schemes in an age of fragmentation and alienation (1923, 483). What one perceptive Jones reader has called the poet's "typological method" appears to serve a purpose analogous to Joyce's myth, replacing linear narrative with another principle of order that draws together apparently disparate materials (Wilborn 1976, 66–69). But while Joyce's method, in Eliot's account, is implicitly the product of an inner, psychological principle, Jones's typological vision provides a way for the modern poet to engage the history and mythology of the past as persistent modes of interpretation applicable to the present. For Jones, de la Taille's phrase "He placed himself in the order of signs" brings together the historic Jesus, the Christian mythos of Last Supper and Mass, and all those human makers who have held up signs in every era— including contemporary poets making their poems. For him, typology is more than a principle of order providing underlying unity for an apparently fragmented stream of consciousness. It is also a principle of continuity, linking the contemporary poet to a community of human sign-makers from the past, a community that his Christian faith also connects to a transcendental order. Hence for Jones, modern poets, pursuing their craft "in a world which offers very little assistance" (Eliot 1923, 483), are participating in an activity fundamental to human historical experience, regardless of its apparent irrelevance to the contemporary world.

Jones acknowledges that the poetic enterprise that he pursues and promotes is an anomaly in his time (*A*, 15). The subtitle of *The Anathemata*, "Fragments of an Attempted Writing," exemplifies this sense of tenuousness. This kind of self-consciousness about the difficulty of poetic making in the twentieth century is common to modernist literature, reflected in writing from J. Alfred Prufrock's "It is impossible to say just what I mean" to the Babel-like linguistic thunderclaps in *Finnegans Wake*. Jones's prose and poetry alike reveal that he participates quite consciously in this modernist tendency to write poetry that reflects on the difficulty, even impossibility, of its own enterprise.

In the preface to *The Anathemata*, Jones stresses the important connections that the poet should seek to establish between a word and the complex of meanings it evokes. His commentary on the temporal erosion of the word *wood* typifies the kind of poetic problem that concerns Jones most deeply

> If the poet writes "wood" what are the chances that the Wood of the Cross will be evoked? Should the answer be "None," then it would seem that an impoverishment of some kind would have to be admitted. It would mean that that particular word could no longer be used with confidence to implement, to call up or to set in motion a whole world of content belonging in a special sense to the mythus of a particular culture and of concepts and realities belonging to mankind as such. This would be true irrespective of our beliefs or disbeliefs. It would remain true even if we were of the opinion that it was high time that the word "wood" should be dissociated from the mythus and concepts indicated. The arts abhor any loppings off of meanings or emptyings out, any lessening of the totality of connotation, any loss of recession and thickness through. (*A*, 23–24)

Jones attributes this erosion of poetic discourse to the materialism and positivism of twentieth-century society, the same impersonal, mechanical culture that romantics, symbolists, and modernists sought to escape by constructing separate worlds of words. Jones's defense against the aesthetic insensitivity of technocratic society is, however, quite distinct from that of the "men of the nineties," as he calls them (*DG*, 64). Many post-Romantic writers and critics have been concerned with draining, purifying, or emptying the signifier, but Jones is eager to fill it, to restore the hidden affinities between words and the experiences they constitute, and to allow the sign-making impulse to enrich contemporary experience.

Yet pervading Jones's search for valid signs is a fear that the pace and character of twentieth-century culture may be undermining the sign-making urge and even the order of signs more fundamentally than in any previous era. The doubts expressed in the preface to *The Anathemata* are given powerful expression in Jones's shortest poem, "A, a, a, DOMINE DEUS," first published in fragmentary form at the end of his essay "Art and Sacrament" (1955), but dating from a manuscript of the late 1930s and early 1940s (see *RQ*, 209–11). In its final form, as published in *The Sleeping Lord* in 1974, the poem reads:

> A,a,a, DOMINE DEUS
> I said, Ah! what shall I write?
> I enquired up and down.
>   (He's tricked me before
> with his manifold lurking-places.)
> I looked for His symbol at the door.
> I have looked for a long while
>   at the textures and contours.
> I have run a hand over the trivial intersections.
> I have journeyed among the dead forms
> causation projects from pillar to pylon.
> I have tired the eyes of the mind
>   regarding the colours and lights.
> I have felt for His Wounds
>   in nozzles and containers.
> I have wondered for the automatic devices.
> I have tested the inane patterns
>   without prejudice.
> I have been on my guard
>   not to condemn the unfamiliar.
> For it is easy to miss Him
>   at the turn of a civilisation.
> I have watched the wheels go round in case I might see the living crea-
> tures like the appearance of lamps, in case I might see the Living God
> projected from the Machine. I have said to the perfected steel, be my sister
> and for the glassy towers I thought I felt some beginnings of His creature,
> but *A, a, a, Domine Deus,* my hands found the glazed work unrefined and the
> terrible crystal a stage-paste. . . . *Eia, Domine Deus.*
>
>   (*SL*, 9)

The question that opens the poem and the wrenching vocatives of the title and last line are addressed to a God who seems to have receded from the poet's world. The quest narrated here presents an accumulation of disappointments, all arising from the poet's inability to discover "His creature" in the things of the technological world. The opening line, "I said, Ah! what shall I write?" echoes the prophet Isaiah's "A voice said, cry, and I said, what shall I cry" (Isaiah 40:6), as if the speaker gropingly identified himself with the biblical prophet, trying to find a way of revealing God's word to an uncomprehending generation. This impression is confirmed in the title and in the closing cry of the poem, *"Eia, Domine Deus."* Both are quotations from Jeremiah 1:6, in the Vulgate: "et dixi, Domine Deus, ecce nescio loqui, Quia ego puer sum" (and I said, "Oh Lord God, behold I do not know how to speak, for I am only a boy") (Hague 1975, 68). The closing lament of the poem answers the question "what shall I write?" as if the opening line had also been the prophet's question. In the interim, the speaker's frustrated search appears as a series of attempts to answer the same question, implying that some evidence of "His" presence is necessary if the poet is to use the things and experiences around him as material for valid signs.

The search for a divine presence is not abandoned in this poem or in any of Jones's work. If "it is easy to miss Him / at the turn of a civilisation," it does not follow that "He" is not there, somewhere. Yet the mere conviction of divine presence is not enough to guarantee the poet material for his work. There must be something in the nature of the things and experiences of the world in his time that will allow the poet to make them into "valid signs." Thus the poet's frustration is not at God's failure to appear but at a human failure to produce the kinds of things that could be adapted to the poet-artist's sacramental activity.

Perhaps the most bitterly ironic lines of the poem are those in which the speaker seeks some analogy between the creations of technology and the image of Christ already present in his mind from past modes of signification. The statement "I have felt for His Wounds / in nozzles and containers" points to a glaring disproportion between the reality to be signified and the material available for sign making. In the final paragraph, the propelling rhythm of "in case I might see" seems to harmonize with the description of revolving wheels and mechanical projectors, but again, the passage depends on a biblical allusion to the "four living creatures" of Ezekiel (1: 5–21) and Revelation (4: 7–10). Its apocalyptic implications seem ludicrously disproportionate to the monotonous revolutions of mechanical wheels. Repeatedly, the poet seeks occasions to use the things of technological society for "extra-utile" purposes, and always they prove inadequate to his sign-making intention. His reversion to the Latin of the Vulgate Bible implies that the impoverishment of contemporary materials forces this poet back into an older tradition, perhaps a dying or dead one, but one that evidently provides the kinds of charged signs needed for a craft that he feels impelled to pursue, even in the twentieth century.

Although Jones worked on this short lyric at several different times in his life, beginning in the late 1930s, the version published in *The Sleeping Lord* represents one of the latest stages of his poetic development. Its commentary on the problem of writing poetry in the mid-twentieth century invites comparison with the later work of Eliot and Pound, where the poets reflect similarly on their enterprise and its conflict with the world in which they live. In Eliot's "East Coker," for example, a fantasy on historical cycles and apocalypse, written in modified sestina form, is suddenly interrupted by the poet's voice, which comments in deliberately prosaic meters on the difficulty of finding a language.

> That was a way of putting it—not very satisfactory:
> A periphrastic study in a worn-out poetical fashion,
> Leaving one still with the intolerable wrestle
> With words and meanings. The poetry does not matter.
>
>   (Eliot 1971, 125)

This passage, like the lament in "Burnt Norton" that "Words strain, / crack and sometimes break, under the burden" (1971, 121), suggests in its own mode a persistent questioning of the adequacy of language to the poet's quest for spiritual order, a theme that runs throughout the *Four Quartets*. The tired resignation implicit in "The poetry does not matter" looks forward to the mystic resignation that will enable the poet to pass beyond both history and language at the end of "Little Gidding." It articulates concisely a central modernist problem recognized by both Eliot and Jones—the need to work with a language that is tied to the past and therefore increasingly unintelligible to the present. *Four Quartets* resolves this problem by shedding language altogether to move beyond "the intolerable wrestle / With Words and meanings" into an inner silence.

Ezra Pound, in contrast, finds little internal refuge from what the later cantos present, often with paradoxically lyric beauty, as the failure of his poetic project. Canto 120 laments:

> I have tried to write Paradise
>
> Do not move
>   Let the wind speak
>   that is Paradise

> Let the Gods forgive what I
> have made
> Let those I love try to forgive
> what I have made.

Although the poet asks forgiveness for the inadequacy of "what I have made," the spare beauty of his language shows that something remains. In demonstrating the impossible contradictions inherent in what he has "tried to write," Pound is summarizing the modern problem of finding a language that can intersect with the contemporary world order.

These later writings of Eliot and Pound show greater resignation and a more ready retreat from the external world than do Jones's works. The agonized cry that closes "A, a, a, DOMINE DEUS" betrays the frustration that accompanies Jones's obstinately affirmative vision of the poet's vocation. He persists in calling on a divine presence for which the modern world seems to offer no signs. He continues the effort to "make it cohere," even though he acknowledges the difficulty, perhaps the impossibility, of the task. The desire to make signs out of materials at hand and the proclamation of a divine presence in the world are inseparable for David Jones. All his work is driven by a need to reveal "things"—events in history, poetic images, myths, and words—as signs that connect humanity to a sacred order. "A, a, a, DOMINE DEUS" insists that the groping search for valid signs and the invocation of a God whose presence remains unquestioned belong to the same poetic gesture. The fuller implications of this gesture, in history and in individual experience, is the focus of Jones's poetic theory, which begins from a carefully delineated analogy between the activities of poet and artist in the secular world and the form and claims of the sacraments in the Christian tradition.

Chapter 2

"Art and Sacrament"

Jones explains his particular view of the nature of *poiesis* most fully in "Art and Sacrament," an essay first published in 1955. He argues that a work of art is at once a material thing, a representation of some reality, and an index of the artist's action—the material evidence that an act of sign making has taken place, and therefore that the creature called "man" has been here. These threads of the poet's argument are woven together almost inextricably in the typically discursive style of the essay, but it is crucial to separate them out to appreciate the full implications of his poetic theory. Although many of the examples and terms Jones employs here are taken from the visual arts, sign making, his central focus, belongs as much to verbal as to visual art, by his account. The argument of "Art and Sacrament" engages some of the most fundamental issues that have preoccupied poetic theorists in our century, and it looks ahead in important ways to postmodern poetics in its analysis of representation, gesture, and temporal process as essential elements of poetic form.

The Work as Thing

One of the most important debates among twentieth-century literary theorists has centered on whether the poetic text should be viewed as an autonomous structure or as a referential medium. The Anglo-American New Critics of the 1940s and 1950s trained a generation or two of scholars to read texts primarily for their intrinsic structure, discounting biography, influence, and reference to social and cultural reality as extraneous to a poem's status as a closed and internally coherent verbal artifact. More radical versions of this view of the text have been propounded by structuralist and poststructuralist critics, who have argued that texts can only be read as intransitive structures of interdependent signs and should be interpreted, not with reference to any external truth—because truth is seen as a textual construct—but as a play of differences and interrelationships among words.[1] At the opposite extreme of the critical debate have been adherents of Marxist and other socially oriented critical schools, who argue that language is necessarily embedded in social and cultural structures and systems and that texts must always be read as referential, pointing beyond themselves to cultural and social reality.[2]

Although these two approaches are usually seen as mutually exclusive, a few theorists have acknowledged that one of the problems and challenges of language as it is used in poetic texts is that it inevitably works both as artifact and as sign. The Prague school formalist Jan Mukařovsky puts the matter with admirable clarity when he points out that the textual and the representational aspects of language interact problematically in poetic texts. Language in literature, he suggests, is "a *material*, like metal and stone in sculpture, like pigment and the material of the pictorial plane in painting." At the same time, Mukařovsky insists, "language in its very essence is already a sign," calling up associations that connect words at once to other words in a self-contained poetic system and to the further connotations and contexts that those words evoke in everyday communication (1977, 9).

Mukařovsky would not have known the work of David Jones, but the connection he makes between the language of poetry and the materials of the visual arts helps to illuminate Jones's poetic theory. Jones first evolved his sense of art as sacrament from his training as a painter and graphic artist.[3] In "Art and Sacrament," he recalls a recurring dispute among postimpressionist theorists between the "abstract" artists, who said "that the work was a 'thing' and not (necessarily) the impression of another thing" (*EA*, 172), and the "representational" artists, who insisted that a work of art always represented some version of reality under new forms. Jones concludes his brief account of this dispute by insisting that "no matter what the situation, we cannot escape the obligation of asserting as axiomatic that all art is 'abstract' and that all art 're-presents'" (173). Drawing on a terminology derived from neoscholastic thought and especially from Jacques Maritain, Jones goes on to argue that all art, poetic and visual, must be seen at once as a "gratuitous" or "intransitive" creation (152–54)—a thing in its own right—and as a transitive "sign," pointing beyond itself to "something other" (157). This fusion of abstract and representational theories of art is essential to Jones's insistence on an analogy between the arts of the secular world and the sacraments of the Christian church.

One important argument of "Art and Sacrament" rests on the scholastic teaching that "the chief mark of man lies in his being capable of the gratuitous" (*EA,* 149). The terminology and the concept of the gratuitous here are drawn from the French neoscholastic philosopher Jacques Maritain, whose work was an important influence on Eric Gill's community at Ditchling in the 1920s. Particularly important to Jones was Maritain's *Art and Scholasticism,* an early translation of which was published by St. Dominic's Press at Ditchling in 1923. As Maritain explains his concept of the gratuitous,

> art is gratuitous or disinterested as such—that is to say, that in the production of the work the virtue of art aims only at one thing: the good of the work-to-be-made, beauty to be made to shine in matter, the creating of the thing according to its own laws. (1962, 89)

Though this definition might at first seem startlingly close to the symbolists' belief in "art for art's sake," with its concomitant disengagement from the moral order, Maritain quickly distinguishes his definition of the gratuitous from the versions offered by Mallarmé, Gide, and other French symbolist and postsymbolist writers. These writers, he argues, view the representational aspects of the work, its "lyrical and intellectual materials," as impurities to be eliminated. Thus they create, according to Maritain, "pure art, art about nothing." This account of their art might actually have pleased the symbolists, and it might also satisfy some formalist and poststructuralist critics. Maritain, however, condemns it as "a sin of idealism with respect to the *matter* of art: in the end, a perfect constructing, with nothing to construct" (90). Maritain values gratuitousness because for him it offers a human analogy for the divine act of creation (87). It attests to an inevitable link between the human and transcendental orders, or in Jones's words, to the "extramundane end" of humankind (*EA,* 150).

Jones extends Maritain's conception of the gratuitous by opposing it to what he calls the "merely utile," the creation of works for purely functional or utilitarian purposes (*EA,*180–85). A central theme of much of Jones's later writing is the dehumanizing threat of a technocratic society that emphasizes utility over any kind of aesthetic value. In his essay "The Utile," published as an appendix to "Art and Sacrament," Jones warns that when human works seek utility only, they become "sub-human."

The characteristic works of our present technocracy *at its best and at its worst* seek the "utile." Thus we have the formidable beauty of the war-planes and of the ballistic devices of various kinds. Thus also the gleaming and exact apparatuses, the beauty of which, being seen, pleases, even when seen from the dentist's chair. All such products of our technocracy derive their beauty from the play of light on shapes which seek an uncontaminated utility. Yet it is this same technocracy which achieves the vacuity and deprivation apparent in the thousand-and-one utensils and impedimenta of our daily lives, domestic or public. There the mediocre, shoddy and slick is no longer a matter for comment. Nor can the search in antique-dealers' shops for a single spoon that does not affront the senses be any longer dismissed as an aesthete's faddishness or as a collector's craze or as an obsession with the past. On the contrary, it is symptomatic of a general, if muddled, nostalgia for things which though serviceable and utile are not divorced from the extra-utile and which, on that account, conform to man's ordinary, normal and proper, if obscured, desires—the fundamental desires of all men, of Man. (*EA,* 181)

Jones's evident appreciation for the beauty of many technological artifacts demonstrates that he is not a primitivist wishing to escape to earlier eras of art and culture. He is concerned with the intention that shapes the art works of his contemporaries. Hence his distress at his inability to find "a single spoon that does not affront the senses" reflects a sensitivity to the process, the human activity that went into the making of the spoon. In the products of industrial society, he sees works that point to a merely utilitarian intention, stripped of the gratuitous. He longs for works whose gratuitous beauty would be the *fecit*-mark of a human maker acting in full accord with his or her humanity—the sign of a lover of play. Jones claims that he is not merely arguing for the restoration of an elitist aesthetic ideal from the past, although he has been accused of taking this position (Ward 1983, 12). His argument is that the pace and priorities of contemporary society are depriving all people, from whatever social position, of a kind of satisfaction that is natural to them, the lack of which leads, sooner or later, to spiritual impoverishment. The metaphysics that defines humankind as a fundamentally artistic species also leads to Jones's sense of a division between the direction of his contemporary society and the more natural appreciation of beauty for its own sake that is so basic to the artist's perceptions.

An Act of Art

By embracing the gratuitous, Jones resists any typically idealist or escapist formalism. Commenting on the aestheticists working in the visual arts, who took their inspiration indirectly from Stéphane Mallarmé and symbolist poetics, Jones writes:

> Like most heretics, the men of the '90's were proclaiming a truth in isolation when they asserted that "art is for art's sake." An act of art is essentially a gratuitous act. It does not have to be justified by metaphysical argument. It is essentially "play." (*DG*, 164)

Jones's notion of art as play differs fundamentally from that of deconstructive criticism because it is grounded in a metaphysical conception of human beings as creative agents. Yet within this metaphysical framework, Jones is fascinated by the interplay of significations and its capacity to generate new signs. His poetry celebrates not simply a fixed transcendental center or even a "still point of the turning world" (Eliot 1971, 119) but an ongoing process of creation that Jones finds basic to the experience of "man the maker." Hence Jones insists on the gratuitousness of the *act* of art, rather than on the art work's autonomy as a completed thing. In contrast to the symbolists or even the imagists, he does not focus on the end product of art, the perfect form that in some way allows an escape from the complexities of the contemporary order. He insists in "Art and Sacrament" that "Ars has no end save the perfecting of a process by which all sorts of ends are made possible. It *is* that process. In so far as art has an end that end is a 'fitting together' and the word art means a fitting together" (*EA*, 151). The principle at the heart of Jones's order of signs is above all else this act of art, the process of fitting together and representing in which humanity naturally engages.

Jones's account of *poiesis* as an activity, a process—and of art works as indices of that process—intersects strikingly with the thinking of literary critics whose work on metaphor and representation reflects some of the central concerns of modern and postmodern poetics. Charles Altieri, writing in another context, sheds some light on this aspect of Jones's poetics in his discussions of the poem as act, a terminology that parallels Jones's focus on the act of art. Altieri identifies five basic tenets of what he calls "presentational theories" of poetry—theories that have been best represented in the writing of American postmodernist poets and critics. According to Altieri's account, presentational theories do not claim simply that the poem imitates an event outside the poem; rather, such postmodern writers as Joyce, Pound, William Carlos Williams, and Charles Olson present a continuous and always unfinished creative activity in their texts. Presentational theories insist on the immediacy of the poem. They view the reader as sharing the poet's speech, and they re-create the author's struggle to give form to feelings. The presentational school claims that the poem's meaning is in what it does. Altieri attempts to fuse with these claims the "mimetic" theories, which hold that a literary text is not a copy or direct expression of reality but a "purposive structuring of experience." He suggests that by combining these two broad approaches to poetics, we can begin to talk about the poetic text as the index of an act. Through the text, we watch the poet in the process of restructuring perceptions of experience (1975, 107–11).[4]

The philosopher Paul Ricoeur has argued analogously that the making of a metaphor should be seen as an act or event. For him, the creation of a poetic metaphor adds something new to discourse, and hence to our experience of the world, by suspending conventional relationships between words and their referents and making possible some other reference. Metaphor enables us to see the world in new and more creative ways. The creation of new metaphors is not a matter of simple ornamentation, nor is it a substitution of one meaning for another, the expression of an old idea in a new way. Metaphor transforms reality by changing the way that we describe and perceive the world. Hence Ricoeur asserts that "the 'metaphoric' that transgresses the categorical order also begets it" (1977, 23). For him, metaphor is not simply a representation of reality; it is also a transforming "event" (1974, 103).

The early work of one prominent postmodernist thinker, William Spanos, explicitly associates the problem of poetic representation—the text's engagement with historical and temporal experience—with the Christian concepts of incarnation and sacrament. In his 1970 essay "Modern Literary Criticism and the Spatialization of Time," Spanos criticizes the "angelism" or "crypto-Gnosticism" of the New Critics, particularly of Joseph Frank's theory of spatial form. Developing from an existentialist perspective a terminology introduced by Jacques Maritain and Allen Tate,

Spanos argues that a criticism calling for the autonomy and formal closure of the literary work necesssarily claims for the critic and for the poet a teleological perspective beyond time, from which the contingencies of human life can be avoided. Spanos points to a widespread effort in modernist poetry and criticism to escape from "the terrifying world of temporal flux" (92) into a "timeless moment of aesthetic contemplation that holds sway both in and out of the academy at the expense of temporal motion and the dialogic process" (98).

Against this teleological tendency, Spanos explores some twentieth-century manifestations of an incarnational aesthetic founded in human action. His study of sacramental time in modern British verse drama is particularly instructive in its definition of the Christian or sacramental aesthetic as a clear alternative to the angelic tendencies of modernism. His focus on British Christian verse drama of the twentieth century leads Spanos to stress primarily the representational choices made by the dramatists he studies, especially Charles Williams, Christopher Fry, and T. S. Eliot. He examines, for example, the perspective that these dramatists present on existential human action in time and their tendency to use naturalistic images that stand as concrete universals—at once fully themselves and fully symbolic. Though he acknowledges that verse is the most effective vehicle for this kind of concrete imagery, Spanos is finally critical of the "neutral style" (1967, 334) of his subjects, their tendency, ultimately, to be more concerned with content than with form. In the style of these British Christian dramatists, Spanos does not find a consciousness of the temporality and historicity of poetic language. A commitment to this material character of words pervades David Jones's approach to poetry and enlarges significantly on the sacramental aesthetic that Spanos describes.

Re-presentation and Re-calling

Jones moves far beyond Spanos by developing the analogy between the "Sacraments with a capital S" and "sacrament with a small s"—the "sacramental" nature of poetic art (*EA*, 177–78). He pursues, in particular, an analogy between the remembering that goes on in poetic works and the gesture of anamnesis, which theologians have defined as central to the celebration of the Eucharist in catholic Christian tradition. The Anglican theologian Dom Gregory Dix defines the term *anamnesis* as "a re-calling, a re-presenting of a thing in such a way that it is regarded as not so much 'absent' as *presently operative by its effects*." Dix also emphasizes the early church's understanding of "the whole rite of the Eucharist as a single action" (Dix 1975, 245). These two aspects of anamnesis—the material work that claims to be a "re-presenting" or "re-calling" and the dramatic action and gesture that are essential to what is made—are the basis of the analogy Jones draws between the arts and the sacraments of the church.

From a theological perspective, this may seem an ill-considered analogy, because sacramental theology insists that the Real Presence of Christ in the Eucharist is a unique mystery. Jones, a devout Catholic, is careful not to deny this uniqueness, and he insists more than once that he uses theological terms only by analogy. Nonetheless, he persists in using theological terms, with all their implications and resonances, and he presses the analogy as far as he can, out of a sense of historical urgency. An example is the language that he uses in concluding his analysis of Hogarth's painting "The Shrimp Girl."

> By the particular working of Hogarth's genius a reality is offered to us. So long as there is not a serious disintegration of the "matter" (the paint) we have whatever is denoted under "Shrimp Girl" really present under the form of paint, remembering that "Shrimp Girl" is but a label only for a complex of realities. Not, needless to say, "really present" in the particular sense used by the theologians, but in a certain analogous sense. I can speak only by analogy and it may be I speak ill-advisedly, but I know of no other way of giving sufficient emphasis to something that I believe to require emphasis, especially in view of our culture-situation and for a number of other reasons. (*EA*, 175)

"The Shrimp Girl" is seen here as the index of an act of sign making— the material result and evidence of the "working of Hogarth's genius." Jones's passing reference to the "matter" of the painting suggests a further reason why he invokes the sacramental analogy. The arts, like sacraments, depend for their effectiveness on material elements—words, paint, clay. The "matter" of a sacrament—the water of Baptism, the bread and wine of Eucharist—are necessary to the celebrations of these rites. Aquinas writes that a serious disintegration in the bread and wine for the Eucharist would make the sacrament void (1914, 315–16), and Jones seems to be adopting this idea in his search for matter for valid signs. We have already seen this in his lament for the erosion in significance of the word *wood* in the preface to *The Anathemata*. But besides being a thing, he argues, "The Shrimp Girl" is also a "re-presentation" of a certain view of reality. He uses the term *re-presentation* deliberately for its echoes of anamnesis and Real Presence. The art work is a thing, but it also makes something else present, because that is what signs do, and that is why people make things that are signs of something other. Jones's concern is that our cultural situation is inhibiting this basic human impulse and thus threatening the character of human life. He turns to the theological analogy to emphasize what he sees as the cosmic urgency of the analysis and celebration of the act of art that motivates all his works.

Jones's use of the term *really present* in his account of "The Shrimp Girl" underscores his conviction that if an act of art is gratuitous and intransitive, the making of signs is, by its nature a transitive, or referential, activity. In making a sign, Jones argues, the artist "holds up this thing and says 'this *is* something other.'" The "is" in this statement has a force that is more than metaphorical. It does not simply indicate the substitution of one idea for another on the basis of resemblance or for the purpose of ornamentation. When Jones says that a work of art "re-presents" a reality, he does mean that it points beyond itself toward something that "has *esse*," or Being (*EA*, 157)—toward the transcendental referent that poststructuralist thought has so insistently deconstructed. [5] "A sign," writes Jones, "must be significant of something, hence of some 'reality,' so of something 'good,' so of something that is 'sacred.' That is why I think that the notion of the sign implies the sacred'" (*EA*, 157).

Jones's assumption that art is always referential has been taken up frequently in Jones criticism. Thomas Dilworth's monumental 1988 study of the "shape of meaning" in Jones presents him primarily as a writer who uses poetic form to shape a broad and original analysis of twentieth-century culture. Thomas Whitaker, in an important and carefully argued essay, insists on the connection between Jones's view of humanity as a sign-making species and his conviction that all signs ultimately point to "the universal ground or act that inheres in them, calls them into being, and can be known imperfectly through them" (1989, 471). Whitaker is right, I think, in his argument that Jones's work is in this sense radically referential, supporting through both its themes and procedures Jones's belief that "a sign then must be significant of something, hence of some 'reality,' so of something 'good,' so of something that is 'sacred'" (*EA*, 157).

"Art and Sacrament" was originally written for an audience of fellow believers.[6] His original readership would have recognized the terms of two statements that Jones presents as equivalent toward the beginning of his essay: "Man must be considered a sign-maker and . . . his art is sign-making," and "Man is unavoidably a sacramentalist and his works are sacramental in character" (*EA*, 154–55). As he puts it in another part of the discussion, "The activity called art is, at bottom, and inescapably, a 'religious' activity, for it deals with realities and the real is sacred and religious." His fellow believers would also have shared his understanding that "*religio* is that which binds man to God" (159). Yet despite the audience and context of "Art and Sacrament," Jones is at pains to extend his understanding of sacramental theology beyond the community of believers, using the analogy between the arts and sacraments to give emphasis to what he sees as a critical problem in the twentieth-century world: the loss of appreciation for the gratuitous elements of art and life. He protests, somewhat disingenuously perhaps, but with great earnestness:

> In this essay, . . . our concern is not with the truth or otherwise of a given theology, that is outside my scope and would not be relevant. What is here relevant is that such a theology exists and that it can be seen as affording, by analogy, a remarkable example of the activities of Ars. I repeat, I speak only by analogy. (171)

Without denying or minimizing Jones's belief in what Whitaker terms the "real presence of the signified in the sign" (1989, 480–81), I focus on the second aspect of Jones's analogy between the arts and sacraments—his assumption that the act of making signs affirms one of the most basic truths about our humanity. It identifies us as human, and therefore, in Jones's belief, as creatures who are connected to God. The continuity of sign making as evidence of our humanity is threatened, in Jones's view, by modern culture and thought. To stress this point, Jones deliberately secularizes a theological analogy, underscoring what he sees as a fundamental connection between the action of Jesus at the Last Supper—when he held up bread and said, "This *is* my body"—and the acts of "man-the-artist." He takes this analogy from Maurice de la Taille, whose account of the continuity between Christ's actions at the Last Supper and those on the cross deeply influenced the poet's thinking and the form of *The Anathemata*. For Jones, the story of the Last Supper and the Passion demonstrates that Jesus shared one of the fundamental qualities of all humanity. He was, as all people are, a sign-maker. In de la Taille's argument, Jesus was also the referent of his own sign, because the offering at the Last Supper became an effective sign of his self-offering at the Crucifixion (see *A*, 225, 233; Hague 1977).[7] But in "Art and Sacrament," Jones is most interested in the incarnate God's participation in the human activity of making signs, his experience of "the joy of signifying" that humanity shares with the Creator (de la Taille 1930, 212).

The foregrounding of the act of sign making in the form and texture of his works constitutes Jones's most important and original contribution to twentieth-century poetic theory, particularly for postmodernist poets and theorists who have seen texts as the indices of an ongoing or open process of imaginative creation. His concern with sign making as act and with humanity as a sign-making species is already implicit in his portrayals of sign-makers and rememberers in *In Parenthesis*. The sacramental analogy finds its fullest poetic expression in the formal procedures and central themes of *The Anathemata*.

Chapter 3

"Singing Where He Walks": Making and Remembering in *In Parenthesis*

Jones's first book, *In Parenthesis*, has become an important part of the canon of literature emerging from the First World War, and it has received its widest critical attention as a war book.[1] Most readers find it more accessible than *The Anathemata*, perhaps because its use of narrative structure and character development are relatively transparent, despite an initially daunting complexity of allusion and language. A number of critics have also praised the painterly quality of its account of life in the trenches (Holloway 1964; Cooper 1979). But Jones claims in his preface that it is not really a war book: "I should prefer it to be about a good kind of peace. . . . We find ourselves privates in foot regiments. We search how we may see formal goodness in a life singularly inimical, hateful, to us" (xii–xiii).

If we look at *In Parenthesis* in the context of Jones's work as a whole, especially in relation to the mature vision that emerges in *The Anathemata*, it becomes clear that the "good kind of peace" that *In Parenthesis* evokes is rooted in what Jones views as humanity's fundamental identity as *homo sapiens, homo faber* (man the knower, man the maker) (*EA*, 184). The war is nearly always a background to the experiences of the men, but the poem focuses on their efforts to hold on to the things that make them human, especially to those impulses that are for Jones the mark of the "sacramentalist" (*EA*, 155). If we read the poem with Jones's "good kind of peace" in mind, these acts, filtered through the consciousness of characters who also represent humankind as sign-makers, emerge as the most important events of the poem. Thus *In Parenthesis*, an important response to the First World War and a masterful example of modernist use of allusion, is also, like Joyce's *Portrait of the Artist* or Woolf's *To the Lighthouse*, a self-conscious reflection and demonstration of the poetic consciousness coming to terms with an alien external world. *In Parenthesis* celebrates not simply the moral values of the past or the heroic war tradition in itself but more particularly the acts by which people recall their forbears and create order, consciously or unconsciously, in surroundings that consistently thwart their most basic needs and impulses.

The early chapters of Jones's book focus on the homely, domestic activities and relationships of a group of Welsh and English soldiers—many of them deeply aware of their historical roots—against the background of the brutal and mechanistic twentieth-century warfare in which they are engaged. Parts 1–4 focus on the particulars of the men's domestic and communal life, lingering over the things and impulses that impart humanity to what one passage calls the "loveless scene" of the war zone (75). The surroundings are described most often by a narrator whose clear and highly visual perceptions identify him as a representative of "man-the-artist" at the front. Early in part 2, for example, the barn in which the men assemble for lectures is described through the eyes of one sensitive both to homely local beauty and to the history of Western architecture: "They were given lectures on very wet days in the barn, with its great roof, sprung, upreaching, humane, and redolent of a vanished order" (13). The observing consciousness here is at once artist and rememberer, and his appreciation of his surroundings endows them with a warm humanity they would otherwise lack.

Similarly, the narrator's perceptions of communal life behind the lines stress the ways in which the men make their surroundings livable and humane: "They rested cosily at night in thick straw. They crowded together in the evening—hours full of confused talking; the tiny room heavy with the haze of smoking, and humane with the paraphernalia of any place of common gathering, warm, within small walls" (13–14). Later, the men pause for a few hours in their march toward the front, and we see some of them hanging up clothes and creating sleeping places of their own, even in these temporary quarters. The narrator comments, "They would make order, for however brief a time, and in whatever wilderness" (24). Even the first view of the trenches stresses not the squalor and disarray of the battleground but the mark that the men have made on these inhospitable surroundings:

And you know the homing perfume of wood burned, at the termination of ways; and sense here near habitation, a folk life here, a

people, a culture already developed, already venerable and
rooted. . . .

And you too are assimilated, you too are of this people—there will
be an indelible characterisation—you'll tip-toe when they name the
place. (49)

The archaic diction here—"the termination of ways," "near habitation"—
and the recollections of primitive folk life connect the experience of
these twentieth-century soldiers to the experiences of their ancestors in
legend and romance. They name their surroundings; they will found a
culture. The purpose is not to sentimentalize this war but to suggest a
continuity of consciousness that enables these men to survive their in-
creasingly incomprehensible surroundings by acknowledging their links
with sign-makers who fought in past battles.

In *In Parenthesis,* the men's natural urge to make order out of the small
details of their lives and surroundings is steadily undermined as the reality
of the war approaches. A first glimpse of this evolution comes at the end of
part 2, when Private John Ball—the character who most closely reflects
David Jones's experience as a soldier—undergoes a shelling for the first
time.[2] For a moment, the artist's vision freezes the tiniest details of the
scene about to be destroyed. Then it too succumbs to the overwhelming
destructive power of a new kind of human artifact (24). This account
stresses the contrast between John Ball's perception of the "small things"
that have made his existence bearable so far and the more sinister exacti-
tude of the human calculations that have created the bombs. The destruc-
tive power of this exactly timed "stinking physicist's destroying toy" has
the effect of destroying particulars, of "saturating all existence" (24). The
choice of words is significant here, because as *In Parenthesis* progresses,
the narrator uses more and more images of saturation, confusion, and
blurring, to show how the approaching battle threatens the world of
ordered particulars in which the men at first find refuge. The gradual
undoing of this order is suggested most clearly in the fog that pervades the
landscape of part 4, "King Pellam's Launde."

Fog refracted, losing articulation in the cloying damp, the word of
command unmade in its passage, mischiefed of the opaque air,
mutated, bereaved of content, become an incoherent uttering, a
curious bent cry out of the smarting drift, lost altogether. (60)

Here the "saturating" power of the shells is literalized in the natural world, as the fog and rain dissipate the orderly articulation previously embodied in the word of command.

As order and clarity disappear, the men become increasingly passive. In describing the experience of trench warfare, the narrator of the second half of *In Parenthesis* relies increasingly on myth and legend to make sense of the men's incomprehensible situation. A few pages later, John Ball's companions are described as "appointed scape-beasts come to the waste-lands, to grope; to stumble at the margins of familiar things—at the place of separation" (70). The boundary image emphasizes the transition from the natural humanity of the men behind the lines—symbolized by the "familiar things" with which they have formerly surrounded themselves—to a dehumanizing world created by the new inventions of trench warfare. The use of myth—which I discuss in greater detail in chapter 5—implicitly identifies this transition with the more universal experience of the age, which the First World War brought to a "place of separation" between a humane and familiar past and an incomprehensible present.

The familiar things left behind on the eve of battle are emphasized with growing poignancy in part 6 of *In Parenthesis,* as John Ball meets for the last time with two good friends.

> They talked of ordinary things. Of each one's friends at home; those friends unknown to either of the other two. Of the possible duration of the war. Of how they would meet and in what good places after-wards. Of the dissimilar merits of Welshmen and Cockneys. Of the diverse virtues of Regular and Temporary Officers. Of if you'd ever read the books of Mr. Wells. Of the poetry of Rupert Brooke. . . . Of whether they three would be together for the Duration, and how you hoped so very much indeed. Of captains of thousands and of hundreds, of corporals, of many things. . . . Of how stripes, stars, chevrons, specialisations, jobs away from the battalion, and all distinguishing marks were better resisted for as long as possible. Of how it were best to take no particular notice, to let the stuff go over you, how it were wise to lie doggo and to wait the end. (139–40)

This passage is similar in effect to the narrator's observation of "the exact disposition of small things" at the moment of shelling (24). It brings together the minutiae that have been important to these men and that will be dispersed and forgotten in battle. These include the details of their personal lives, the political events of their day, the platitudes of soldierly exchange, and even allusions to Malory, as in the title of part 6, "Pavillions and Captains of Hundreds." The trivial conversation of these men thus becomes a catalog of their cultural awareness on the brink of the battle's "unmaking" (24).

In the battle, the human contacts stressed during this interlude in part 6 are blurred into unintelligibility, and the narrator of the poem, as if increasingly conscious of his role as a survivor of the battle, laments above all the violations of the natural rituals by which the men desire to honor and remember the dead. When a companion dies in John Ball's arms the poem laments not only this death but the way in which war prevents the ritual impulses that Jones holds essential to the human nature:

> And get back to that digging can't yer—
> this aint a bloody Wake
> for these dead, who soon will have their dead
> for burial clods heaped over.
> Nor time for halsing
> nor to clip green wounds
> nor weeping Maries bringing anointments
> neither any word spoken
> nor no decent nor appropriate sowing of this seed
> nor remembrance of the harvesting
> of the renascent cycle
> and return
> nor shaving of the head nor ritual incising for these *viriles* under each tree.
> No one sings: Lully lully
> for the mate whose blood runs down.
>
> (174)

The lament for the dead is typical of war literature in any period, but here the allusions to neglected rituals, to the ancient connection between the hope of resurrection and the natural cycle of birth and regeneration, reminds us that modern warfare brings about an even more radical severance from the natural order. For Jones, the impulse to sing elegies for the dead connects humanity to this natural order. John Ball is indulging a basic human desire when he pauses to commit his comrade to the cycle of death and rebirth.

The poet as rememberer is embodied most fully in Lance Corporal Aneirin Lewis, the most thoroughly Welsh character in the poem.[3] In the work as a whole, Aneirin Lewis comes to reflect the crucial role of the poet as the one who discerns connections between a dehumanizing present and a more humane past. When we meet him on the first page, he has a priestlike function, bringing "baptism, and metaphysical order, to the bankruptcy of the occasion" (1–2). A brief but haunting passage in part 2 connects him at once to Shakespeare's Captain Fluellen, the Welsh devotee of "the disciplines of the wars," and to the ancient folk tradition of Wales (*Henry V* 3.2). A description of bursting shells in the night march to the front is interrupted by this brief observation: "Lance-Corporal Lewis sings where he walks, yet in a low voice, because of the Disciplines of the Wars. He sings of the Hills about Jerusalem, and of David of the White Stone" (42). This allusion to Captain Fluellen points to an important aspect of Lewis as maker. In Shakespeare, Fluellen's devotion to the "disciplines of the wars" is presented as an endearing, if perhaps misplaced, devotion to the modes of order that are imposed by battle. But as John Barnard acutely points out, the part of Shakespeare's play that centers on Fluellen and the common soldiers and their officers "catches the mingling of brutality and nobility under the 'disciplines of war'" (1979, 19). Jones's use of the allusion also respects the link between Fluellen's "disciplines" and the Latin *disciplina*, a term he uses often in his discussions of humanity's natural inclination to make things that are also signs. One of these *disciplinae* is military strategy (*EA*, 159–60), which for Jones remains an expression of the sacramental impulse in the strategist, even when it is directed toward immoral ends. This is also true of military discipline as experienced by the common soldiers of *In Parenthesis* and *Henry V*. Hence it is significant that the Queen of the Woods honors the memory of Lewis by being "careful for the Disciplines of the Wars" (*IP*, 186).[4]

The incongruity of Lewis singing Welsh folk hymns in the midst of shelling turns out to be a source of strength for his men. A few pages later, when John Ball begins to lose his way and panics in the "fluid mud" of the trenches, the lance corporal's singing provides guidance and a kind of metaphysical order for this individual soldier.

John Ball cies out to nothing but unresponsive narrowing earth. His feet take him upward over high pilings—down again to the deep sludge. . . . Beneath his feet, below the water, he feels again the wooden flooring, and round the next bend in another light's rising the jogging pack of Aneirin Lewis—and heard him singing, very low, as he went. (45)

For Ball in this moment, Lewis is a prophetic figure, quietly affirming life even when he and his men are nearly buried in "unresponsive . . . earth." His song carries forward things secure and familiar, despite the general disintegration of the surrounding world. His role is akin to the poet's function as Jones describes it later in "Past and Present." His song is the song of the exiled psalmist who goes on singing the Lord's song in a strange land, reminding the people of an order of value that persists.

But the poem's portrayal of "man-the-sign-maker" at work extends beyond its development of characters who display the poetic consciousness. The form of the poem seems calculated to make us aware of its maker at work, elaborating his bardlike tale. *In Parenthesis* has a fundamentally diachronic narrative, organized around key events in the life of Jones's regiment as they move from the camp behind the lines, toward the front, and finally to the battle of Mametz Wood. Yet though the narrative formed by the retelling of the chief events in the men's progress toward the front is linear and chronological, Jones deliberately fragments these events in the service of the poem's underlying synchronic structure, the intricate pattern of allusion and cross-reference by which the men's present actions are connected to their mythic and historical roots.[5] The narrative pauses frequently to meditate—often through the consciousness of a specific character, and usually in verselike, metric forms—on the details of the men's experience. From time to time, it stops to spin out a lyric excursus on the relation of this war to others or on connections between these men and their forbears. In this way, the events of the narrative become a structural pretext for the poet's lyric improvisations, which slow the chronological and linear progress of events and suspend temporal flow for extended moments of lyric introspection. These interruptions keep the reader continually aware of what structuralist critics have called the textuality of the text, reminding us at every point that this is the work of a modern writer who is trying to make what the preface calls "a shape in words" out of his experiences (x).

This deliberate foregrounding of the poetic text of *In Parenthesis* is particularly remarkable in part 4, "King Pellam's Launde." Paul Fussell has suggested that this section could be called "A Day in the Trenches," and he complains of the slow progress of its narrative (Fussell 1975, 149–50). Nonetheless, the overall structure of part 4 shows Jones exploiting narrative and lyric modes together to reflect both the suspense and the monotony of the routine days preceding the battle of Mametz Wood and to uncover the deeper cultural and historical resonances of these prepara- tions for battle. Though the diachronic narrative line of this section moves slowly, it is carefully and symmetrically constructed, beginning and ending with the "stand-to" that ritually defines the soldiers' day, and interrupted—in the exact center of the section—by the long excursus of Dai's boast, a key passage that constitutes the structural and thematic center of *In Parenthesis.*

Part 4 opens with stand-to at dawn, and we hear the men being roused from sleep by their officers (59–63). At daybreak, they "stand down" to clean rifles, and the search begins for oil and hot water. Mr. Jenkins and Sergeant Snell come to inspect the weapons (63–65), while John Ball takes morning sentry duty, watching for enemy movements near Biez Copse. It is Christmas morning, and he and his mates hear the German soldiers singing *Es ist ein Ros' entsprungen.* They respond by drowning out the carol with a raucous chorus of "Casey Jones" (65–68). The officers come by again for inspection, and afterward the men sit and smoke and curse the weather and the surrounding conditions (69–71). The tea and rum ration arrives (71–74). John Ball finishes his sentry duty and goes in search of breakfast (75–76). At about mid-morning, a party goes out to inspect enemy fortifications, marching toward Pioneer Keep. The various stages of this march form a chronological sequence punctuated by gossip about the war ahead and signs of the surrounding enemy presence. The men hear shelling in the distance and react to reports of casualties (84– 89). They meet a warden of stores who has been living in the trenches so long he seems to have become a part of the landscape. He issues supplies and warns them of what to expect in the trenches ahead (89–93). They return to their first quarters for a midday rest, followed by a long after- noon relieved only by occasional work details, which they greet eagerly as relief from boredom (93–96). The day ends, as it began, with the stand- to, as dusk falls (96–99).

This sequence of events is true to the actual routine of a day on the western front, and some of the events it records, notably the account of the German soldiers' Christmas caroling, are based on Jones's actual memories.[6] The most striking portions of this section, however, are not the events themselves but the poet's lyric elaborations on them, which offer a pretext for the deeper symbolic and mythic connections made by the language of *In Parenthesis.* Frequently, these elaborations begin from

John Ball's observations of the "loveless scene" around him (75). For example, following his breakfast, we see the men of his company through his eyes, engaged in their routine morning tasks and conversations. This descriptive passage stresses the disharmony between human nature and trench life.

> Men-bundles here and there in ones and twos, in twos and threes; some eating, others very still, knee to chin trussed, confined in small dug concavities, wombed of earth, their rubber-sheets for caul. Others coaxed tiny smouldering fires, balancing precarious mess-tins, anxious-watched to boil. . . . All their world shelving, coagulate. Under-earth shorn-up, seeled and propt. Substantial matter guttered and dissolved, sprawled to glaucous insecurity. All sureness metamorphosed, all slippery a place for the children of men, for the fair feet of us to go up and down in. (75–76)

The technique of this highly impressionistic description is reminiscent of the interior monologues of modern lyrical novels, for example the reflections of Leopold Bloom at Paddy Dignam's graveside in Joyce's *Ulysses* or of Mrs. Ramsay at supper in Woolf's *To the Lighthouse*. In Jones, however, the rhythms and rhymes are more deliberately poetic and verselike. Sentence rhythms and alliteration recall the Welsh-inspired sprung rhythms that Jones so admired in Gerard Manley Hopkins, as in "únder-éarth shórn-úp, séeled and própt," or "for the fair feet of us." The abbreviated poetic diction of "anxious-watched to boil," the fragmented syntax, and the unusual verbal adjectives in "all their world shelving, coagulate" identify this passage as a poetic elaboration on the scene, a transmutation of lived experience into poetry that is self-consciously lyrical.

The role of this improvisatory technique is clearest in two lyric set pieces in part 4 that interrupt the linear progression of the narrative to offer a display of poetic inventiveness, connecting chronological events to the synchronic structure of *In Parenthesis*. The first of these lyric digressions begins from John Ball's meditation as he sits on sentry duty, surveying Biez Copse. The narrative voice of the poem soon takes over, spinning out a meditation on the role of groves in the mythic and cultural history shared by these men—indeed by all men. The lyrical feeling of this sequence marks it as a literary performance—an aria or set piece—that interrupts, ornaments, and elaborates on the main action.

To groves always men come both to their joys and their undoing. Come
lightfoot in heart's ease and school-free; walk on a leafy holiday with kin-
dred and kind; come perplexedly with first loves—to tread the tangle frus-
trated, striking—bruising the green.
Come on night's fall for ambuscade.
Find harbour with a remnant.
Share with the prescribed their unleavened cake.
Come for sweet princes by malignant interests deprived.

(66)

The incantatory repetitions of *come* in this passage and the inverted, poetic
syntax of "to groves always men come" give it the quality of a ritual incanta-
tion, as if it were an invocation to the genius loci. The passage is filled with
allusions to the myths and legends that determine the poem's synchronic
structure, evoking as it does Frazer's *Golden Bough,* the ill-fated battle of
Camlann, the death of Llewelyn, and the unleavened cake of the Passover
feast and the Mass. In moving from John Ball's contemplation of the few
patches of green left in "King Pellam's Launde" to a self-consciously
poetic celebration of the natural order and the historic roots of these
men, this meditation breaks out of the narrative mode of the poem to
display the poetic consciousness at work, making connections and
discovering order even in the devastated landscape of the war.

   This passage is one of a number of digressions or set pieces that break
out of the narrative theme and sequence of *In Parenthesis,* interrupting the
temporal flow to elaborate on some small detail of the narrative, almost in
the way that a medieval scribe might illuminate part of a manuscript from
the past. These embellishments usually arise organically from the narra-
tive situation—originating in the consciousness of a character or in an
event, such as Dai Greatcoat entering a general boasting contest. But they
wander far from the original narrative pretext, and they ultimately draw
attention to the act of making that is at work whenever people make these
associations. These lyric digressions mark *In Parenthesis* as the work of a
sign-maker who was present in the battle and who is now remembering it,
in keeping with his nature. In this way, they are the earliest instances of a
more self-conscious form that Jones later develops in *The Anathemata,*
where the process of elaboration and digression becomes a theme as well
as a technique.

   The most significant lyric digression in the poem is Dai's boast, which
interrupts the narrative of part 4 for six pages (79–84). Vincent Sherry has
shown how this boast, which begins "My fathers were with the black Prince

of Wales" and ends with the Great War song "Old soljers never die / They simply fade away," recapitulates the history of the heroic tradition in the West, using a traditional form from Welsh heroic literature. Dai is a symbol of continuity. Nonetheless, there is irony in his boast, which stresses at key moments the passive role of the men sent to battle. It summarizes the themes of futile battles, of the violation of life and land, that *In Parenthesis* attempts to bring together. In contrast to the groves sequence, Dai's boast is connected to the main narrative by only the most tenuous of logical ties. Dai is not developed as a character elsewhere in the poem. His main role is to appear here and deliver this speech.[7]

The form of Dai's monologue is borrowed from the boast, a set genre in the Welsh oral tradition and in Malory. The convention is that the boaster claims to have been present, either in his own person or in the person of an ancestor, at key events in the history of his community.[8] Dai, who claims to have witnessed a series of violent scenes, beginning with the murder of Abel, immediately separates himself from the realistic dimension of the narrative by claiming to be an immortal embodiment of the connection between these men and soldiers of the past. His boast summarizes in lyric form the key themes underlying the narrative of *In Parenthesis*. Dai frequently adopts songlike meter and rhyme, as in "I was the spear in Balin's hand / that made waste King Pellam's land" (79). He also quotes from folk and nursery rhyme, alluding, for example, to the poem "Who Killed Cock Robin" in his account of the Passion (83) and to nursery rhyme and folk song throughout the boast. The incantatory repetitions of "I heard," "I saw," and "I was with" connect the historic and mythic events Dai narrates to the oral tradition he personifies. The continuity of that tradition into the present of *In Parenthesis* is suggested through his quotation, at the end of the boast, from the Great War song "Old soljers never die / they simply fade away"—a song that also justifies the immortality Dai claims. A repeated refrain in the boast, "Oh blessed Bran . . . hold the striplings from the narrow sea" (82–83), implicitly connects the present-day battle of the Somme to ancient Welsh accounts of battles fought on French soil, across the "narrow sea," invoking an ancient tutelary deity of Britain to protect the twentieth-century soldiers.

A digression from the main text of the poem, Dai's boast presents the kind of historical poetic consciousness that makes *In Parenthesis* possible. Coming as it does in the exact center of the poem, it underscores the poet's role as a person conscious of history yet speaking to a present-day audience. This emphasis is particularly clear toward the end of the boast, when Dai alludes to *Peredur ap Evrawc*, the Welsh version of the Grail myth, in which the drying-up of the land is caused by the hero's failure to ask the dying king where he has been wounded. Dai says:

> You ought to ask: Why,
> what is this,
> what's the meaning of this.
> Because you don't ask,
> although the spear-shaft
> drips,
> there's neither steading—not a roof-tree.[9]

(84)

This paragraph deviates from the series of boasts—all beginning "I was," "I am," "I was with"—by turning to the audience with an exhortation— "You ought to ask." By implication, the question that the audience "ought to ask" about the experience is precisely the poet's question: Why? What is the meaning? How is this experience connected to others? In an essay written some years later, Jones suggests that the Grail hero's question is the poet's question. The failure to ask the question results in the wasteland (*DG*, 184–85). The urgency with which Dai exhorts his audience suggests the need for them to remember, to maintain the poet's insights into the causes and consequences of events, to resist discontinuity and affirm connections, to say with Dai, "I was there." Dai is calling on the audience to ask, not to answer, a question. In this he is a prime example of what several insightful critics have called the interrogative character of Jones's writing.[10]

The significance of this interrogative quality in Jones's writing is precisely what Thomas Dilworth misses in his characteristic reading of this passage as part of the poet's analysis of culture—particularly of war. He reads Dai's question in part as a call for the reader to decide on the morality of warfare. "The choice" in Dai's boast, Dilworth writes, "is whether to ask a question, but it is also, in the most profound of spiritual senses, the choice of which side to take in the first of all wars, which began in heaven and is not over yet" (1988, 116). It seems to me that this part of Dilworth's reading misses the point of the Grail hero's question in Jones and diffuses unnecessarily the rhetorical impact of Dai's exhortation to the reader. It also imposes a moral frame of reference that is not the poet's. We have some evidence that Jones did not see this poem as an antiwar poem or himself as an antiwar poet. William Blissett notes that Jones protested mildly after reading an earlier interpretation of *In Parenthesis* in which Dilworth stressed what he saw as the poem's concern with the immorality of war. "David Jones does not regard himself as an anti-war writer," Blissett writes in this context; "war for him is simply the world in one of its ways" (1981, 58). This argument seems consistent with Jones's disclaimer in the preface that *In Parenthesis* is not a war book but a book about "a good kind of peace" (xii–xiii). Similarly, in letters belonging to the period of *The Sleeping Lord*, he insists on the confusion of goodness and badness that characterizes the experience of all who participate in military activity. Jones is less concerned with the issue of the morality of war than he is with the need for the modern poet and his listeners to bear witness to dehumanizing historical experience and to ask "Why?" Dilworth is right when he writes that Dai's exhortation is important because it places the crux of *In Parenthesis* "outside the poem in the reader, who is free to respond—and in a way that would make a real difference to the world he lives in" (1988, 93), but I think he is wrong in his implication that the poet is asking for a response to the moral issues raised by this or any battle.

Beginning with the death of Lance Corporal Aneirin Lewis and the wounding of John Ball in part 7, the narrator of *In Parenthesis* gradually assumes the lance corporal's role as rememberer. Even as he laments that there is "no one to care there" for the fallen officer, the poet sings his elegy using the Welsh matter that was closest to Lewis's heart.

No one to care there for Aneirin Lewis spilled there
who worshipped his ancestors like a Chink
who sleeps in Arthur's lap
who saw Olwen-trefoils some moonlighted night
on precarious slats at Festubert,
on narrow foothold on le Plantin marsh—
more shaved he is to the bare bone than
Yspaddadan Penkawr.
     Properly organised chemists can let make more riving power than ever Twrch Trwyth;
more blistered he is than painted Troy Towers
and unwholer, limb from limb, than any of them fallen at Catraeth
or on the seaboard-down, by Salisbury,
and no maker to contrive his funerary song.

                                                            (155)

Despite the last line of this passage, there *is* a maker to contrive Lewis's funerary song and to lament the others killed in battle, and the lament here is precisely the kind Lewis would have liked—filled with allusions to the myths of his Welsh past and recalling the way that his Welshness transformed the wasteland of the front. That maker is the surviving poet— the speaker of *In Parenthesis*.

The poem ends by giving a contemporary bite to the closing lines of *The Song of Roland*, another war song contrived by a survivor. Like *The Song of Roland* and the Welsh poem *Y Gododdin*, which supplies the epigraphs to each section of *In Parenthesis*, Jones's poem is written out of an urgent need to remember the dead and their past in a time when that legacy may no longer be appreciated. The narrator speaks as a witness, making the memorial that there was "no one" to make there on the field. But the narrator of *In Parenthesis* recalls not the individual heroism of men fighting in a noble cause, the traditional subject of war literature, but the ways in which his companions tried to salvage some remnants of order and humanity from the chaos of the western front. The poem as a whole shows the poet at work as he consciously fashions a shape out of these remnants—the matter of Wales, the "humane . . . paraphernalia" assembled by the men (14), the memories and conversations and recollections that kept their lives tolerable in impossible circumstances. Jones refers to this process when he writes in the preface that he is making a "shape in words" (x).

Although *In Parenthesis* offers no solutions to the modern dilemma of "past consciousness living in the present," it also refuses to accept as inevitable a change in human consciousness that corresponds to some overwhelming external decadence. In this sense it contrasts significantly with Eliot's *Waste Land*, a work whose influence on *In Parenthesis* Jones acknowledged (*DGC*, 188–90). The uniqueness of the act of remembering that *In Parenthesis* presents can be seen clearly if we compare his use of the common modernist technique of allusion with Eliot's use of a similar technique in *The Waste Land*.

In lamenting the decay of civilization, *The Waste Land* depicts a corresponding shrinking of humanity's capacity for communication and love. The characters and speakers in *The Waste Land* are the "hollow men" of the modern world. Their isolation—both from past tradition and from one another—is often highlighted by Eliot's use of literary allusion. The beginning of "The Fire Sermon" (ll. 173–84), for example, depends on an allusion to Spenser's "Prothalamion," and in evoking this poem and the cultural attitudes toward love that fostered it, *The Waste Land* shows how irrevocably the Spenserian vision has been altered by twentieth-century consciousness. The allusion here to the "Prothalamion," a song in praise of ordered courtly love and marriage, stresses the squalor of the modern London landscape and the bankruptcy of broken human relationships, two themes that haunt Eliot's poem (Eliot 1971, 42). It underscores a radical change in human sensibility. Spenser's refrain "sweet Thames! run softly, till I end my song" (l. 18) anticipated a marriage, so the allusion to his "sweet Thames" evokes a whole body of conventions that once ordered human lovemaking from courtship through marriage. In contrast, the speaker of *The Waste Land* looks for evidence of love in the littered industrial river, and the "nymphs" of the Spenserian pastoral tradition, now transformed into London shopgirls courted by "the loitering heirs of city directors," "are departed" (ll. 179–81). By juxtaposing the mythic figures with the bureaucratic stamp "Departed: left no address," Eliot stresses the utter disappearance of past sources of value from the modern scene (l. 181). In short, the allusions in this passage point to the contrast between the refined courtship traditions of the past and the sordidness of modern broken relationships—a theme played out later in the same section in Teiresias's account of the encounter between the typist and the "young man carbuncular" (ll. 215–55). The biblical allusion at line 183, "by the waters of Leman I sat down and wept" (which evokes Psalm 137, the same psalm mentioned in Jones's "Past and Present" as epitomizing the modern sense of exile), conflates the theme of exile with the speaker's more personal alienation from love. By bringing together the consciousness of his generation and the literature of the past, Eliot uses the past to criticize the decadence of human relationships and emotions in his time.

Jones, a great admirer of *The Waste Land*, also uses allusion to comment ironically on the modern predicament. Like Eliot, he recognizes the "new and strange direction of the mind" that the modern world seems to require (*IP*, xiv). The irony of *In Parenthesis*, however, is directed not against human relationships but against a civilization that inhibits the basic and still persistent human impulses to make signs and to remember the past. Jones focuses on the contrast between a human consciousness that continues almost unchanged from past to present and a present environment that threatens and ridicules any sense of continuity. Allusions to past heroic literature in Jones's poem often point up the impersonal character of this war as compared to other wars, but the men's historical sense appears as a kind of desperate, perhaps futile, effort to maintain some sense of a persistent and coherent human consciousness. Sometimes this leads to striking, deliberately incongruous associations.

In "King Pellam's Launde," for example, the evils of chemical warfare evoke the Boar Twrch Trwyth, a legendary evil from Welsh folklore described in *The Mabinogion*. By evoking Twrch Trwyth and comparing the destruction he brings to that brought by mortar shells, Jones successfully conveys the horror of experience in the trenches. Yet the allusion is also somehow bleakly reassuring, if only because the tradition has provided an image to express this horror. The allusion to the Boar Trwyth shifts rather suddenly from describing the twentieth-century battle scene to evoking this legend from the distant Welsh past, which is curiously appropriate to the present scene. Beginning in the manner of a tale from the oral tradition, "They say that . . . ," the speaker tells of the Boar from the story *Culhwch ac Olwen,* in *The Mabinogion,* who rooted up the land and, in so doing, released poisons that indifferently destroyed innocent men:

> They say that when the Boar Trwyth broke the land, by Esgier Oervel, with a fifth part of Ireland; who in his going by destroyed indifferently, men and animals, and the King's son there, Llaesgeven who was good for no one, got off without a scratch, to come safe home again. The ingenious Menw, despite his craft, was a sick man all his life after because of the poisons loosed. The two auxiliaries who were swift and useful were not seen again after that passage, when the quiet came again with the sudden cessation—in the tensioned silence afterwards you couldn't find a rag of them—only someone complaining under a broken revetting-frame. (86)

The Boar represented a destructive natural force in the world of Arthurian legend, and he was defeated by the men of Britain under Arthur's leadership, in a legend that in some ways parallels better-known folk tales and fertility myths about the restoration of the land.[11]

By comparing the natural destructive forces represented by the Boar Trwyth with the unnatural destruction brought about by human-made shells, *In Parenthesis* underscores at once a break and a continuity between past and present consciousness. On the one hand, the juxtaposition of the chemical shell with the poisons released from the land relies on a questionable parallel, much like the one in Jones's preface (*IP,* xiv) that attempts to link "Mr. X adjusting his box-respirator" to Shakespeare's "young Harry with his beaver on." On the other hand, the human experiences in the two stories remain analogous, just as Jones sees a continuity between Bardolph's farewell to Mistress Quickly in *Henry V* and the soldiers leaving Victoria Station in 1914. In both the Arthurian myth and the contemporary battle, we experience the indifferent destruction of good men by forces beyond their control. The illness of Menw, who was "a sick man all his life after because of the poisons loosed," foreshadows the illnesses, both physical and psychological, that plagued many survivors of the First World War, including David Jones. The juxtaposition of the two stories also reminds us of the difference between the magical and ultimately natural evils of legend, over which no humans had control, and the evils of the contemporary world order, which are largely human-made, yet which violate our nature.

Stephen Spender insists that an important part of the modern consciousness is the sense that contemporary changes in civilization are unprecedented and that if this presents cause for despair, it can also lead to the creation of totally new poetic forms. The war as described in Jones's *In Parenthesis* is an odd mixture of the unprecedented and the familiar, and this mixture is one source of its power as a response to its time. Modern warfare is portrayed as releasing all kinds of destructive forces, unprecedented in their power. Yet at the same time, the use of parallels between the past and present experiences of war suggests that if the circumstances are radically different, the men engaged in battle are much the same as they always have been. The end of the passage on Twrch Trwyth accordingly blends what the poem has been presenting as the soldier-languages of past and present. The heroic language of the tale-teller, who uses epithets to refer to "the two auxiliaries who were swift and useful," blends back into the colloquial report of the twentieth-century soldier telling his own story—"you couldn't find a rag of them—only someone complaining under a broken revetting-frame."

In Eliot's *Waste Land*, allusions to past literature and history tend to be ironic. Characters are portrayed as isolated from the past, trapped in a bankrupt present culture. In contrast, the characters of *In Parenthesis*, though equally alienated from their surroundings, are accompanied in their exile by some sense of continuity with previous generations whose experience has been like their own, despite radical differences in external circumstances. In contrast to Eliot's ironic and desolate portrayal of human experience in the modern wasteland, Jones's vision remains quietly, almost perversely, affirmative.

In his memoir of David Jones, William Blissett recalls seeing in Jones's room an inscription quoting Bernard of Cluny. It read "Hora novissima, tempora pessima sunt, vigilemus" (The latest hours are the worst times: let us be vigilant). In this inscription, the last word, printed in red, was nearly erased. Jones recalled a priest friend who had once remarked, "Best not lose sight of that last bit."[12] Jones heeds this advice, against all odds, in his poetry, where his response to the contemporary scene is imbued with what one essay calls the "optimism of the saints" (*DG*, 159). Discerning clearly the evils of the surrounding order, Jones nonetheless continues to pursue the poet's vocation, without seeing what (if anything) may come of it. For Jones, the poet's role recalls the exiled psalmist who searches for ways to "sing the Lord's song in a strange land." It is reflected in Aneirin Lewis, who "sings where he walks," slogging through the human-made mud of the western front. The vision that *In Parenthesis* presents of the poet who sings and remembers, lamenting the dead and observing "the disciplines of the wars" in the most barren contemporary situation, becomes increasingly self-conscious in Jones's later work. Its implications are explored with a new depth and subtlety in *The Anathemata*.

Chapter 4

"Making This Thing Other":
The Anathemata

The makers and rememberers of *In Parenthesis* focus our attention on the acts of people who are expressing their fundamental nature as sign-makers or sacramentalists. Their actions anticipate the central theme and the dominant poetic mode of *The Anathemata*. In its core of themes and in its formal procedures, this poem repeatedly displays itself as material and sign shaped by the history of humanity as a sign-making species. Everywhere, it bears the mark of its maker as a member of humanity and even of its audience as members of a human community of sign-makers, a "we" aware of "our" nature as sacramental creatures.

This is indisputably a demanding poem, and it requires time and patience to appreciate the form that Jones builds out of his particular *materia poetica*. The copious notes provided, as the poet says, "to elucidate a background" (*A*, 42) seem intimidating at the outset.[1] To appreciate the originality of this poem as an expression and exploration of the nature of *poiesis*, the reader needs to move beyond the initial impression that this is an ostentatiously erudite poem that demands detailed explication and a thorough understanding of its contents. The impression that the reader needs a vast store of knowledge of Western culture, of Catholic theology, of Welsh mythology, even to approach this poem has been supported, often unintentionally, by a number of commentaries and detailed readings of the poem, many of which enhance our understanding of the materials with which Jones was working. An unfortunate and largely unintended result of all this explication has been a somewhat limited focus among Jones scholars on what the poem is about, at the expense of the more interesting question of what the poet is about in producing a text of this kind at his particular moment in history.

Jones warns against this approach to his work in his preface to the poem.

My intention has not been to "edify" (in the secondary but accepted and customary sense of that word), nor, I think, to persuade, but there is indeed an intention to "uncover"; which is what a "mystery" does, for though at root "mystery" implies a closing, all "mysteries" are meant to disclose, to show forth something. So that in one sense it is meant to "edify," i.e. "to set up." (*A, 33*)

If he is not trying to edify or to offer an exhaustive intellectual and cultural analysis, why does Jones use materials that seem to require great erudition and education? He claims that he is using the "things" that have shaped his experience. The material with which he works is curiously accidental, even personal. The poem, he insists, is about

one's own "thing," which *res* is unavoidably part and parcel of the Western Christian *res,* as inherited by a person whose perceptions are totally conditioned and limited by and dependent upon his being indigenous to this island . . . a Londoner, of Welsh and English parentage, of Protestant upbringing, of Catholic subscription. (11)

The content of *The Anathemata,* in this account, comes out of the poet's own idiosyncratic choices. It consists of

pieces of stuffs that happen to mean something to me. . . . Things to which I would give a related form, just as one does in painting a picture. You use the things that are yours to use because they happen to be lying about the place or site or lying within the orbit of your "tradition." (34)

He makes this point repeatedly, in different ways, in his preface to the poem (see also 9, 24, 32, 42).

One quality that distinguishes Jones from other modernists with whom critics have tried to associate him is this peculiarly personal stamp that he puts on the cultural material found in his work. Jones catalogs and celebrates the things of his own culture, in *The Anathemata* and in his other works, but he avoids apology and edification. The poet, he says, must work "within the limits of his love" (*A,* 24). His chief concern is to use what he calls his *materia poetica* as material to be shaped into works of art, not necessarily to preserve or promote these materials for their own sake. The "mystery" that this text discloses, then, emerges in the processes of composition and reading, not simply in a deciphering of the poem's various extrinsic references. The text presents itself as both a record and a particular instance of the activity of sign making that in Jones's view defines us as "sacramental animals" (*EA*, 155).

Jones gives clues in his explanation of the poem's title. *Anathemata*, the plural of *anathema*, has a double meaning. The anathemata of this poem are

> the blessed things that have taken on what is cursed and the profane things that somehow are redeemed: the delights and also the "ornaments," both in the primary sense of gear and paraphernalia and in the sense of what simply adorns; the donated and votive things, the things dedicated after whatever fashion, the things in some sense made separate, being "laid up from other things"; things, or some aspect of them, that partake of the extra-utile and the gratuitous; things that are the signs of something other, together with those signs that not only have the nature of a sign, but are themselves, under some mode, what they signify. Things set up, lifted up, or in whatever manner made over to the gods. (*A*, 28–29)

As Jones points out, his definition of anathemata as "things set up" corresponds to the strict sense of "to edify" that he acknowledges as part of his intention. Two aspects of anathemata deserve closer attention in a reading of the poem. First, Jones's choice of the term *anathemata*—a choice encouraged by the classicist W. F. Jackson Knight (Jones, *DGC*, 130)—stresses what Mukařovsky would have called the "material" character of this poetic text. It is a collection of linguistic and cultural "things"—set aside to be blessed or cursed—that the poet has put together as a kind of sign, and the text of the poem is a self-consciously material "thing." Second, the poem thematizes and presents the action of the poet, what he does to the things he has assembled, in ways that mark it as a poem on the edge of modernism, concerned with issues of form and poetic process that have preoccupied poets of the later part of this century.

The self-consciously material quality of the text of *The Anathemata* is underscored in the opening pages of the poem.[2] The first two pages consist of an inscription by Jones on the page facing the title and of a variety of typefaces on the first page of the poem. The inscription, "PARENTIBUS MEIS ET PRIORIBUS EORUM ET OMNIBUS INDIGENIS

OMNIS CANDIDAE INSULAE BRITTONUM GENTIS" (To my parents
and their forbears and to all the native people of the bright island of
Britain), printed in two contrasting tones of ink and marked by Jones's
distinctive style of lettering, functions primarily as a dedication. But it also
reminds us from the beginning that words are the physical materials of
this poet's work, as they are the materials for the inscriptionist. The
heading on the first page of the poem has a similar effect:

THE ANATHEMATA

TESTE DAVID CVM SIBYLLA

The Roman V in "TESTE DAVID CVM SIBYLLA" identifies this text as
another inscription, one of the many verbal "things" that the poet is
bringing together in this offering of anathemata. As René Hague has
pointed out, this particular epigraph also points to many of the sources or
deposits from which Jones constructs *The Anathemata*. This line from the
medieval Latin poem "Dies Irae" translates roughly "as witnessed by David
and the Sibyl." It points at once to the presence in this poem of material
from the Roman Catholic liturgy, the classical mythic tradition that in-
cludes the Sibyl, and the Old Testament roots of Christianity, especially
the psalms of David. At the same time, the line functions as the contempo-
rary poet's *fecit*-mark, identifying the text that is to follow as the testimony
of "David" Jones (Hague 1977, 1–4).

These opening inscriptions demonstrate Jones's conception of lan-
guage as a part of the corporeal and temporal world to which human sign-
making activities belong. The recurrence of inscriptions, of variations in
typeface, and of elaborate plays on the etymologies and sources of key
words reminds us at every moment that the poet is working in the con-
crete, the material world, and that words, quotations, and allusions to
myth and legend all belong, for him, to incarnate experience. Themat-
ically, the poem describes a series of makings and offerings that have
identified "man-the-sign-maker" at various stages of history, and all these
"makings" are related typologically, in the intricately crafted structure of
this work, to the Last Supper and Passion of Christ. But even before the
structure of the poem becomes evident, the reader is aware of a series of
opaque and apparently disconnected fragments, each offered and
developed for its own sake at the same time that it participates in the act of
sign making that the poem as a whole records and enacts.

David Jones's favorite section of *The Anathemata* was part 7, "Mabinog's
Liturgy," which consists in large measure of a series of narrations about

the Incarnation of Christ, as celebrated in different epochs of British history. In Welsh tradition, a *mabinogi* is the tale of a hero's infancy. Hence the title here refers to the "mabinogi Iesu Christi"—the story of Christ's infancy. But one of Jones's notes also identifies the *mabinog* as a "tyro bard" who is learning the craft by which the culture's oral tradition is passed along to the next generation (*A*, 200 n. 5). This mabinog's liturgy celebrates the Incarnation by describing a series of Christmas celebrations held at various times and places in Western history. Its catalog of folklore about Christmas night and its references to various Christmas masses in Britain and in Rome emphasize not only the events of the Nativity story but the different manners in which these events have been recalled and re-presented.

At one striking moment in this sequence, the poet inserts his account of a celebration of Christmas in the trenches of the First World War. In this passage, "he" refers to the enemy, the Germans, a convention of Great War literature that Jones also follows in *In Parenthesis*. The account immediately follows a group of "fanciful" folk legends about Christmas night, which it dismisses as "but allegory." In contrast, the speaker here offers an example of the "scientific" language of Jones's century, speaking "factually," "from observed data."

> If this, though sure, is but allegory
> at all events
> and speaking most factually
> and, as the fashion now requires, from observed data: On this night, when I was a young man in France, in Gallia Belgica, the forward ballista teams of the Island of Britain green-garlanded their silent three-o-threes for this I saw and heard their cockney song salute the happy morning; and later, on this same morning certain of the footmen of Britain, walking in daylight, upright, through the lanes of the war-net to outside and beyond the rusted trip-belt, some with gifts, none with ported weapons, embraced him between his *fossa* and ours, exchanging tokens.
> And this I know, if only from immediate hearsay, for we had come on this mild morning (it was a Green Christmas) back into the rear, two to three thousand paces behind where his front *vallum* was called by us, the Maiden's Bulge, and ours, the Pontiff's Neb, between which parallels, these things, according to oral report reaching us in this forward reserve area, were done,
> BECAUSE OF THE CHILD.
> (216)

The speaker blends the objective style of an on-the-scenes reporter with the heightened style of a bard, who speaks of "Gallia Belgica" and "teams of the Island of Britain"—phrases resonant with Malory and Roman chronicle—and who relishes the peculiar place names that the men have given to their surroundings. By thus adapting "factual" discourse to more traditional heroic narrative, the passage emphasizes the gestures of these twentieth-century soldiers. They garland their guns, they "exchange tokens," and these things are all done as signs, "because of the child." Moreover, the incongruity between "speaking most factually" and the heroic style marks this speaker's discourse as part of the poem's overall celebration of the act of sign making in all its variety.

Another passage from "Mabinog's Liturgy" acknowledges more self-consciously the status of this text as artifact and as sign. Near the end of the section, we come on an account of a midnight Christmas mass at which the appointed gospel is being read aloud. The text is the second chapter of Luke, beginning in Latin, "Exiit edicto a Caesare Augusto" (There went out a decree from Caesar Augustus that all the world should be taxed). The deacon is reading from a palimpsest on which the gospel text is written over the words from Virgil's Fourth Eclogue: "Iam redit virgo, iam regnat Apollo" (Now the Virgin returns. . . . Now Apollo reigns)—lines that Christian typologists from the fourth century on read as a prophecy of the Incarnation. On the facing page is an inscription by Jones in which the two texts are joined together as a part of the same graphic artifact. This inscription, echoed by the typeface of Jones's poetic text, works like a piece of concrete poetry, focusing attention on the text as made thing. The poem, meanwhile, embeds the English version of the same gospel text in a densely ornamented and thickly textured paragraph.

> And then he must (after he has joined his hands together) relate in a clear high voice from this Aramaean brut, of how that within six months from the beginning of the Sixth Age of the World, our divine Ymheradawr Octavian, ever august, of the Blood of the progenitress the Purifier, Turner of Hearts, and of Mars Pencawr (the *old* Pantocrator) seated in curia, in his ivory chair, with his cushion under him, in the apsed hall of his *palas* on the Caelian heights that surmount the earth, sent out a decree, demanding his heriots, man-fees and entertainment-dues from the free-trevs and the bond-trevs of all the cantrevs of the whole universal orbis, and of how the wolf-

watch on the lower field (for it was winter calends) because of
certain marvels, understood where to find the Maban.

(219)

Here the familiar words "sent out a decree" are almost obscured by layers
of bardic ornament that multiply Caesar's titles and accoutrements and
translate the circumstances of the enrollment into Welsh, Latin, and
archaic English.

Jones's introduction of Welsh words—*Maban* for "boy," *Pencawr*, the
Welsh title for Mars, and especially Welsh words whose derivations are
obviously Latin (*Ymheradawr*, "emperor"; *palas*, "palace")—brings to the
foreground the poet molding his materials. This effect is particularly clear
when the passage is read aloud. For anyone who has been accustomed to
hearing this text read on Christmas Eve, the words "sent out a decree,"
translating the gospel text ("There went out a decree from Caesar Au-
gustus that all the world should be taxed" [Luke 2:1]), emerge as some-
thing familiar and universal embodied and celebrated under the new
form of an intricately wrought poetic language. This simultaneous pre-
sentation of the gospel word as timebound material and as timeless uni-
versal sign, elaborated by a human artist, is an important aspect of Jones's
sacramental technique.

I chose these examples to illustrate some of the most obvious ways in
which the text reminds us that it is constructed of "things." Jones's pref-
ace, however, insists that these things become "anathemata" or offerings
only through what a human agent *does* to them.

> . . . the *donated* and votive things, the things *dedicated* after what-
> ever fashion, being "laid up from other things" . . . . Things *set up,
> lifted up*, or in whatever manner *made over* to the gods. (29; my
> emphasis)

I emphasize the verbs in this passage to show the close relationship be-
tween Jones's concept of anathemata and his commitment to the activity
of sign making as the defining mark of humanity. The poem as a whole
thematizes and demonstrates the act of offering up selected things and
impressions from the poet's culture, consciousness, and memory, both
personal and historical. Though *The Anathemata* is formally "closed" in the
sense that it returns to its beginning, it also unfolds in linear time. It takes
place during a contemporary celebration of the Mass, between the eleva-

tion of the consecrated host and the consecration of the wine (Dilworth 1988, 157). At the same time, the poem attempts, chiefly through the use of the pronoun *we* and through its copious and often conversational notes, to engage the reader in the time-and-matter-bound act of offering that it displays. In this sense, the meaning of *The Anathemata* lies not only in what the poem imitates or represents—though the theme of sacramental offering is central to the poem's particular assembly and offering of anathemata—but, equally, in what it does with the materials it assembles. This is true of many poems, but Jones's work is unique because an act of sign making is also the ultimate referent of the poem.

The Anathemata opens with the description of a poetic act: "making this thing other," a phrase Jones uses often to define sign making or sacrament. The agent is a figure called "him," whom the poem gradually reveals as simultaneously the priest at a twentieth-century celebration of the Mass, Jesus presiding over the Last Supper, and the poet as maker of signs. Moreover, "we," the assembly of participants at Mass and also the assembled readers, are introduced from the beginning as witnesses whose response is necessary for the completion of this poetic act (see Whitaker 1976, 52–55). As the poem unfolds, the simultaneous cooperation of "him" and "us" in a gesture of offering emerges as a central action. The opening lines focus on the celebrant's gesture and the words accompanying it: his hands operate "under modes and patterns altogether theirs," doing something that only human hands do. The main clause of the first sentence is interrupted by "already and first of all," and the second by "if we attend," mimicking the hesitant, heavily qualified sentence structure of the priest's words in the Latin liturgy. "Groping syntax" also describes well one consistent feature of Jones's own thickly textured poem, reflecting a congruence between the words and actions of poet and priest, whose common task is to lift up "efficacious signs" (49).

The Anathemata begins and ends with the poet-priest's gesture of offering and returns to it frequently as a key point of reference connecting the poem's materials and themes. Thus part 1, "Rite and Fore-Time," elaborates the connection between the Christian sacrament and the rites and sacraments of earlier eras, going back to the earliest men of Europe and to the *fiat lux* of Genesis. It also presents the emergence of the geological phases of the earth and the evolutionary precursors of man as an elaborate masque or harlequinade directed by the Creator. In parts 2–6, the poem conflates the anamnesis of the Mass with the voyage myth of the

Western tradition, where the "he" of the Mass becomes an archetypal wanderer passing through various phases of British history. Part 7, "Mabinog's Liturgy," narrates several versions of the story of the poem's "him," using changing voices and temporal perspectives. Part 8, "Sherthursdaye and Venus-Day," returns to the story of the Passion and reveals again the continuities among Jesus' self-offering on Calvary, his offering of bread and wine at the Last Supper, the gesture of the priest at Mass, and, by implication, the gestures of all poets and sign-makers who work in the material and temporal orders.

This connection between past and present gestures of offering is celebrated in the climactic account of the Crucifixion in "Sherthursdaye and Venus-Day." In keeping with de la Taille's belief in the continuity between Last Supper, Passion, and Mass, this account portrays the Crucifixion as a human gesture that sums up, repeats, and revalidates previous and future gestures of offering that human artists have made and may make. This final section of *The Anathemata* emphasizes simultaneously the specific time and place of the Crucifixion and the essentially human gesture of the crucified Christ as he participates in the order of signs. Associating Jesus with Odin, inventor of the runic alphabet, the poet muses:

> ("Nine nights on the windy tree?
> Himself to himself?
> Who made the runes would read them—
> wounded with *our* spears.)
>
> (225)[3]

In René Hague's words, this passage implies that "on Calvary the God who inaugurated the vision (the coming of the Messiah) is also he who realises it in person (or 'reads' the runes)" (1977, 238).

A related passage near the end of part 8 calls Golgotha the "rune-height," again suggesting that this action involves the making of a sign.

> On rune-height by the garbaged rill
> the scree-fall answers the cawed madrigals
> and there are great birds flying about.
> And (to sustain his kind)
> the mated corbie
> with his neb
> forcipate, incarnadined—

                    prods at the dreaming *arbor*
                                    ornated *regis purpura*
            as his kind, should.

                                                            (240)

This passage is based on an allusion to the Anglo-Saxon poem *The Dream of the Rood*, in which the Cross speaks with a human voice and bleeds like a human body. Jones adds to this text his description of the birds of the air taking their nourishment from the living tree, according to nature. On the facing page, an inscription by Jones of a passage from *The Dream of the Rood* helps identify Jones's text as a construct made up of other texts that we must see both as mediators of the tradition and as material instances of it in their own right. The allusions and Latinisms in this text have a similar purpose and effect. "*Arbor*" and "ornated *regis purpura*" come from the Good Friday hymn *Vexilla Regis,* a favorite text to which Jones alludes at a number of key moments in *The Anathemata.* "Incarnadined," a word associated with Shakespeare's *Macbeth,* evokes other references to that work in *The Anathemata* and points to the place of Jones's text in a long British literary tradition. As the Crucifixion represents a human act of the Incarnate God who made it significant, so the inscription and the allusions here ask "us" to see this modern poet and artist as a participant in an ongoing tradition of sign making. In this limited sense, the poem, like a sacrament, claims to do what it signifies.

In addition to emphasizing its own textuality, *The Anathemata* develops the connections between Passion, Mass, and poem by portraying the Crucifixion as an action performed in time, whose effects continue into the present tense of poet and reader. The Crucifixion takes place

            Here.
            Where?
                            Here when?
            Here at the spoil-dump
            at a war's term
            where the high-flyer stalls
                            after his concentric
            and exact reconnaissance.

            . . . .

            In the wasted land
                            at jackal-meet

<blockquote>
at the division of the spoils
with his hands stretched out
he continues.
</blockquote>

(231)

The Crucifixion takes place "at the division of the spoils," "at a war's term," a reference to the division of Christ's garments on Calvary and to the analogous political situations of Roman Jerusalem in the first century A.D. and Britain at the end of the Second World War, the period during which Jones was composing *The Anathemata*. The military language depicting the high flyer's "concentric and exact reconnaissance" may also evoke the sound of bombers over London during the blitz, which were part of Jones's daily experience during part of the time he was working on this poem.[4] The reference to a "jackal-meet" in the "wasted land" seems to pay homage to Eliot's vision of declining Western culture in *The Waste Land*. Here Jones adds to the typically modernist lament for a dead tradition a sense of continuity of action and intention within poetic discourse. The passage conflates the actions of Christ on the cross with those of the priest following the rubrics: "With his hands stretched out, he continues" (*et extensis manus prosequitur*—see *A*, 231 n. 2). It stresses not a final sacrifice but a continuing poetic gesture.

As a long poem written during the Second World War and invoking Christian imagery and typology, Jones's *Anathemata* invites comparison with Eliot's *Four Quartets*, to which the theme of incarnation is also central. The contrast in emphasis between these two major twentieth-century Christian poems illustrates dramatically the originality and the persistently affirmative character of Jones's poetics. This contrast is perhaps most evident in Eliot's reflections on Good Friday in "East Coker," one of the few passages that Jones marked in his copy of *Four Quartets*. Here Eliot takes the Crucifixion as an emblem for the physical and spiritual purgation that the individual must undergo to reach beyond the temporal to a timeless order. This view is the central paradox of Eliot's mystic vision: true wholeness is achieved by passing through and beyond the experience of the temporal and corporeal order. According to the poem, "we" are not simply "sound, substantial flesh and blood" (Eliot 1971, 128). We are something more (and something less—as suggested by the image of "garlic and sapphires in the mud" in "Burnt Norton" [Eliot 1971, 118]). Yet the only means of access to the spiritual dimension is through the flesh. Hence the paradox of Good Friday is that bodily suffering, which would seem to contradict the existence of a spiritual order, becomes the means to that order.[5]

Characteristically, Jones chooses to refer to the day of the Crucifixion not as "Good Friday" but as "Venus-Day," translating the Welsh name for the day, "Dydd Gwener y groglith"—"Venus day of the lesson of the cross." The title "Sherthursdaye and Venus-Day," the final section of *The Anathemata,* presents the Passion as both mythic and historic event, associated with the goddess of love, and also identified as "venersday" or "Venus-day" by the Roman calendar, the calendar under which the events of the Passion took place historically. The Crucifixion, together with the Eucharistic ritual of the poem's opening lines, is presented as the climax of a love story acted out by the "cult hero," Jesus, within time.

Eliot's poem presents "sound, substantial flesh and blood" as the means of purgation, something humanity must move through and beyond, but Jones's poem stresses the bodily beauty of the Redeemer/quest hero himself, as man born of and beloved of woman—he is "beautiful in his shirt . . . his limbs like pillars" (224). The Redeemer figure is presented as part of cultural memory through his associations with the quest hero of the Grail myth—"signed with the quest sign" (224). Thus, for Eliot, Good Friday reflects the divine presence that can be discovered by moving beyond personal fleshly and temporal experience, but Jones is fascinated by the Crucifixion seen as a historic and mythic event in which the Godhead joins human flesh and validates "what is done in many places," within time and the body, by sign-making creatures (243). It follows, for Jones, that every human act of sign making—including the act that produced this poem—in some way repeats and affirms Incarnation as a historical event and proclaims itself an anamnesis.

Accordingly, *The Anathemata* closes not with a gesture beyond its powers of expression but with a summarizing repetition and conflation of all the acts of sign making and ritual celebration and the "things offered up" (anathemata) that have been its subject. The end of "Sherthursdaye and Venus-Day" returns to the "cult man" of the opening pages, the priest who lifts up "the stemmed dish" at Mass (242). Bringing us back to the Mass table of the opening lines, this closing sequence also marks the culmination of the poem's account of "him" as Grail hero, completing his voyage and quest. Jones insists here on both the particularity and the typological significance of the places where he believes the historical Incarnation and Passion took place—on Golgotha and in Jerusalem, in the Upper Room ("Salem cenacle") of the Last Supper, and "on Uru mound," a metonymy for the "tumuli," or ancestral burial mounds, of pre-Christian Britain.[6] The Last Supper, of which the present offering of the Mass is an anamnesis, was performed "according to the *disciplinae*" of one particular people—the people of Israel—but repeats itself in all cultures—"et *gentium, cenhedloedd,* and *Volker /* that dance / by garnished *Baum /* or anointed stone" (241–42). This polyglot translation of *people* conveys in the very texture of Jones's language his sense of the particularity of the Latin, Welsh, and German cultures that have celebrated analogous rituals. Jones takes these peoples as types of the contemporary Western participants in the Mass, and perhaps also as types of the contemporary readers of this highly self-conscious text.

At the end of Jones's poem, as in Eliot's *Four Quartets,* we "arrive where we started / and know the place for the first time" (Eliot 1971, 145). But *Four Quartets* makes its discovery primarily through the mystic's paradoxical renunciation of the temporal order. Jones's sacramental method calls for a gathering in of the beloved things and rituals of past and present. The poetic language that for Eliot becomes "epitaph," recording a passage from time to the timeless, functions for Jones as anamnesis, transfigured matter that makes present again, in its dense texture and allusive resonances, the sacramental acts of the past.[7]

The Anathemata closes where it began, in the Upper Room of the Last Supper and of the Mass, and with the "he" who offers up the "stemmed dish." The closing lines of this poem once again stress the action being performed "here, in this high place" and within time (243). As the priest lifts up the host in the Mass, the speaker comments:

> He does what is done in many places
> what he does other
> > he does after the mode
> of what has always been done.
> What did he do other
> > recumbent at the garnished supper?
> What did he do yet other
> > riding the Axile Tree?
>
> > > > (243)

The key words in this passage are obviously "he does"; and what "he does" is presented as an open and continuing action, not a closed, final, or apocalyptic one. The ending of *The Anathemata* insists that there is something constant in the gestures of offering that Christ, priest, and poet have made and make "at all times," regardless of the products of that gesture. By celebrating the continuing vigor of the poetic gesture, *The Anathemata* at once affirms and demonstrates what might be called the central tenet of Jones's sacramental poetics. It shows how even in a world that *In Parenthesis* called "singularly inimical" to the production of art works, human artists, including the one who made this poem, continue to fashion and to offer up their "efficacious signs."

Part 2

"Rite Follows Matriarchate": Reenvisioning Myth

In the name of Annah the Allmaziful, the Everliving, the Bringer of Plurabilities, haloed be her eve, her singtime sung, her rill be run, unhemmed as it is uneven.
—James Joyce, *Finnegans Wake*

In the December of our culture ward somewhere the secret seed, under the mountain, under and between, between the grids of the Ram's survey when he squares the world-circle.
Sweet Mair devise a mazy-guard
in and out and round about
double-dance defences
countermure and echelon meanders round
the holy mound
    fence within the fence
        —David Jones, "The Tutelar of the Place"

Introduction to Part 2:
The Maker and the Myth

To read Jones's poetry is to enter a world that is shaped and conditioned by myth. Like the work of Joyce, Yeats, Blake, and Shelley, it directs its readers toward a knowledge of and provisional assent to a whole fabric of mythoi—of plots or stories having archetypal meanings.[1] Some of the most insightful writers on the nature of Jones's myth have identified his use of myth with the formal impulses that shape his work. Jeremy Hooker (1989) has noted the correspondence between the meandering, labyrinthine quality of poetic form in Jones's work and his assimilation of such mythic patterns as the labyrinth and the initiation rituals associated with it. John Peck (1989) has captured well the elusive connection between such rhetorical patterns as litany, naming, and questioning and the archetypes on which Jones's work draws. Jones's status as a mythological or mythmaking poet has raised problems, however, for his critics and for his advocates, ranging from Elizabeth Ward's now familiar dismissal of him as a mythmaker who escapes into an unreal or mythic world of his own constructing[2] to René Hague's characteristic uneasiness with the way in which Jones "by his use of *myth* and *mythus* in connection with the Mosaic and Christian tradition, blurs the essential distinction (to which he was fully alive) between pagan myth and Christian *revelation*" (Hague 1977, 11).

Thomas Dilworth recognizes what is at issue in many discussions of Jones and myth when he insists on the priority of "the Christian assimilation" in Jones's work. He warns that

> Jones is not, like Shelley, a myth-maker. . . . He has no deep affinity with the syncretic mythology of the eighteenth century that influenced Blake and Shelley and survives chiefly in the writings of Jung. Myths are not interconvertible for David Jones since, for him, history determines that one myth takes precedence over and absorbs the

others. Because the Christian Word was made flesh, it assimilates the pagan "words," which otherwise remain mere fantasies—as they do, I think, in Pound's *Cantos* and the poetry of Robert Graves. Whatever the reader's personal beliefs in our culture—even in an unbelieving age—the Christian assimilation is imaginatively possible and, in Jones's poetry, it provides a unifying thematic synthesis which is a major imaginative achievement. (1988, 363)

Like Hague, Dilworth wants to preserve an awareness that Jones, for all the typological cross-referencing and mythological conflations we find in his work, remains committed to a Christian view of history and human experience and reflects this in his poetry. I agree that in this he is significantly different from mythmaking poets like Blake, Shelley, and Yeats, who construct their original myths without referring to any authoritative tradition or revelation outside their work. But it is easy to oversimplify the connection between the unfolding of mythological meaning in Jones's work and his Catholic Christian belief.

Dilworth's description of "the Christian assimilation" in Jones as an "achievement" may be misleading in its implication that the priority of the Christian revelation is a central argument of Jones's poetry, a synthesis that he worked to "achieve." Jones insists that his aim is not to "edify" or "persuade" but to "set up," "offer up," "make over," and in and by this process, to "uncover a mystery" (*A*, 33). The mystery expressed in the Christian concept of the Word made flesh and in the mythoi of the Incarnation and Passion is not a matter for argument or apologia in the work of David Jones. It is the starting point and the ultimate end of his own "making," which he also views as reflecting the common vocation of all humanity. In his poetic and his visual art, however, he reenvisions and reimagines key moments in the Christian story, rediscovering and sometimes inventing new connections among the many diverse elements that make up the tradition of the West.

Jones's re-visions of traditional mythoi evolve and become more complex through his poetic career, reaching toward a greater maturity and deepening historical insight. In the later poetry especially, his mythic vision is ordered around vivid personifications of powerful and unresolved oppositions that have pervaded the culture of the West. In Jones's work, these oppositions often correspond to the complementary orders of value that our culture conventionally defines as "masculine" and "feminine." Jones's experience as a soldier in the Great War and his abiding interest in European military history lead to persuasive depictions of characters and civilizations enmeshed in the "masculine" activities of conquest, assimilation, and imperialist politics that he views as the chief concerns of his era. At the same time, in keeping with his view of the poet as an outsider in contemporary culture, Jones's sympathies gravitate toward the sphere of influence that his work defines as "feminine"—an order that cherishes memory, poetic activity, a love of place and particularity, and a persistent hope of regeneration and renewal in the face of arbitrary destruction. The ongoing dialogue between these masculine and feminine impulses throughout Jones's work provides a key to the evolution of his mythic world and reflects his unique response to his historical moment "at the turn of a civilisation" (*SL*, 9).

At the outset, Jones's mythological imagination draws on many of the sources used by his fellow modernists, especially Sir James Frazer's *Golden Bough* and Jessie L. Weston's *From Ritual to Romance*. His presentation of feminine cosmic forces is further shaped by careful readings of the Catholic historian Christopher Dawson and of the anthropologists W. F. Jackson Knight and G. Rachel Levy, all of whom he acknowledges in the preface to *The Anathemata*. During the late 1940s, when he began undergoing psychoanalytic treatment for his recurrent neurosis, Jones told several friends that he was reading Freud's *Totem and Taboo* with more appreciation than he could have summoned formerly, and his growing understanding of Freud's Oedipus complex is reflected in his portrayals of feminine figures who are at once mothers and lovers.[3] An equally important influence on Jones's mythic imagination comes from James Joyce's *Finnegans Wake*, especially the Anna Livia Plurabelle section, which was an important part of Jones's *materia poetica* as early as the late 1920s.[4]

Jones's three published works reflect distinct phases in the evolution of his mature mythological vision. *In Parenthesis* reshapes in its own way mythic material from his Welsh background and some of the anthropological sources that other modernists used and admired, notably Frazer and Weston. The decisive turning point between *In Parenthesis* and the later poetry comes with Jones's careful reading of Oswald Spengler's *Decline of the West* in the 1940s, coupled with rereadings of Joyce's "Anna Livia Plurabelle." Jones's re-vision of these two thinkers is brilliantly realized in *The Anathemata*'s celebration of the feminine principle in history. It culminates in *The Sleeping Lord*, with a kind of open dialogue between the Spenglerian mythos of history and the "essential Celticity" that Jones admired in James Joyce (*DG*, 58).

Letters and essays of the period reveal that the reshaping and maturing of Jones's mythic vision in the 1940s coincides with his careful rereading of Oswald Spengler's *Decline of the West*.[5] The role of Spengler in the mythic structure of Jones's later work is comparable in importance to the role of Giambattista Vico in Joyce's *Finnegans Wake*. The German philosopher's cyclical view of history provides a poetic structure and a mythic-historical frame of reference for Jones's explorations of the conflicts between the poetic impulse and the utilitarian credos of political empire-builders at various moments of Western history. It also leads to Jones's consistent presentation of his own era as a late moment in the evolution of Western civilization. At the same time, the example of Joyce appears to have strengthened Jones's sympathy for the marginal, but nonetheless powerful, forces that in his view oppose the imperialistic high history featured in Spengler. Partly in imitation of Joyce, Jones evolves the linguistic and poetic techniques that place the female speakers in *The Anathemata*—especially Elen Monica, his "Lady of the Pool"—among the most impressive poetic speakers in modernist poetry.

The last stage in the development of Jones's mythological vision is reflected in the unresolved dualities that pervade *The Sleeping Lord and Other Fragments*. This work presents side by side the harsh "Roman" world of Spengler's late civilization and a nurturing and revivifying "Celtic" world built out of Jones's love for Wales and influenced by his careful reading and rereading of parts of *Finnegans Wake*. The uneasy juxtaposition of these two conflicting, yet overlapping, world orders makes *The Sleeping Lord* a more open and inconclusive work than *The Anathemata*. But this openness reflects the fullest development of Jones's work as a response to what he saw as the deepening cultural crisis of his time.

Chapter 5

The Wasted Land and
the Queen of the Woods:
From *In Parenthesis* to *The Book of*
Balaam's Ass

In Parenthesis uses the heroic tradition to emphasize what Jones sees as a continuity of human experience, especially in the men's ability to make anamnesis of the things they value from their cultural heritage. But beyond the literary heroic tradition, *In Parenthesis* also uses myth—especially the Malorian and Arthurian versions of the Grail legends, which Jessie L. Weston and Sir James Frazer associate with ancient Mediterranean and European fertility rituals—to contrast the creaturely nature of the soldiers with the impersonal and mechanistic conflict in which they are engaged. Especially in the later parts of *In Parenthesis,* the allusions to fertility myths expose trench warfare as a violation of the land and look to a self-regenerating natural order that will survive the local conflict, though most of the individual men will not. The mythic structure of *In Parenthesis* thus insists on a hidden but vital connection between the creaturely order that the war violates and the violent conflict that men pursue in trenches that are also the womb of mother earth.

The basic myth, familiar to any reader of Frazer's *Golden Bough* or Eliot's *Waste Land,* tells of a god associated with the life-spirit of crops and vegetation who is sacrificed and buried so that the land may bloom again. Frequently, the death of the god is accompanied by the mourning of a female deity who represents the earth, for example, Isis, who mourns for Osiris in the Egyptian myth, or Mary, the *mater dolorosa* mourning for the crucified Christ. According to Frazer, the god's resurrection in the spring was celebrated in northern Europe and the Celtic lands by such spring-

time rituals as the dance around the Maypole or the ceremony of Jack o'
the Green, where a villager dressed in leaves and flowers led a ritual
celebration of the return of spring to the forest (Frazer 1959, 121–22).
Jessie Weston, whose work Jones knew well before he had read *The
Waste Land* (see *DGC*, 46; Blissett 1981, 96), argues for a connection
between the dying and reviving god myths and the "maimed king"
of the Grail romances, whom the hero must heal before the "Waste Land"
can bloom. *In Parenthesis* frequently associates the fertility myths from
Frazer with the Waste Land myth, which he knew best from Malory and
from the Welsh story *Peredur ap Evrawc* in *The Mabinogion*. Although much
of the poem turns on the identification between the deaths of the men
and the deaths of cult heroes from Frazer's fertility myths, Jones presents
the men not as sacrificial lambs or redeemer figures but as victims of
a perverted fertility ritual, in which human sacrifice takes place with-
out a consequent renewal of the land, and where the experience of
war, far from being integrated into the cycles of nature, takes place in a
realm apart from and in conflict with the natural cycles of birth and
renewal.[1]

This disharmony between the men's function as modern soldiers and
their human connection to the cycles of nature is evident in the narrator's
meditation on groves, which I have already discussed in connection with
the lyric form of *In Parenthesis*. This meditation associates Biez Copse with
the more universal role of groves in the men's lives and cultural memory.
Thus, he reflects, "To the woods of all the world is this potency—to move
the bowels of us," and "To groves always men come both to their joys and
their undoing." Dominating this passage is the sense that the grove, which
normally represents life, sexuality, and fertility, can also become a locus of
distraction and madness. To groves they "come lightfoot in hearts' ease
and school free; walk on a leafy holiday with kindred and kind: come
perplexed with first loves—to tread the tangle frustrated, striking and
bruising the green" (66). But the groves also recall Merlin, who was driven
mad, at an ancient Welsh battle, "for the pity of it; for the young men
reaped like green barley" (204). Similarly, it is to woods that men "come
on night's fall for ambuscade" or "come, for sweet princes by malignant
interests deprived"—primarily an allusion to the death of the Welsh
prince Llewelyn.[2] Ironically, the passage ends by associating the strategic
importance of the wood in this battle with the plucking of the "golden
bough," which signals a ritual human sacrifice in Frazer's account of the
ancient grove at Nemi.

Keep date with the genius of the place—come with a weapon or
effectual branch—and here this winter copse might well be special
to Diana's Jack, for none might attempt it but by perilous bough-
plucking.

Draughtsmen at Army made note on a blue-print of the signifi-
cance of the grove as one of his strong-points; this wooded rise as the
gate of their enemies, a door at whose splattered posts, Janus-wise
emplacements shield an automatic fire. (66)

This juxtaposition underscores the striking contrast between the medita-
tor's perception of the grove as a sacred place, which "none might at-
tempt . . . but by perilous bough-plucking," and its strategic role for his
superiors as an enemy stronghold, made perilous by the trip-wire and
automatic fire of modern warfare.

The last section of *In Parenthesis* presents the battle for Mametz
Wood—part of the larger Somme offensive of July 1916—as a fertility
ritual that perverts the renewing sacrifice of the vegetation-god into a
series of nonredemptive and purposeless human deaths. Here the image
of the young soldiers being "reaped" or "mowed" opposes the war to the
lost fertility of the men, which belongs to the natural order rather than to
the newer order of technological warfare, ruled by the "draughtsmen at
army." The allusion to these distant technicians also stresses the distance
between the immediate, tactile experience of warfare and the abstract
conceptions of those who direct it. The men going into battle are aware
that they are being forced to participate in a perverse ritual, associated in
this passage with the sacrifices of Adonis and of the maimed king. Signifi-
cantly, this sacrifice is "neither approved nor ratified nor made acceptable
but lighted to everlasting partition" (162). It thus contrasts explicitly with
the sacrifice in the Mass, which is "adscriptam, ratam, rationabilem" (*A*,
49)—approved, ratified, and reasonable—and with the sacrifice of Christ
that the Mass recalls.

This perverse sacrifice is presented from the point of view of the victim,

Who under the green tree
had awareness of his dismembering, and deep-bowelled damage; for whom
the green tree bore scarlet memorial, and herb and arborage waste.

(162)

The image of the bleeding tree, associated with the sacrifices of Adonis
and Odin, also evokes the Crucifixion as described in the Anglo-Saxon

poem *The Dream of the Rood*. It becomes gruesomely concrete several pages later, when John Ball wounds a German soldier and watches his blood dripping down the tree. This event is presented both as a violation of the land and as a travesty of human sacrifice linked with the "bleeding tree" of myth.

> You huddle closer to your mossy bed
> you make yourself scarce
> you scramble forward and pretend not to see,
> but ruby drops from young beech-sprigs—
> are bright your hands and face.
>   And the other one cries from the breaking-buckthorn.
> He calls for Elsa, for Manuela
> for the parish priest of Burkersdorf in Saxe Altenburg.
>
> (169)

The German soldier's blood drips from the tree as if the tree itself were bleeding, so this passage clearly associates the "forcing of the groves" (169) with the sacrifice of the young god who embodies the tree-spirit. In myth the sacrifice of the god renews the land and makes the wood bloom, but in this context, the bleeding tree represents the pointless death of young men.[3]

This view of warfare as a perversion of the rituals by which ancient peoples reconciled themselves to nature is also implicit when the assault on Mametz Wood is compared to the May rites of Jack o' the Green. As the men move forward, using cut boughs as camouflage, the narrator notes:

> And now all the wood-ways live with familiar faces and your mate moves like Jack o' the Green: for this season's fertility gone un-pruned, & this year's renewing sap shot up fresh tendrils to cumber greenly the heaped decay of last fall, and no forester to tend the paths, nor strike with axes to the root of selected boles, nor had come Jacqueline to fill a pinafore with may-thorn. (168)

Vincent Sherry (1982a) has shown how the pruning of natural vegetation neglected here recurs in the poem as an image for the heroic "restraint" or "mesure" of the Malorian cycle, which the excesses of this war have overrun. But a more insidious kind of neglect is also implied. Normally, the Jack o' the Green and Maying rituals are meant to welcome the spring and to celebrate a harmony between human and natural orders. But here the boughs "gone unpruned," the absence of Jacqueline and the forester, and the unrestrained growth, like the unratified human sacrifice on the bleeding tree(162), stress the disharmony between human and natural orders on this battlefield. At the same time, this passage implies that despite human neglect, the vegetation grows back in its own way "to cumber greenly the heaped decay of last fall." Without the harmony established by ritual, the natural order renews itself regardless of humanity, growing over the fallen leaves and the dead men alike. The men are incorporated into the natural cycle of death, decay, and renewal, but without the human acquiescence that would be implied by ritual.

In Parenthesis embodies this inevitably triumphant natural order in a series of mythic female figures who incarnate both the redemptive and the demonic aspects of the natural cycle of life and death. The poem's frequent use of sexual imagery and fantasy may reflect the enforced celibacy of military life (see Dilworth 1988, 83–84), but the most powerful feminine influences in the mythic world of *In Parenthesis* are those who offer maternal and nurturing protection rather than explicitly sexual comfort. Most prominent among these are the moon, whose maternal presence dominates the night march of part 3, "Starlit Order," and the Queen of the Woods, who appears at the end of part 7 to honor the men killed in battle. By opposing these maternal figures to the masculine activities of warfare, Jones manages to emphasize again the men's creaturely characteristics and their sacramental impulses, as opposed to the mechanical order of the trenches in which they serve, and in which many will die. In the Queen of the Woods, he reveals a connection between the creaturely order, dominated by feminine presences, and the poetic impulse reflected in the songs of Aneirin Lewis and in the commemorating gesture that closes the poem.

The silver moonlight pervading "Starlit Order" recalls the "moving moon" of Coleridge's *Rime of the Ancient Mariner* (l. 263), whose light initiated the Mariner's redemption. In Jones's poem, the moonlight evokes a maternal presence that transfigures the wasted land, even though the flickering of this light as the moon moves among clouds is also taken as a sign of her capriciousness. This dual conception of the moon reflects the men's sense of their own insecurity in this wasteland, away from mothers, sisters, and other beneficent female figures of whom the moonlight reminds them. One passage contrasts the moon's transfiguring and redeeming properties with the harsher reality of the war gear that her light illuminates.

She drives swift and immaculate out over, free of these obscuring waters;
frets their fringes splendid.
A silver hurrying to silver this waste
silver for bolt-shoulders
silver for butt-heel-irons
silver beams search the interstices, play for breech-blocks underneath the
counterfeiting bower-sway; make-believe a silver scar with drenched tree-
wound; silver-trace a festooned slack; faery-bright a filigree with gooseber-
ries and picket-irons—grace this mauled earth—
transfigure our infirmity—
shine on us.

                                                              (34-35)

The moon sustains the childlike and imaginative side of the men, which
their role as soldiers requires them to suppress. Like a mother soothing a
frightened child, she transforms the paraphernalia of war into a benefi-
cent make-believe world. The prayer to "transfigure our infirmity" recog-
nizes in her a grace-bringing power, associated, like the Ancient Mariner's
moon, with the Virgin Mary. The next line, "I want you to play with / and
the stars as well," echoes a remembered lullaby, once again stressing the
moon's maternal role from the men's point of view.

The moon, however, is not a reliable presence. She appears and disap-
pears capriciously. A few lines before this passage, when the moon is
hidden behind a cloud, John Ball reflects, "There's no kind light to lead:
you go like a motherless child" (34). Later, a soldier praises the mother or
sister or lover who has made him a comforter: "The precious—she's
made it of double warp" (35). "Starlit Order" is filled with nostalgic
evocations of nurturing figures left behind in England. Even their of-
ficers, as if sensing this nostalgia, coax the soldiers along with mothering,
if ironically intended, words: "not far now little children—try to keep the
pace" (41). John Ball's musings also connect the moon to the pre-
Christian earth goddesses described by Frazer (1966) and depicted here
as foreshadowings of the cult of Mary in the Christian West.

Once when her capricious shining, when she briefly aided them,
John Ball raised up his head:
In the cleft of the rock they served Her in anticipation—and over
the hill-country that per-bright Shiner stood for Her rod-budding
(he kept his eyes toward the swift modulations of the sky, heaven
itinerant hurrying with his thought hasting)—but that was a bugger
of a time ago. (39)

The association of female mythic figures with caves, and of pre-Christian cave rites surrounding the birth of gods with the tradition of the Nativity, is described in Christopher Dawson's *Age of the Gods* (1928; see also *IP,* 196 n. 22). But from a masculine point of view, the goddess has other qualities that are less reassuring. One is the inscrutable mystery of female sexuality associated with the Sibyl. Another is the status of mother earth not only as a place of birth but as a place of death (180–81), which makes her seem a sinister and arbitrary power to the celibate men who face death in battle throughout *In Parenthesis.*

Part 7 stresses this darker side of the female power by associating the trenches themselves with the womb of mother earth, alluding at the same time to her sexual receptiveness as the "maiden of the digged places" (176). Thus, "Ball pressed his body to the earth and the white chalk womb to mother him" (154). Elsewhere, the men caress or "curroodle" mother earth (176). In battle, the soldiers pray for a refuge that for most turns out to be death itself.

> Maiden of the digged places
>   let our cry come unto thee,
> *Mam,* moder, mother of me
> Mother of Christ under the tree
> reduce our dimensional vulnerability to the minimum—
> cover the spines of us
> let us creep back dark-bellied where he can't see
> don't let it.
> There, there, it can't, won't hurt—nothing
> shall harm my beautiful.
>
>   (176–77)

Here, as in every one of Jones's published volumes, men in situations of extremity pray for protection to a goddess associated with nurture and the cycles of nature. Here the "maiden" is at once *Mam,* the mother of each man, and the Mother of Christ. Their prayer to her ironically echoes the stiff language of military jargon: "reduce our dimensional vulnerability to the minimum." The prayer's tone is plaintive, childlike: "let us creep back dark-bellied where he can't see." Yet the promise, "nothing / shall harm my beautiful," seems treacherous, because the very next verse-paragraph records the same men dying in an assault of shells. What appears to be a prayer for protection is answered as a prayer for a benevolent kind of death, in which the men are hidden in the depths of mother earth. The womb of mother earth and the graves of the dying soldiers turn out to be the same, and in this sense the mother who bore them is the mother to whom they return. The womb of mother earth and the tomb of the soldiers are united in the image of the trench, dug in the earth for protection and shelter, which becomes a common grave for most of the men.[4]

During the battle of Mametz Wood recounted in part 7, the wounded John Ball must discard his rifle to save his life. John Ball's military training has taught him to view his rifle as a surrogate wife, mother, and mistress. He has learned to sublimate his sexual desire and his boyish wish for feminine comfort and protection into a will to protect and defend. Wounded and encumbered by his rifle, John Ball nonetheless hesitates to cast off his burden, though it hangs around his neck like the Albatross in Coleridge's poem (ll. 141–42) — "the Mariner's white oblation" (*IP,* 184). He recalls his training sergeant's speech about the rifle.

> Marry it man! Marry it!
> Cherish her, she's your very own.
> ·
>   Fondle it like a granny—talk to it—consider it as you would a friend. . . .
>   You've known her hot and cold
> You would choose her from among many.
> You know her by her bias, and by her exact error at 300, and by the deep scar
> at the small, by the fair flaw in the grain, above the lower sling-swivel—
> but leave it under the oak.
>
> (183–84)

This passage recalls the soldier's deep and genuine attachment to his rifle, even as it demonstrates the sublimation of sexual desire into battle readiness that war demands. To leave the rifle behind entails a kind of surrender and abandonment. But the passage also presents the rifle as a female figure that the men could control, cherish, and even marry. In that sense, its companionship was supposed to give them a sense of control over the field of battle, a control that the men have lost at this stage of the conflict in Mametz Wood.

The soldiers' ambivalence toward a female power who simultaneously embodies maternal solace and death finds more pointed expression in the complimentary figures of Sweet Sister Death and the Queen of the Woods, who haunt the battlefield at the beginning and end of part 7. These two figures correspond to the polar images of demon and angel that feminist criticism has recognized as a commonplace among Western representations of femaleness.[5] In Jones, both figures are also associated with the inevitability and randomness of death in battle, and both connect this manner of death to the persistence of the natural cycle and to images of renewal and continuity that transcend the paltry concerns of a "masculine" war.

The demonic aspect of this natural cycle is personified in the figure of Sweet Sister Death in part 7, the harlot who snatches men impudently and capriciously from life.[6]

> . . . —howsoever they may howl for their virginity
> she holds them—who impinge less on space
> sink limply to a heap
> nourish a lesser category of being
> like those other who fructify the land
>
> (162–63)

Paradoxically, the strumpet death is also allied with more positive processes of renewal and continuity associated with the ancient earth goddesses. "Those other who fructify the land" include the heroes of Arthurian romance—Tristram, Lamorak de Galis, Balin and Balan,

> and all the rest—so many without memento
> beneath the tumuli on the high hills
> and under the harvest places.
>
> (163)

The dead here join the buried heroes of Celtic legend, who will return one day to restore the ancient ways. This Welsh myth rests on a faith in the cycles of nature, which continue unimpeded by human history, and which are suggested here by the "harvest places." Despite the men's revulsion as they "howl for their virginity" before Sweet Sister Death, she remains at once mistress and mother. Her embrace draws them, despite themselves, into a cycle of renewal that transcends the fortunes of battle and the arbitrary victories of the war.

The Queen of the Woods, who mourns the dead at the end of *In Parenthesis,* connects this female-dominated cycle of renewal to the mission of the poet, as represented by Dai Greatcoat and Aneirin Lewis. Unlike her demonic counterparts Sweet Sister Death and Life the Leveller (185), who mark men indiscriminately for death, the Queen of the Woods recognizes the individuality of each soldier.

> She speaks to them according to precedence. She knows what's due to this elect society. She can choose twelve gentle-men. She knows who is most lord between the high trees and on the open down. (185)

Some of the Queen's tributes are surprising: "that swine Lillywhite has daisies to his chain. You'd hardly credit it." Others imply unexpected recognition, as she "plaits torques of equal splendour for Mr. Jenkins and Billy Crower"—officer and unsung enlisted man together (185). The Queen of the Woods sequence, which ranks with the hymn to groves and Dai's boast in part 4 as one of the most carefully crafted lyric digressions in the poem, culminates in the Queen's effort to reward Dai Greatcoat and Aneirin Lewis, the poets and rememberers of *In Parenthesis:*

> Dai Great-coat, she can't find him anywhere—she calls both high and low, she had a very special one for him.
> Among this July noblesse she is mindful of December wood—when the trees of the forest beat against each other because of him.
> She carries to Aneirin-in-the-nullah a rowan sprig, for the glory of Guenedota. You couldn't hear what she said to him, because she was careful for the Disciplines of the Wars. (186)

The Queen of the Woods cannot find Dai Greatcoat, who appeared in the poem only to give his boast and then faded away like the generations of old soldiers for whom he speaks. Aneirin Lewis, however, is given special attention "for the glory of Guenedota," and like him, the Queen remembers Lewis's favorite Welsh parallel to today's hopeless battle.

These dead Welshmen are associated with the mythic complex that included, for Jones, the death of Christ, the dying god of Frazer's mythology, and the death of Llewelyn, the last great Welsh prince, in a "December Wood" in 1282. Like the poet, the Queen of the Woods remembers. She is "mindful of the December Wood" associated with Aneirin's and Dai's Welsh past and also with the *Corpus Christi Carol* (*IP,* 211–12 n. 42). Honoring Lewis for his love of the past, she speaks, as he sang on the battlefield, in a low voice, respecting with him Fluellen's "disciplines of the wars." A few lines later, when the poem ends with the poet's act of remembrance, we recognize the Queen of the Woods as the poet's ally, sustainer of the "good kind of peace" that Jones's preface (xii) identifies as the real subject of *In Parenthesis*.

The Queen of the Woods is the fullest embodiment of the feminine principle in *In Parenthesis*. In the masculine world of warfare and disaccommodation, recorded most self-consciously in Dai's boast, she embodies all that the soldiers miss and desire.[7] In view of the subsequent development of Jones's mythic vision, it is illuminating to look at the complementary actions of Dai and the Queen of the Woods as sign-makers, because together they illuminate one aspect of the dialogue between masculine and feminine aspects of human experience that emerges in Jones's later work.

Like the soldiers we later meet in *The Sleeping Lord,* Dai Greatcoat presents himself chiefly as an instrument, rather than an agent, of war. In the poem, he remembers and tells the tale of what he has seen and experienced. His boast is in this broad sense an anamnesis of crucial moments in the public history of human conflict, especially in British history. In remembering the tragic battles of history and legend, Dai speaks, like the poet, as "the man who was on the field" (*IP,* 187), and his act of remembrance results in a call to understand and make sense of the historical experience of warfare. "You ought to ask: Why, / what is this? / what is the meaning of this" (84), says Dai. "The man who does not know this has not understood anything" (187), concludes the poem's speaker, quoting the *Song of Roland.*

While Dai deals with the public and historical record of warfare, the Queen of the Woods makes anamnesis of the individual soldiers who have died in battle. Though this kind of memory is not exclusive to women any more than eyewitness recollection is exclusive to men, it is associated in *In Parenthesis* with the feminine side of human experience, with the "naturally" human impulses of the men themselves, which the rules of battle have resolutely excluded. In the midst of battle there is no "time for halsing . . . / nor weeping Maries bringing anointments. . . . No one sings: Lully, lully / for the mate whose blood runs down" (174). Dai and the Queen of the Woods together reflect the action of the poet at the end of the poem. The closing act of remembrance by "the man who was on the field" combines Dai's eyewitness recollections of the public history of warfare with the Queen's individual mementos of particular men and their experiences of life and battle. By bringing together both "masculine" and "feminine" modes of memory and remembrance, *In Paren-*

thesis anticipates a deepening and more problematic dialogue between masculine and feminine cultural forces in Jones's subsequent work.

A link between the feminine principle in *In Parenthesis* and the more complex vision of "femaleness" that informs *The Anathemata* is evident in a set of manuscripts on which Jones was working in the late 1930s and early 1940s. Only two fragments from these manuscripts were ever published. They are "A, a, a, DOMINE DEUS" and "From *The Book of Balaam's Ass*," the opening and closing poems of *The Sleeping Lord and Other Fragments* (1974). The manuscripts of *The Book of Balaam's Ass,* now available in *The Roman Quarry,* represent an important stage of development in Jones's thought. They tell us much about the emerging mythic and historical sense that would find its fuller expression in *The Anathemata* and *The Sleeping Lord.*

The published fragment from *The Book of Balaam's Ass* conveys a profoundly disillusioned picture of the later phases of the First World War. In comparison, *In Parenthesis,* with its recollections of heroic tradition and its confidence in the persistence of memory, seems almost idyllic. Jones mentions this contrast between the earlier and later phases in the preface to *In Parenthesis,* but the tone of "From *The Book of Balaam's Ass*" reflects far more bitterly than the earlier work what Paul Fussell describes as the image of "time divided abruptly" that pervades the poetry of the Great War (1975, 81). Parts of the published fragment, and an even greater portion of the unpublished manuscripts, show Jones struggling with conflicting portrayals of the feminine powers that condition the poet's intolerable historical situation.

Jones's brief introductory note to the published fragment explains that it was written in the 1930s and 1940s and that it "evokes conversations of 1919–20" and shows connections between *In Parenthesis* and *The Anathemata* (*SL,* 97). Some longer and much more informative drafts of this introductory note have survived, many of them depicting vividly the desolation of the muddy landscape where Jones's unit was involved in part of the disastrous Passchendaele offensive in 1916. One draft explicitly contrasts Jones's reaction to that later phase of the war with the ambience and the mythic motifs that *In Parenthesis* associates with the battle of the Somme.

There was no "Queen of the Woods" to garland the dead at Passchendaele but no doubt her equivalent found a way for Villon reminds us that the Queen of Heaven and Mundi domina is also Imperatrix of the infernal marsh.[8] (*BA* MS.)

One wonders why Jones excluded this illuminating comment from the published version of the introductory note.

The contrast between the battlefield of *In Parenthesis* and that of *The Book of Balaam's Ass* corresponds to Jones's belief that the poet's isolation from the contemporary world was worsening in his time. One passage from the published fragment explicitly associates the waste and folly of the assault on the mill at Passchendaele with the war's destruction of the Western European tradition, especially of the heroic tradition that still afforded some hope of continuity to the men of *In Parenthesis*. The speaker is a woman named Lavinia, who sees through the heroic trappings of the battle story and sarcastically compares it to a magician's tale and a "bloody lie."[9]

> Tilly-vally Mr. Pistol that's a petty tale of y'r Gallia wars. Gauffer it well and troupe it fine, pad it out to impressive proportions, grace it from the ancients. Gee! I do like a bloody lie turned gallantly romantical, fantastical, glossed by the old gang from the foundations of the world. Press every allusion into your Ambrosian racket, ransack the sacred canon and have by heart the sweet Tudor magician, gather your sanctions and weave your allegories, roseate your lenses, serve up the bitter dregs in silver-gilt, bless it before and behind and swamp it with baptismal and continual dew. (*SL*, 99–100)

This skeptical female voice first emerges in a manuscript dating from 1938 or 1939 (see *RQ*, xxvi–vii; *DGC*, 86–90). It may be the earliest example of David Jones's effort to endow a female figure with her own particular voice and perspective, challenging the "masculine" thought-world that has built Western military and political history.

Lavinia presents a sardonic view not only of warfare but of art about warfare, which she characterizes as "a bloody lie turned gallantly romantical." Her association of old soldiers' war stories with a perverted liturgy suggests a profound disillusionment with this war and perhaps even a mistrust of the kindlier vision that Jones had developed in *In Parenthesis*. (In one letter of this period, alluding to *In Parenthesis*, he writes to Grisewood, "My book seems already about the Zulu war" [24 September 1938; *DGC*, 86].)[10] A few lines later, another speaker alludes to the men who died in the battle as "a million and a half disembowelled yeanlings," and remarks, "There's a sight for you that is in our genuine European tradition"; and this line introduces a long list of individual soldiers, many of them bearing the names of writers, poets, and heroes of the Western tradition, for whom there was "no help . . . on that open plain" (*SL*, 104, 111; *RQ*, 197, 202). The tone here is remarkable for its anger, coming as it does from a poet who served in the war and tended to look back on his war experience as in various ways formative and ultimately positive (*EA*, 28; *DGC*, 58). It is closer than anything else in Jones's recollections of the war to Pound's bitter lament in "Hugh Selwyn Mauberley": "There died a myriad, / and of the best, among them / for an old bitch gone in the teeth, For a botched civilisation" (Pound 1957, 64).

Though Jones uses a female speaker to question the value of art emerging from war, other portions of the published fragment associate feminine powers with a more traditional appeal for redemption made by the dying men at Passchendaele. Much of the fragment stresses the lack of cover during that conflict and thus the hopeless position of the men in this new, grimmer wasteland. As they are trapped in the "infernal marsh" of this battlefield, we overhear these soldiers praying, and many of their prayers are addressed to feminine powers.

Only three men survive the conflict: Privates Lucifer, Shenkin, and Austin. Of these three, "Pick-em-up" Shenkin is evidently a reflection of Jones (see Blissett 1981, 133). Shenkin is "the least surefooted of men, and the most easily confused of any man of the island of Britain," and he runs from the battle, the poem suggests, out of cowardice (*SL*, 106, 108). Hiding from the battle, Shenkin overhears the prayers of dying men. As he describes the men drowning in the mud churned up by a still more mechanized form of warfare, the poet laments, "Not a rock to cleft for, not a spare drift of soil for the living pounds of all their poor bodies drowned in the dun sea" (101). The position of these men contrasts markedly with that of the men of *In Parenthesis* who prayed to mother earth to "hide you in her deeps" (176) and whose bodies were decorated and mourned by the benevolent Queen of the Woods. Nonetheless, like the soldiers of *In Parenthesis*, these men continue to pray for protection.

Shenkin overhears a litany of the powers to whom the soldiers appeal for deliverance.[11] The soldiers call on Christ for various reasons, mostly having to do with His human, bodily suffering—"On the Lamb because he was slain, / On the Word seen by men because He was familiar with the wounding iron," and "On the Son of Mary, because, like Perédur, He left

His Mother to go for a soldier, for he would be a *miles* too" (107). These prayers are finally summed up in a revealing passage near the end of the prayer sequence, where the men call

> on all the devices of the peoples, on all anointed stones, on fertile goddesses, that covering arbours might spring up on that open plain for poor maimed men to make their couches there.
>
> On her that wept for a wounded palm that she got by a mortal spear—that she might salve a gaping groin that the race might not be without generation.
>
> On the unknown God.
>
> Each calling according to what breasts had fed them—for rite follows matriarchate when y'r brain-pan's stove in. (110)

Like *In Parenthesis*, this passage associates the maiming of the men with the wounds of the maimed king in the Grail story. But the emphasis at the end of the litany is on the female figure who salves this wound.

The final line, "for rite follows matriarchate when y'r brain-pan's stove in," summarizes well the poet's consistent association of femaleness with refuge amid the chaos of the western front, though with a sarcasm appropriate to the men's apparently irredeemable state. The phrase alludes to the patristic formula "rite follows patriarchate," which refers questions of ritual and canonical observance in the Roman Catholic church to the writings of the church fathers (see *SL*, 110 n. 1). Here the spiritual and moral authority associated with "patriarchate" is displaced by an alternative order, a "matriarchate" that sympathizes at once with the deepest spiritual needs and the most intimate bodily memories of these individual men as they face death. The phrase stresses the desperation of the men's fear and need, and it underscores subtly their status as bodied creatures ("each calling according to what breasts had fed them"), even as they reach for a metaphysical sustenance that seems to be the only kind of hope remaining to them. In its context, the formula "rite follows matriarchate" summarizes Jones's persistent, if here almost absurdist, affirmation of bodily experience and of the sacramental impulse that makes possible this litany in extremis. By its acknowledgement of the creatureliness of these men, this part of their litany also works against any tendency of this poem to leave the world behind in favor of a purely spiritual or mental redemption, as Dilworth suggests it does. In this regard, the narrator's acknowledgement that "rite follows matriarchate" prevents this fragment

"From *The Book of Balaam's Ass*" from becoming what Dilworth has called "a Catholic's Protestant poem" (1988, 356). As a reflection on the fuller significance of the feminine principle that is explored in the drafts of *The Book of Balaam's Ass*, the "rite follows matriarchate" formula also indicates an important direction in David Jones's evolving poetic myth.

In the published *Balaam's Ass* fragment, few of these prayers for deliverance seem to be answered. Private Lucifer survives by apparently supernatural powers of his own, amply suggested by his name. "Pick-em-up" Shenkin survives because of his cowardice. Most significantly perhaps, Private Ducky Austin—whose name evokes St. Augustine, aided by the prayers of his mother, St. Monica—escapes "by reason of the suffrages of his mother who served God hidden in a suburb, and because of her the sons of the women in that suburb were believed to be spared bodily death at that time, because she was believed to be appointed mediatrix there" (*SL*, 110–11). The theme of the mothers at home praying for their sons has already been sounded by *In Parenthesis,* where "all the old women in Bavaria are busy with their novenas, you bet your life" (149). In *The Book of Balaam's Ass,* the saving feminine power suggested by Mrs. Austin—and probably associated in Jones's mind with the love of his own mother—is similarly limited in its effect, and the poem concludes starkly, "But for all the rest there was no help on that open plain" (111).

Despite the bleakness of the final lines in the published fragment, Jones evidently regarded the manuscript of *The Book of Balaam's Ass* as making a kind of affirmation. His working title suggests the nature of this confidence. The story he alludes to here, found in Numbers 22 and 23, tells of a prophet, Balaam the Son of Balak, who sets out on a mission to curse the people of Israel. Along the way, the angel of the Lord stops him and blocks his path. Balaam does not see the angel, but his ass does, and as a result of the encounter, the ass speaks to Balaam in a human voice, persuading him to change his curse to a blessing. Jones associates this story with the poet's desire to curse the contemporary world. His curse, like Balaam's, is transformed into a blessing, because the poetic act is an affirmation in the face of civilizational decay. The only clue to the title's meaning that we find in the published fragment comes in the litany, where the dying men call on the Holy Spirit, "who spoke by Balaam and by Balaam's ass, who spoke also by Sgt. Bullock" (*SL*, 107). The transformation of curse into blessing implicit in Jones's title is evident here. The mention of a "Sgt. Bullock" in conjunction with Balaam's ass also exemplifies the poetic playfulness that is part of this manuscript's affirmation. In a letter to his friends H. S. and Helen Ede, written while he was still working on *The Book of Balaam's Ass*, Jones explains this more clearly.

> I think it is really about how if you start saying in a kind of way how *bloody* everything is you end up in a kind of *praise—inevitably—*I mean a sort of Balaam business. Yes perhaps it will be called *The Book of Balaam* or *Book of Balaam's Ass*. A spot of Job, too! It started off by talking about how things are conditioned by other things—a person comes into a room for instance and all the disorder and deadness takes shape and life—but it has wandered into all kinds of things— got a lot more "religious" than I anticipated in a way. (11 April 1939; *DGC*, 91)

The explanation given to the Edes applies more clearly to the un-published draft of *The Book of Balaam's Ass* than to the published fragment, which confines itself to the assault on the Mill at Passchendaele. In these drafts, Jones seems to have been experimenting with different embodi-ments of the feminine principle in association with his praise of the creaturely and natural order. At the beginning of the manuscript, for example, he introduces a female figure whose presence, as suggested in the letter to the Edes, transforms the surrounding landscape.

> SHE'S BRIGHT WHERE SHE WALKS SHE
> DIGNIFIES THE SPACES OF THE AIR AND MAKES AN AMPLE SCHEME
> ACROSS THE TRIVIAL SHAPES. SHE SHAKES THE PROUD AND ROT-
> TEN ACCIDENTS; SMALL CONVENIENCES LOOK SHRUNK SO THAT
> YOU HARDLY NOTICE THEM (*RQ*, 187)

René Hague identifies this section as an homage to Prudence Pelham, one of Jones's closest friends during this period, who visited him often at Sidmouth and Devon. In Hague's view, this friendship was "the most important personal relationship in David's life" (*DGC*, 65). Although one must be cautious about seizing autobiographical explanations in Jones's poetry, it is interesting that the experiments with the theme of "female-ness" in the *Balaam's Ass* fragments coincided with a particularly diffi-cult time in Jones's relationship with the most important woman friend of his life. The connection between Jones's actual feelings about women and sexuality and his mythic presentation of femaleness con-tributes much to the power of his poetic myth, especially as it develops in *The Anathemata*.

Prudence Pelham first met Jones at Piggots, where she came to study stone carving with Eric Gill in 1929–30. Jones's letters from 1935 to 1939 mention long visits and letters from "sweet, bright Prudence," and their friendship rested on a familiarity and camaraderie unusual between an unmarried man and woman of the period. One gets a sense of this in the one letter from Prudence Pelham that René Hague includes in *Dai Great-coat*. The letter was written in August 1935, during a somewhat oppressive stay at Rock Castle in Northumberland, home of Jones's patron Helen Sutherland.

> Dearest René and Joan, It wouldn't half be a marvellous thing to see you both indeed. I am nigh to bursting. I feel criminal impulses of the worst kind welling up—Christ I could do with a spot of booze. May I really come next week? This is a house of "utter prevention" you know. . . .
>
> *Later.* Evening when everyone feels like cats on red-hot bricks—half the chaps waited in the library and the other half in the drawing room—each waiting for each—going to and fro before dinner. Helen was just *fuming.* It *was* awful and only cold rabbit to cheer you.
>
> There are many religious discussions mixed up with communism and good works. David leaps to doors and for coffee-cups. I have never seen him so agile.
>
> We sit by a small nice pond for a bit nearly every day and complain and are happy in turns—I do think it *awful* that David is to stay here so long. I'm sure it will make him ill.
>
> Too fed up to go on. (*DGC*, 78)

The frankness of this letter, with its irreverent sense of humor and affection for "David," conveys something of the quality of understanding that existed between the two friends. In a letter written after Prudence's first marriage, Jones recalls "I *leaned* on her in some obscure kind of way although we seldom spent time together—we were so very alike in a lot of ways, however incredible that sounds" (*DGC*, 91).

Although theirs was not a sexual relationship, Jones loved Prudence and was devastated by her marriage in 1939 to Guy Branch, a friend of her brother's whom she had known since school days. The same letter to the Edes that explains the title of *The Book of Balaam's Ass* reports with misleading detachment the news of Prudence's marriage.

Dear Prudence got married *very sudden* the other day to a man called Guy Branch. I hope it will be nice and happy for her and make her weller than she has been—she's been ill so long with all my kind of neurasthenic stuff. I love her very very much and her friendship has meant everything to me. So naturally, however much this may be a "good thing," I've naturally had a twisting, trying to get all the tangled delicate emotional bits and pieces tied up and sorted out. (*DGC*, 90)

A letter of the same period to Harman Grisewood, a more intimate friend than Ede, reports the pain of this event more frankly: "Oh dear, this old romantic love, the only type I understand, does let you down. I do see why Lancelot ran 'wood mad' in the trackless forest for four years so that no one might know him . . . , but all one does is to smoke cigarettes and drink an extra whiskey or something" (*DGC*, 93).

Hague and other friends report that Jones exaggerates the suddenness of Prudence's marriage. Obviously he had not prepared himself for it, and it represented the lessening of an important friendship, even though he kept in sporadic touch with Prudence throughout her life. Jones saw much less of Prudence following her marriage, though he still mentions her in his letters to other friends, reporting on her life from letters he has received. During the war, he visited her in the hospital when she was suffering the first symptoms of what was later diagnosed as disseminated sclerosis, and the two met frequently in London during the war years. When Guy Branch was reported missing and later lost on an air mission, Jones shared Prudence's distress and grief. He lost touch with her after her second marriage, to Robert Buhler, and heard of her death in 1952, just as he was about to send her a copy of *The Anathemata* (*DGC*, 156).

Since Jones's work as a whole returns repeatedly to the influence of female forces and figures in the myth and history of the West, it is a matter of some interest that he never married, indeed that he consciously chose a life of celibacy, as he claimed, in service to his art. All three important relationships with women in his life changed when the women married someone else, and at least two of these relationships evidently caused the poet considerable pain, despite his avowed commitment to celibacy. His engagement to Petra Gill, daughter of Eric Gill, was broken off in the late 1920s, and Jones's friends of the period tend to feel that the broken engagement was not particularly devastating to either party (see *DGC*, 41–42). Prudence Pelham's friendship and marriage affected Jones deeply.

His third such friendship, with the Welsh actress Valerie Wynne-Williams (Valerie Price), is recorded in letters of the 1960s, in which Jones seems to see in "Elri," as he called her, qualities that corresponded to his ideal of Welsh womanhood. Her marriage in 1959 occasioned a painful sense of loss that lasted a number of years, despite Jones's intellectual acceptance of her marriage, and despite their continuing friendship (*DGC*, 176–78).

Beginning with his second breakdown in 1946, Jones underwent psychoanalytic treatment with Dr. William Stevenson at Bowden House, Harrow-on-the-Hill, and he continued weekly sessions with Dr. Stevenson for the next two decades (see Dilworth 1988, 205). He was grateful to his analyst for encouraging him to pursue his art to "beat the unconscious in open war," and he felt that his treatment had enabled him to return to work on his art; the preface to *The Anathemata* specifically thanks the doctors "who, by the practice of their arts, aided me to re-continue the practice of mine" (*A*, 39). Hague publishes in *Dai Greatcoat* a series of fragmentary notes that Jones wrote for the doctors during the Bowden House period, and some of these show Jones confronting ambivalent feelings about relations between the sexes. In one note, he writes that the treatment has helped him more in his drawing than in the realm of "ordinary affairs"; then he adds, "But I understand far better the ramifications of the sexual impulse and how the fear of assuming the 'father figure' position works in the most unexpected conjunctions, and I see how all my life I've avoided such a position in innumerable and subtle ways" (*DGC*, 140). Nonetheless, he defends his choice of celibacy in a note that suggests long and careful thought about the relationship between his vocation as an artist, his psychopathology, and his religious faith.

> I do not question the findings [of the doctors] at all about my fear etc. with regard to sex—but I do emphatically say that over and beyond those symptoms of imbalance in my own makeup there is the concept of "not marriage" as a perfectly rational desire in order to pursue what appears to this or that person to be a greater good. . . . It seems to me (and I have all my life been aware of it) that at the breakdown of a culture (bringing great abnormality at all levels and very great divergence of standards of every sort, and economic pressure—all detrimental to mating and normal marriage even for tough and resilient persons) many people who otherwise in a normal world would get married, quite logically avoid doing so if

they feel they have some vital work to do, because the conditions of their time make it virtually impossible for them to marry and bring up a family without at the same time prostituting (or something like it) the work they do. A Catholic at all events cannot marry except with the primary intention of building up a family. Rightly or wrongly, I have *always* known this not to be my job—from my teens I have had this in mind. This *may* be a "rationalization" of my inhibitions and fears of sex, but, discounting those, the attitude seems to me to be completely defensible and reasonable. (*DGC,* 136–37)

Without more information on Jones's biography and the details of his psychiatric treatment at Bowden House, it is probably futile to speculate about the biographical details underlying the fears and inhibitions he mentions here.[12] Nonetheless, Jones's poetic myth plays freely and fruitfully with conflicting and sometimes troubling relationships between male and female, mother and son, woman and lover. Perhaps the richest example of this aspect of his myth occurs at the climactic opening of "Sherthursdaye and Venus-Day," the last section of *The Anathemata,* which portrays Jesus simultaneously as a young warrior leaving his mother for battle and as a hero delivering and embracing his beloved. Here, Jesus on his way to the Crucifixion becomes the Grail hero who "frees the waters" of the wasteland. The imagery here stresses the hero's quest as a rite of passage from childhood to sexual maturity, as he transforms himself from the Son of Mary to the lover of all humanity.

> He that was her son
>   is now her lover
>   signed with the quest-sign
>   at the down-rusher's ford.
>   Bough-bearer, harrower
>   torrent-drinker, *restitutor.*
>   He, by way of her
>   of her his gristle and his mother-wit.
>   White and ruddy her
>   beautiful in his shirt
>   errant for her now
>   his limbs like pillars.
>
> . . . .
>
>   from her salined deeps
>   from the cavern'd waters

> (where she ark'd him) come.
> His members in-folded
> like the hidden lords in the West-tumuli
> for the nine dark calends gone.
> Grown in stature
> he frees the waters.
>
> (A, 224–25)

This account of the hero's transformation stresses his mortal beauty, echoing the love poetry in the *Song of Songs* and praising the beauty of "this flesh" that his mother has passed on to the Incarnate God. All the hero's deeds are recast in terms of his relation to the feminine principle. His physical strength and beauty come "of her," and they are part of his transformation from son to lover. The baby's freeing of his mother's amniotic waters ("the nine dark calends gone") is conflated with the Grail hero's rescue of the wasteland, in an image that identifies the Incarnation as typological fulfillment of the Grail romance. The Oedipal quality of this passage's confusion of mother and beloved, son and lover, may reflect Jones's appreciation for Freud's account of the Oedipus myth as described in *Totem and Taboo,* or it may manifest, as Dilworth has suggested (1988, 204–6), the poet's awareness of his Oedipal feelings toward his mother. Whatever it may tell us about Jones's psychological makeup—a matter that deserves more careful exploration than I can offer here—his keen sense of woman both as mother and as lover leads to an innovative and provocative mythic vision. In the myth that informs Jones's poetry, woman—seen simultaneously as mother, lover, and muse—becomes a fundamental source of moral and spiritual power. Her beauty reflects the greatest glory of life in "this flesh," even as she occasionally embodies the temptations and weaknesses inherent in human mortality. In Jones's work as a whole, "femaleness" emerges as a quietly subversive power, guardian of those qualities in human nature that resist the power struggles and material "progress" of "masculine" history.

Poetry is not merely autobiography—least of all poetry with the objective commitments one finds in Jones. Nonetheless, it seems likely that some of Jones's struggles with the depiction of female figures in *The Book of Balaam's Ass* were intensified by his feelings about Prudence Pelham during that period and by the deeper ambivalences that he was able to articulate later while at Bowden House. The early part of the unpublished *Balaam's Ass* manuscript, in particular, develops the power of the beneficent lady, "bright where she walks" (*RQ,* 187), whose presence transforms

the landscape. Later in the manuscript, the same feminine power is associated with Holy Wisdom and sacramental *poiesis*. The landscape
described here corresponds to many of Jones's seascape paintings done at
Sidmouth in the 1930s, where he spent time with Prudence Pelham.
Other portions of the manuscript sketch female figures who embody the
modern world as alien from the poet, notably the "weave-the-woof-
prophetess" Mrs. Balaam (202) and the harlot "sterility," who mocks the
poet at the end of the manuscript, in a discarded passage that is remarkable for its evocation of sexual rejection and frustration (210).

The opening description of a transforming female presence, "bright
where she walks," blends into further accounts of natural and artistic
beauty—to the majestic tiger seen in the zoo, the statue of a "Northumbrian Bride" in a stucco church, a sail coming into harbor, in a sequence filled with appreciation for the beauty of the everyday, physical
world (187–88). Next, "she" merges with a cow in the manger scene at
Bethlehem, and the cow in turn is compared to Balaam's ass, the dumb
beast who revealed to the recalcitrant Balaam the presence of the angel of
the Lord. Here the feminine presence is the poet's muse. Like Balaam's
ass, she bullies him good-naturedly into "seeing the angel."

> She'ld make a Balaam of you to narrow your path, she'ld drag you
> down on Christmas night into an appropriate attitude till your arse
> reflected the nine Choirs shining. She'ld teach you manners; for she
> has part in the patrimony, her brindled coat and mild eyes sheafed
> and penciled to make your bowels turn like a dark lady, and twice as
> natural, are His idea of her. He hung the creases round her strong
> neck turned like you twist amber beads for Agatha and crystal for
> Lucy and Perpetua. (189)

The association between the cow and the shining lady of the opening
lines is at best startling; it may be too incongruous to be successful poetically. But Jones's point is to praise the artistry of creation in all its forms.
Thus he presents the folds around the cow's neck as artefacture, which
God created as a man creates necklaces for a beloved woman, to adorn
her creaturely beauty.

This connection between the feminine principle and artefacture becomes clearer toward the end of the unpublished manuscript, where the
feminine presence returns as a composite of Holy Wisdom and the muse.
Hers is a transmuting power, like that which transforms the curse of
Balaam into a blessing.

Whichever way you take it, her black's his white—You have to be agile to
trace the fleet-foot doubling Influence. The tare is wheat within your prun-
ing fingers. In the twinkling of an eye the leaden echo wakes for shepherds
and bar-tenders the
Song: Sela.

(205–6)

Here the feminine presence performs the office of Balaam's ass—she
recognizes the angel in the world of accursed things, and she transforms
Hopkins's "leaden echo" of despair to the psalmist's hymn of praise,
"Sela." A bit further on, the same feminine figure is presented as a teasing
muse, whose attractiveness corresponds to the gratuitousness of poetic
making even as she eludes the poet's attempts to capture her archetypal
meaning: "We turn to find Her gone whose types and shadows we served
so straitly," he complains.

But heap the parti-coloured hedge-yield, weav for hair-twine and
for bright limbs bind stars of the field. Compare this fair with that
delight, sing a song of journey's-end. . . . Make harmony your friend
and let her witch you with the jocund sights she can discover. She
knows where secreted, beneath her sister's mantle. She'll draw back
this broidery and you'll agree the mystery is amiably tabernacled.
She'll show you deftly God should be pleased with his latest artistry.
(206–7)

More explicitly than anything in the published work, this passage points
to a close association in Jones's mind, during the period of *The Book of
Balaam's Ass*, between *eros* and *agape*, between bodily love and the divine
love to which human making responds.

The sexual appeal of the feminine principle has a more disturbing,
even sinister, effect in other parts of *The Book of Balaam's Ass*. This is
evident in the treacherous prophet Mrs. Balaam. For Jones this femple
figure seems to reflect the contemporary world's view of reality. She mocks
and opposes the transmuting figure who opened the poem, and who
reappears, as "wisdom's sign" (204), in the section following the "Mrs.
Balaam" sequence. René Hague writes that Mrs. Balaam, like Balaam
himself, "cannot see the angel." She looks squarely at the modern world
and sees only "a mockery and a grim futility" (*RQ*, 227–28). Her role as a
prophet who sees the things of the world as a sham and cause for disillu-
sion is clearest at the end of the fragmentary manuscript. The poet in-
vokes her as he contemplates the grimness of the "Zone," a desolate

landscape corresponding to the industrial civilization that thwarts the artist's search for inspiration (*RQ,* 207–9, 280). This passage, an early version of "A, a, a, DOMINE DEUS," looks at the Zone and sees it as an even greater wasteland than the battlefields of Passchendaele.

> O Mrs Balaam if you want a long thirst to quench after a long burden of prophecy—go to the Zone, you won't be troubled by the sweet influence in the Zone.
>
> Pilkem heath seems fragrant to the memory: her disarray is lovely with the urgent squalor of union—the terrible devastations sing: it would be difficult to think meanly of King Pellam's Launde. But what shall we say of this place?
>
> I said: Ah, what shall I write I enquired up and down. (209)

The passage continues with what became, with only minor changes, the first 18 lines of "A, a, a, DOMINE DEUS."

The passages describing the Assault on the Mill have demonstrated, in this very text, that even the devastation of warfare can be transmuted into poetry, transforming the curse of technological warfare into a kind of praise, even though the "sweet influence" of poetry, or the Queen of the Woods, seemed absent, and the degree of human suffering intolerable. But the industrial landscape poses a greater problem for the poet, because he sees it as ruled by a debased and unresponsive female presence personified as "sterility." Like Sweet Sister Death, she is a harlot, but she has no creaturely appeal to draw men to her. The early version of "A, a, a, DOMINE DEUS" continues:

> It is easy to miss him at the turn of a civilization. I have been on my guard not to condemn the unfamiliar. I have refused the tests of theorists who come with manuals. I have opened my heart to sterility when she said: Ain't I nice with me functional flanks—the sockets of my joints go free of your handiworked frills: you can, given the equation, duplicate me any number of times. I'm very clean very good. All the merchants adore me. I'm bought and sold in the whole earth. (210)

The spirit of the modern world, here personified as "sterility," overthrows the transmuting feminine power with which the draft began, by denying the particularity, the ornament ("handiworked frills"), the uniqueness by which "she" transforms the landscape in the opening pages. This new female figure is universally mass-producible, "bought and sold in the whole earth." She embodies the industrial aesthetic, and her voice echoes the poet's disillusionment.

The manuscript of *The Book of Balaam's Ass* as published in *The Roman Quarry* ends with this earliest version of "A, a, a, DOMINE DEUS," a passage that the poet altered significantly in the later published versions of that poem. The early draft looks to a feminine genius in the industrial landscape. At first the poet sees her as an inaccessible beloved, imprisoned behind the things of the industrial world. Gradually, however, she becomes a taunting mistress, willfully hiding herself from her would-be lover.

> I have said to the perfected steel: Be my sister, and to the glassy towers: Bend your beauty to my desire. Indeed for the glassy towers I thought I felt some beginning of his creature. But my hands found the glazed-work unrefined and the terrible crystal a stage paste if you presume to come to a lover's length of her, no love on nearer acquaintance.
>
> I have howled at the foot of the glass tower. I took hold of her glistening rods and travailed for her adamant surfaces. (211)

This extraordinary use of sexual longing to image the poet's artistic frustration is deleted from the final version of "A, a, a, DOMINE DEUS." The revision eliminates an illuminating metaphor that has important implications for Jones's later work. The figure of the bright lady, a kind of incarnation of poetic wisdom—"We make her wisdom's sign. We honour her for Minerva's special pet. Does she overthrow the nature of a sign, because she incarnates the thing signified?" (204)—indicates the close association in David Jones's scheme between the feminine principle and the poetic impulse. This connection is already implicit in the Queen of the Woods, but the benevolent female figure in *The Book of Balaam's Ass* is connected more explicitly to Holy Wisdom, the beauty of this world, and creatureliness, through the comparisons to the cow and to Balaam's ass. Her opposite, the feminine genius of industrial architecture's "adamant surfaces," is presented as a perversion of creatureliness, a violation of the incarnational principle, which thwarts the poet in his task of transmuting the curse of the industrial landscape into a kind of praise.

But "the profane things which are somehow redeemed" is one of the primary meanings of *anathemata* (A, 28–29), and in his long poem, which he took up after abandoning *The Book of Balaam's Ass,* Jones uncovers deeper connections between femaleness, the creaturely and bodily orders, and the poetic impulse. In the transition from *The Book of Balaam's Ass* to *The Anathemata,* the feminine principle is embodied in a number of speaking female presences whose vitality is greater and whose poetic and mythic implications are more complex than any of the female figures in *The Book of Balaam's Ass.* This transformation, which marks the maturing of Jones's myth, was shaped significantly by his reading and rereading of Oswald Spengler's *Decline of the West* and of James Joyce's "Anna Livia Plurabelle."

Chapter 6

Imagining History: Spengler, Dawson, and Joyce

In his letter of 26 February 1942, Jones writes to Harman Grisewood:

> I would like, in heaven or wherever such things are possible, to hear Joyce and Spengler have a long conversation. Wouldn't you. I expect they will turn out to be the two stars of this period (as people who wrote) on one of those tables of comparative events and persons you get in books for the benefit of learners, in a 100 years time. I wonder if they ever met.[1]

The conjunction of Joyce and Spengler suggested in this letter is not as incongruous as it might appear at first. The authors of *Finnegans Wake* and *The Decline of the West* both offered historical myths that explained and elaborated the sense of cultural lateness felt by many in Jones's time. In his copy of Campbell and Robinson's *Skeleton Key to "Finnegans Wake,"* which he received in 1954 and read at various times in the 1950s and 1960s, Jones marks approvingly a passage that summarizes what he had already discovered about Joyce and Spengler.

> Oswald Spengler's *The Decline of the West* . . . presents a fourfold cycle of history comparable to that of Joyce. . . . The Spenglerian and Joyceian analyses of modern times essentially agree, though the attitudes of the two men toward the inevitables of history greatly differ. (14n)

The same can be said of the Spenglerian and Jonesian views of history, though important distinctions exist between Jones's and Joyce's responses to Spengler.

Northrop Frye has argued that although few people now take *The Decline of the West* seriously as history, its argument has become a part of our sense of culture in the late twentieth century, so that most of us share on some level Spengler's belief that Western civilization is playing itself out in politics, art, and literature. Frye points out that Spengler's vision in *The Decline of the West* is not strictly cyclical. Unlike Yeats's *A Vision*, where history returns and repeats itself inexorably, Spengler's model is organic, allowing room for the randomness of historical accidents and cultural cross-fertilizations. Nonetheless, Spengler's scheme shares with other modernist historical myths—including Yeats's *A Vision*, Toynbee's *A Study of History*, and the cycles of thunderclaps and resurrections in Joyce's *Finnegans Wake*—a keen sense of the "lateness" of twentieth-century civilization. Though many of its "facts" and conclusions may be questionable from a historian's point of view, *The Decline of the West* remains an important work of twentieth-century mythmaking. As Frye puts it, "What Spengler has produced is a vision of history which is very close to being a work of literature. . . . If *The Decline of the West* were nothing else, it would still be one of the world's great Romantic poems" (1976, 187). Though the general direction of Spengler's argument was in some ways part of the modernist zeitgeist, Jones is unique among modernist poets for the close and serious study that he devoted to the German thinker.[2]

Spengler absorbed Jones's attention in the early 1940s. He writes to Grisewood in February 1942: "I've been immersed in Spengler. I'm battling with him. I've not measured him up yet! (if I may say so without appalling presumption). He's *so right*, and, as I think, *so wrong*" (*DGC,* 115). Jones's copy of *The Decline of the West,* a one-volume edition published by George Allen and Unwin of London, has inscribed on the flyleaf, in the poet's hand, "David Jones, August 19th, 1941." His copious annotations in this copy of Spengler's work, now housed with the rest of his books at the National Library of Wales in Aberystwyth, corroborates his description of himself as "immersed in Spengler" and "battling him" in the early 1940s.[3]

The Decline of the West argues that the history of civilization has always followed a cyclical pattern, beginning with the first stirrings of culture growing out of a primitive peasant society, and evolving through a golden age in the arts, political structures, architecture, and religious life of a people. Ultimately this lively culture declines into what Spengler calls a megalopolitan civilization, where the power struggles of imperialist rulers take precedence over all other concerns. In this period, the arts, religion, and social structures of the past decline into mere lifeless shells, recalling, but no longer recapturing, the achievements of the past culture. They become, in Jones's words, the "cramped repeats" (*A,* 45) or the "dead limbs" (*SL,* 64) of a once lively culture. Ultimately, in Spengler's account, the rigid hierarchies of late civilization give way to a chaotic, almost tribal or feudal, military order, the period of Caesarism, led by the soldier-emperors. Amid the disorder of this last phase of civilization, a new culture emerges out of the primitive life of the peasantry, whose "plantlike" existence has until then resisted the cycles of historical change (Spengler 1926, 1:435).

Spengler's cycles follow a seasonal pattern, beginning with the spring-time of culture, when arts and institutions remain closely tied to the rhythms of the earth and the artistic instincts of a particular people, blossoming into the summer of a mature culture, and waning into the autumn and winter of "civilization," cultural decadence, and the mega-lopolis. For Spengler, Europe of 1918 was entering the late autumn and early winter of a civilization that began with the emergence of Gothic culture in the twelfth century. The springtime of this culture was reflected not only in what Jones calls the "living floriations" of Gothic architecture (*A,* 49) but also in the dominance of a fully realized Catholic Christen-dom and in the ordered hierarchies of feudal society and court life. This culture waned into late summer in the Renaissance and Reformation. For Spengler, it entered its late phase in what he calls the Faustian era, which began after the Reformation and extended to the early twentieth century. In Faustian culture, intellect and the scientific method replace the old religion, and people become conscious of history and destiny for the first time. In his time, Spengler sees this Faustian phase giving way to an age of imperialism dominated by political pragmatism and by moral and cultural bankruptcy.

The Decline of the West appeared during Germany's defeat. Its popularity outside Germany reflects a more general postwar feeling that the First World War had brought defeat not only for Germany but for Western culture as a whole. Though Spengler was not a supporter of Adolf Hitler, much of his work seems to prophesy as inevitable the rise of the Third Reich in Germany, and the Nazis could easily have found support for their programs in many of the racial and national stereotypes that Spengler outlines in *The Decline of the West,* especially in its portrayals of the Magian nation of the Jews. A later work by Spengler, entitled *Hour of Decision* and published in 1932, advocates conformity to the national socialist pro-gram, though without explicitly supporting Hitler or the Nazis. Jones was repelled by the propagandistic and brutal style of this work, which he describes to Grisewood as "less concerned with an analysis of history than with hinting as to how chaps better behave now and in the future if they are to be worth anything." As with *The Decline of the West,* he still felt drawn by Spengler's account of the inevitable decline of Western culture, and in that sense, he found it "enormously interesting and full of true things." But he objected to its overall tone, "cheap and a little sixth-form" (*DGC,* 116–17).

David Jones evidently recognized in Spengler a historical imagination equal to his own, and Spengler's formulations enter Jones's work as poetic myth. The poet adapts for his purposes Spengler's account of the "lateness" of contemporary civilization, his parallels between late imperial Rome and mid-twentieth-century Europe, and the oppositions he discerns between culture and civilization, between "truth men" and "fact men," and between masculine and feminine cultural principles. His annotations to these portions of Spengler's argument, taken together with scattered published remarks about Spengler, help to explain the attraction that so absolute and deterministic an argument could have held for the far more catholic and flexible temperament of David Jones.

Jones's myth intersects most obviously with Spengler's in its development of a parallel between the world of first-century Rome and the civilization of his time. A note on the flyleaf that reads "26, Greeks-Romans" refers to Spengler's italicized comment "*The break of destiny that we express by hyphening the words Greeks=Romans is occurring for us also, separating that which is already fulfilled from that which is to come*" (1:26; Spengler's emphasis). According to Spengler, the classical civilizational cycle had its springtime in the Attic culture of the fourth and fifth centuries B.C. By the time of Christ, under Roman rule, it had begun to harden into a civilization that would ultimately give way a few centuries later to early Latin Christian culture—the first phase of the Faustian West. A Spenglerian view of first-century Rome as a civilization parallel to that of the mid-twentieth century is implicit in *The Anathemata,* particularly at the beginning of "Mabinog's Liturgy," where the short-lived Pax Augustae of the Romans is connected to Europe of the 1930s through an allusion to Neville Chamberlain's vain hope that the Munich accords guaranteed "peace for our time" (cf. *A,* 186). This view is also clear in a well-known letter to Saunders Lewis written in April 1971, in which Jones recalls his trip to British-occupied Palestine in 1934 and conflates the British troops of that period with the Roman soldiers who occupied Jerusalem at the time of Christ. The same letter insists on the obvious importance of this insight for both *The Anath-emata* and *The Sleeping Lord* (*DGC*, 56–57).

Jones's appreciation of Spengler puzzled and even embarrassed many of his friends and early commentators. The poet and the German philosopher-historian differ radically in their allegiances and personalities. Spengler's philosophical orientation, influenced by German idealism and the romantic traditions of Goethe and Nietzsche, often conflicts with Jones's Catholic sacramentalism. Moreover, Spengler's positivistic insistence on the "facts" of history dismisses as futile any pursuit of an artistic or religious vocation in an age that has replaced art and religion with military and technological might. This stance puts him at odds with Jones, the advocate of "man-the-artist" in all times. Probably because of such obvious incongruities, Jones's friend and commentator René Hague repeatedly minimizes Spengler's influence on Jones, dismissing it as an irritating eccentricity in Jones's work. He refers somewhat patronizingly, for example, to Jones's "magpie-like borrowings from the loquacious German" (1977, 485) and to the poet's use of Spengler as an "endless supply of gold bricks" (*DGC*, 115). Hague is particularly eager to dissociate Jones from the racism implicit in Spengler, which such commentators as Christopher Dawson and W. T. Albright criticized vehemently (Hague 1977, 18, 196). Hague is right that the aspects of Spengler that most appealed to Jones "were abstracted from a background that is fundamentally abhorrent to the poet" (1977, 18). Unfortunately, however, Hague's effort to absolve Jones of objectionable views inevitably undervalues the fundamental role of Spengler's cyclic model of history in Jones's vision. More seriously, it overlooks the challenges to Spenglerian ideology that inform Jones's poetry and thought, often in the places where the poet seems to be adopting most faithfully Spengler's terms and models.

Some of these challenges find expression in Jones's marginal notes to *The Decline of the West*. Jones, whose intellectual outlook was formed by a love of the arts and by Roman Catholic theology, could not accept Spengler's determinism, which called for "true men" to adapt themselves to the inevitability of the coming military and technocratic age. His reading of Spengler seems to have challenged Jones to work out a response to his age that would be consistent with his vocation as artist and writer. We see this in a marginal note to the introduction, where Spengler counsels a stoic resignation for all men of his age, the "early winter" of a full civilization. This passage typifies Spengler's disdain for any who refused to con-

form themselves to their "destiny," an attitude that particularly irritated
Jones. Spengler writes:

> We cannot help it if we are born as men of the early winter of full
> Civilization, instead of on the golden summit of a ripe Culture, in a
> Phidias or a Mozart time. Everything depends on our seeing our own
> position, our *destiny*, clearly, on our realizing that though we may lie
> to ourselves about it we cannot evade it. He who does not acknowl-
> edge this in his heart, ceases to be counted among the men of his
> generation, and remains either a simpleton, a charlatan, or a ped-
> ant. (1:44)

Jones seems to recognize himself in Spengler's disdainful account of
the man who refuses to accept the dominant trend of his own age. He
takes exception, however, to Spengler's suggestion that such a man must
be "a simpleton, a charlatan, or a pedant." He writes in the bottom margin
of this page, "He might be merely an intelligent person who knows that he
is living in a kind of hell." He articulates this even more clearly when he
criticizes what he calls "the main contradiction" in Spengler—his appar-
ent belief that "Culture" is better and more natural to humanity than
"Civilization," weighed against his insistence that men of the contempo-
rary age must suppress their longing for culture and embrace the civiliza-
tion of their own late age. Thus on page 353 of volume 1, Jones
underscores Spengler's statement "Culture and Civilization: the living
body of a soul and the mummy of it." At the bottom of the page, he writes,
"If this is true and I think it is, it seems to follow that "man" will be
nostalgic and wretched in any 'civilisation'—Yet S. urges in the introduct.
and elsewhere that one is a third-rate person if one has such nostalgia for a
'culture.' He can't have it both ways."

On the next two pages, Spengler develops this discussion using parts 1
and 2 of Goethe's *Faust* to show how the creative man of a cultural spring-
time inevitably dwindles into "practical" man, interested only in facts and
applied theories. Jones's response to this extended discussion again
seems to be an effort to justify his own commitment to the sacramental
impulse that for Spengler belongs only to the early stages of culture. Jones
writes, "All this again seems to show plainly that men *must* be nostalgic in a
'civilisation.'—only the bastards can feel otherwise. You can't have 'mo-
rale' if you are living a 'mummified' existence—except the will to see the
end of it—to hope for its collapse. It seems to be his main contradiction.

but see 363–4." Pages 363–64, which seem partially to satisfy Jones's objection, acknowledge that the "late Faustian" man of his own time feels still "the mere pressure, the passionate yearning to create, the form without the content." This acknowledgement recognizes what Jones frequently characterizes as the difficulty facing the twentieth-century artist. Nonetheless, Jones's primary reservation regarding this argument appears to stem from Spengler's exclusion of the artist from any major function in the contemporary world. When Spengler writes with typical absoluteness, "Let a man be either a hero or a saint. In between lies not wisdom, but banality" (2:274), Jones counters, "There is the third condition of the great artist detached from 'the world as history' but not in the same mode as the saint, but not 'making history' like the hero."

It is as an artist that Jones most frequently takes issue with Spengler's pronouncements about the process of cultural decline in the West. For example, in the chapter of volume 1 entitled "Act and Portrait," Spengler uses examples from recent German art to show that the characteristic "late Faustian" art is utterly derivative and devoid of the freshness of the Gothic "springtime" (1:295). Jones cannot reject this formulation entirely—he uses the contrast between the declining architecture of the late age and that of the gothic "young time" as a starting point for his *Anathemata*. However, in his notes to Spengler's text, he objects strenuously to Spengler's dismissal of all modern art.

> It is a pity the examples chosen are Germans, because the contemporary, however temporary, "vitality" of W[est] E[uropean] *painting* is to be found more in France and England. It does not of course invalidate his main argument as to the general eclecticism and decay—but it is a foolish mistake and lack of understanding not to admit the real vitality of some painting in the last 50 years—however doomed to fruitlessness the movement may be and however much it is a hot-house growth. "Contemporary" painting has produced some quite "new" beauties which *could only* belong to this particular "late" stage. But the main argument stands.

Jones also feels moved to qualify Spengler's absolute opposition between "fact men" and "truth men," epitomized in the confrontation between Pilate and Jesus in the gospels, and in Pilate's question, "What is truth?" A note on the flyleaf—"216: Jesus and Pilate"—indicates that he was attracted by Spengler's distinction between the "fact man" of the declining Roman empire and Jesus, the "truth man," whose cult marked the beginning of the new Christian "Faustian" culture in Europe. Jones is uneasy, however, with Spengler's assumption that "truth men" and "fact men" of necessity belong to different historical epochs and cannot exist in the same historical moment, let alone in the same man. Thus on page 368 of volume 2, he marks the paragraph that begins "But in the historical world there are no ideals, but only facts—no truths, but only facts." Jones responds to this paragraph in a note that reads:

> These reiterated and vital distinctions which Spengler makes *so clearly* are in all men so merged—I feel he himself is "doctrinaire" and "theoretic" in speaking of *any* given man as wholly of one or the other. Not even the Cecil Rhodes of this world are only men of facts and not even St. John of the X only a man of "truths"—but he's right enough in saying that in our "contemporary" world and more so in future the top boys will be those of the "fact" world.

This note conveys well Jones's overall response to Spengler. Though he appears to accept Spengler's bleak account of the direction in which the contemporary world is moving, and though Spengler's schematic account of the history of civilization holds a certain attraction for him, he is unwilling to adopt the German writer's deterministic assent to the "decline of the West." Instead, he wishes to find ways of preserving and restoring the links that tie poets of any epoch to the values that Spengler associates only with "Culture." Kathleen Raine offers a good summary of Jones's attitude in this regard. "If he refused to worship the modern gods of progress," she writes, "it was not because he was unaware of their advent" (1975, 101).

Jones's reaction to Spengler is illuminated by the writings of the Catholic metahistorian Christopher Dawson, a good friend of the poet and an acknowledged influence on his work. The sympathy that Jones felt with "Kit" Dawson in both temperament and religious sensibility is reflected in his remark to Grisewood in a letter of 1 June 1942. "It's nice to talk to someone whose brain is the right *kind*," he writes of Dawson, " . . . the disagreements don't matter—but the *temper*—the *kind*—the *sort* of thing a chap regarded as *significant*—that's what one wants—and that is hard to come by" (*DGC*, 119). Many of Dawson's ideas found their way into Jones's work.

The title of Dawson's *Age of the Gods* (*AG*) echoes Giambattista Vico's statement "First comes the age of the gods, then comes the age of the heroes" (Dawson 1928, 240). Jones alludes to this in his essay "The Dying Gaul," where he makes Dawson's point that a conquering culture always assimilates aspects of the culture it has defeated. In this sense, the Dying Gaul of Celtic tradition survives in aspects of the English culture that has defeated it. Jones also acknowledges *Age of the Gods* as an important source for his "Rite and Fore-Time" (*A*, 54 n. 1). The sequence on "oreogenesis" and geography in *The Anathemata* (55–80) can be read as a poetic improvisation on Dawson's observation in *Age of the Gods* that "not only the oceans, but the 'eternal hills' themselves rise and fall in obedience to the cosmic law, so that the mountain ranges rise from the flow of the ancient seas, and in their turn fade away again like snow wreaths under the sun and rain" (4). Jones's essay "Art in Relation to War" (1944), written in part as a response to Spengler, begins its main argument by quoting Dawson's distinction between Spenglerian "high history" and what might be called the "hidden history" of defeated peasant cultures.

> History as a rule takes account only of the warrior peoples and the conquering aristocracies, but their achievements were only made possible by the existence of a subject peasant culture of which we seldom hear. Underneath the successive changes in the dominant element, the peasant foundation remains intact, with its own culture and its own traditions. (*AG*, 59; cf. Jones, *DG*, 125)

Dawson regards this hidden peasant culture as the guardian of the most fundamental human values, and in particular as the custodian of religious tradition, which he regards as vital to the survival of any civilized society. Jones obviously sympathizes with Dawson's conviction that true "culture" has its foundation in religious sensibility and that this sensibility is fundamental to "man" (see *AG*, 23).

This premise is the point of departure for Dawson's influential book *Progress and Religion* (1929), a work that T. S. Eliot acknowledges in his *Notes toward the Definition of Culture*. Here Dawson attacks what he calls the "religion of progress" in the West, the dissociation of material from spiritual concerns, which for him characterizes postwar liberalism. Jones marks approvingly Dawson's introductory premise that "every culturally vital society must possess a religion" (viii) and Dawson's assertion that "a society which has lost its religion becomes sooner or later a society which has lost its culture" (233). In this volume, Dawson argues at some length against the historical and philosophical relativism that directs Spengler's inquiry. For Dawson, Spengler's argument is seriously weakened by its rejection of moral and cultural absolutes and by its tendency to isolate one culture from another in world history (31–43). He also quarrels with Spengler's determinism, insisting that because of humanity's fundamental spiritual orientation, vital changes in culture must always originate from within the human mind, not as a reaction to blind external events. In one quibble with Spengler that Jones particularly appreciates, Dawson writes, "If man is essentially a tool-using animal, the tool is from the beginning that of the artist, no less than that of the labourer" (72). He goes on to argue that cultural change begins from the human spirit and is only assimilated into the external technological and material order if it also fits into the spiritual worldview of the people who live in a society.

Dawson's book may have been Jones's earliest introduction to Spengler. The poet's reservations about Spengler share much in common with Dawson's. But the fundamental agreements between Jones and Dawson regarding the spiritual foundations of cultural change also point to important differences between them. Dawson's chief purpose in attacking Spengler's relativism is to support his argument for a general return to some modern version of the medieval cultural synthesis—a new "Western Christendom" led by a revitalized church and overthrowing the pallid materialism of both contemporary liberalism and Marxism. As I suggested in my discussion of Jones's political views, Jones is far more skeptical than Dawson or Eric Gill about the possibility of returning to an older culture. He seems more inclined to agree with Spengler that the value structure that once organized a "culture" in the West has departed from the contemporary public world. As he implies in his essay on Gill, a person cannot "make a culture exist" (*EA*, 289). His annotations to *The Decline of the West* and the allusions to Spengler in his work show that Jones's primary concern is with the contemporary role of "man-the-sign-maker" in the midst of a civilization in decline.

A Spenglerian atmosphere of civilizational "lateness" pervades all of Jones's later work. It is implicit in the setting of *The Anathemata*, "at the sagging end and chapter's close" of Western culture (49). It is even more pronounced in the poems of *The Sleeping Lord:* a Roman tribune declares to his men, "We are men of now and must strip as the facts of now would have it. Step from the caul of fantasy even if it be the fantasy of sweet Italy" (*SL*, 51–52); and a representative of waning "Culture" prays for protection "in all times of *Gleichschaltung,* in the days of the central economies" (*SL,* 63). Yet Jones's poetry and the myth informing it show no sympathy for Spengler's conclusion that "true men" of the time must submit themselves to the inevitable destiny of the coming civilizational phase. And Jones does not subscribe to the racial stereotypes or to the often crude aesthetic and moral oppositions that pervade Spengler's work, despite his adoption of many of the German philosopher's terms. This resistance to Spenglerian determinism is already evident in several passages from *The Anathemata* that allude directly to *The Decline of the West.*

The Anathemata begins in Spengler's declining West, adopting his sense of the derivative and "empty" character of late Faustian art forms that imitate the body, but not the spirit, of the Gothic springtime. The speaker in these opening pages adopts an elegiac tone reminiscent of Spengler to describe the architecture of the neo-Gothic chapel in which the Mass is being celebrated.

> between the sterile ornaments
> under the pasteboard baldachins
> as, in the young-time, in the sap-years:
> between the living floriations
> under the leaping arches.

(Ossific, trussed with ferric rods, the failing numina of column and entablature, the genii of spire and triforium, like great rivals met when all is done, nod recognition across the cramped repeats of their dead selves.)

(*A,* 49)

The passage is unmistakably Spenglerian in its evocation of the "failing numina" of Gothic architecture, once-living spirits of a young culture who now inhabit the hardened and belated forms of a late civilization. Nonetheless, Spengler's account of civilizational lateness here represents not the end but the starting point for the poem's celebration of "the makers of anathemata," who are almost completely excluded from Spengler's vision.

As if to correct Spengler's devaluation of the artist in history, the first two sections of *The Anathemata* adapt the cyclic structure of Spenglerian history to an account of the earliest emergence of human artefacture. Instead of beginning with the major civilizational phases of Spengler's "world as history" and tracing their origins and declines, "Rite and Fore-Time" uncovers the hidden history of humanity as a sign-making species, showing the continuity between this history and the cosmic cycles of building up, tearing down, and renewing that formed the earth itself. Using many of the details from Dawson's *Age of the Gods,* "Rite and Fore-Time" traces human beginnings back to the first example of "man-master-of-plastic," the sculptor of the Venus of Willendorf, a primitive sculpture of a fertility goddess, dating from 20,000 to 25,000 B.C. (*A,* 60n). This passage stresses the particular humanity of this man and of later artists as makers in the Thomist framework "whose works follow them" (65) and who are commemorated in the celebration of Mass that is the poem's ultimate focus. Thus the poem wonders about this early "form-making proto-maker."

> Who were his *gens*-men or had he no *Hausname* yet
> no *nomen* for his *fecit*-mark
>   the Master of the Venus?
> whose man-hands god-handled the Willendorf stone
>
>   (59)

The picture of the "man-hands" that "god-handled the Willendorf stone" stresses the association of "man-the-artist" with what "Art and Sacrament" terms the "supernatural end" of humankind, and the link between the artist and a sacred order beyond "high history."

Another passage, from early in "Middle-Sea and Lear-Sea," suggests how the poem's revision of Spenglerian determinism might affect the twentieth-century poet. The poem's speaker has been tracing the rise and fall of classic and Faustian cultural phases, using Spengler's examples of artworks that marked the height of these two cultures. The speaker watches the emergence of the classical sculptures of sixth-century Greece, the "second Spring," when "man-limb stirs / in the god stones / and the kouroi / are gay and stepping it." Following Spengler, the speaker goes on to reflect that this cultural springtime will not occur again until the early middle ages, "when the Faustian lent is come / and West-wood springs new / (and Christ the thrust of it!) "; and he hails the flowering of Gothic architecture, "when, under West-light / the Word is made stone" (92–93).

Then, in an unusual moment for *The Anathemata,* the poet seems to speak in his own voice and from his own historical moment, a moment devoid of any cultural freshness. He implores "*Spes,*" or Hope, for assurance that another cultural spring will come after his own time.

> Not ever again?
>   never?

After the conflagrations
        in the times of forgetting?
in the loops between?
before the prides
        and after the happy falls?
Spes!
        answer me!!
How right you are—
        blindfold's best!
        But, where d'you think the flukes of y'r hook'll hold
next—from the *feel* of things?

(93)

According to Spengler's model, the last flowering of culture in the West was the medieval era. In keeping with this, the speaker wonders what will come after his era, the time of "conflagrations," the "times of forgetting." The echoes of Catholic Christian tradition in the reference to *felix culpa,* or "happy fall," and the phrase "Answer me" (*responde mihi*), attributed to Christ in the "Populi Mei," one of the most solemn moments of the Latin Good Friday liturgy, suggest the poet's tendency to view the modern problem on a cosmic scale. From this perspective, the present cultural decadence may be part of a larger order that he cannot see. Hope, here portrayed playfully as a mythological figure who refuses to answer, reflects the poet's ambivalent relationship to his time. He is inclined to implore Hope for an answer about the future of the West, but he receives none. He longs for assurance that the poetic activity will once again be vindicated at some future historical moment. Yet he knows that he must work without this assurance—"blindfold's best."

This passage represents the most explicit response to Spenglerian determinism in *The Anathemata.* Instead of conforming to the necessity of the age, as the German philosopher counsels, the poet here resolves to continue blindfolded, though he longs for reassurance about the future. Here we have some of the stubborn poetic persistence that governed *The Book of Balaam's Ass:* the assurance that some kind of blessing must come out of any poetic activity, however grim its subject matter. The blindfold represents not a passive acquiescence to the necessity of the times, but a resistance to it.

The kind of art Jones chooses to pursue in his historical circumstances owes much, by his account, to the work of James Joyce, especially to

Finnegans Wake (FW). Jones's appreciation for *Finnegans Wake* separates him in important ways from his modernist contemporaries. Eliot, while enthusiastic about *Ulysses,* was reserved and somewhat mystified in his evaluation of the *Wake.* Jones, however, says almost nothing about *Ulysses* or *Dubliners* in his essays or letters; he reserves most of his praise for what he calls the objective and incarnational use of language and myth in the *Wake.* Two comments in the unpublished correspondence with Grisewood summarize well Jones's identification with Joyce over and against other modernist trends. In a letter of 19 March 1940, he laments his lack of expertise in languages, particularly Latin, which prevents him from contributing more fully to what he sees as a Joycean tradition.

> I believe I could be a good writer if I knew all about these root languages but it's hard otherwise. What I don't understand is why more has not been done with this language thing—why are there not a whole lot of leaders-up-to-and from-Joyce—I mean the pleasure is endless and the possibilities infinite.

In January 1954, commenting on a *TLS* review of Jacques Maritain, Jones expresses dismay at the "subjectivism" that dominates modernist art and thought: "It is all quite fruitless this subjectivism . . . and, I think, at bottom it's the trouble with Tom E[liot] also. In fact, in one form or other, it holds the field. At base, I suppose, it is this subjectivism that separates them all from Joyce." (Jones, *HJG*)

In an essay on the 1930s, Jones cites the work of Joyce as the most significant poetic response of his time to the problem of cultural lateness that preoccupied intellectuals of the period. He describes Joyce as "an artist of unique qualities and of enormous stature, though so 'cosmopolitan' a figure and highly 'contemporary,' and *thought of* by many as 'a rebel' destructive of standards of all sorts, an enemy of tradition, etc" (*DG,* 45–46). Jones praises Joyce for his linguistic virtuosity and for his breadth of vision, which includes anthropology, archaeology, psychiatry, and what Jones sees as a Thomist appreciation for the particular and the concrete, especially for places and historic sites: "It was from the *particular* that he made the *general* shine out. That is to say he was quintessentially 'incarnational'" (*DG,* 46). Jones appreciates the play of language in Joyce as a supreme modern example of the gratuitous in poetic art, and he attempts in parts of *The Anathemata* to adapt the linguistic techniques of Joyce's playful and parodic *Wake* to his own more solemn quest for cultural continuity. He is particularly attracted by Joyce's cyclic myth, with its returns to the renewing "riverrun" of history (*FW*, 3). In Jones's reading, Joyce offers a corrective to Spengler both by stressing the feminine principle's role as reconciler and healer and by showing how signs of cultural continuity can be discovered in language itself, even where Spengler would see only discontinuity and lateness. Such a sense of continuity may have been far from Joyce's purpose, but it made a deep impression on Jones and contributed to the idiosyncratic linguistic style that serves his mythic vision in *The Anathemata* and *The Sleeping Lord*.

Jones knew Joyce's "Anna Livia Plurabelle" before he read Spengler. He recalls that René Hague first read it to him "in about 1928" (*DGC*, 188), and it remained an important part of his *materia poetica* throughout his life. Jones writes to Grisewood in 1939 to thank him for a "second copy" of "Anna Livia," noting that he has found his first copy after all but is glad to have both a "house copy" and a "travel copy" of the work. He listened frequently to the Caedmon recording of Joyce reading from this fragment, and in an unpublished letter of 14 April 1939, he tells Grisewood that he has "got 'Anna Livia' by heart." Again, in May 1942, he mentions that he has been rereading "Anna Livia." Joyce's text was in Jones's mind when he was annotating Spengler and writing the beginnings of *The Anathemata*.

The qualities Jones most appreciated in Joyce come together in a passage near the end of the "Anna Livia Plurabelle" section that identifies the feminine principle with historical renewal. Two Dublin washerwomen are gossiping about the life and loves of Anna Livia Plurabelle (ALP). Joyce's historical cycle repeats itself in a series of identical returns, always beginning with the thunderclap that marks the Fall of cosmic "man" (*FW/HCE*) and ending with the "riverrun" of history, which is humanity's origin and destiny, and which Joyce identifies with the female principle. The washerwomen's conversation takes place toward the end of a cycle, when the consequences of ALP's and HCE's indiscretions have played themselves out and history has reached a period of moral and linguistic chaos, reflected in the washerwomen's increasing difficulty in hearing one another as the course of the river of life (also Dublin's Liffey) runs out to sea. At this point of historical entropy, their conversation recalls the innocent beginnings of the serie of "falls from grace" they have been recounting and looks forward to the beginning of a new mythic cycle. Evoking the influence of Giambattista Vico on Joyce's cyclic myth, they at once recall and prophesy "Teems of times and happy returns. The seim anew. Ordovico or viricordo. Anna was, Livia is, Plurabelle's to be. North-men's thing made South-folk's place" (*FW,* 215).

Writing in an essay of 1948 about the need for "nowness" in literature that deals with the past, Jones quotes Joyce's "Northmen's thing made South-folk's place" and adds, "I cannot recollect words from another source to express so briefly what I mean. . . . Joyce's five words . . . include also 'how then became now,' and also they include the change of people on the unchanged site" (*EA,* 210). He goes on to explain that the phrase alludes to Suffolk (South-folk's) place in Dublin, which in earlier times was the site of a council or "Thing" for the Norse invaders of Ireland (*EA,* 210; *DG,* 48). The word *thing* is also associated in Jones's mind with the Latin word *res*—he speaks of "The Welsh thing" or "the Welsh *res,*" or the "Latin Christian *res,*" using *res* to suggest the whole body of myths and historical "deposits" associated with a given culture. Hence Joyce's words are for him a concrete expression of historical and cultural transformation.

As is typical of the language of *Finnegans Wake,* the washerwomen's dialogue is filled with erudite allusions and wordplay that reveal that their conversation is not simply about a promiscuous woman. They also reflect on the course of the river Liffey as it runs out to the sea and on the infinite fertility embodied in the river and in its genius, Anna Livia Plurabelle. The identity of Anna Livia with the river Liffey—which is both the Dublin river and the river of history—is stressed through frequent puns on the names of rivers, which continue throughout the chapter regardless of the subject of the surface conversation. A passage toward the end of the chapter typifies the blend of earthy dialect, wordplay, allusion, and quotation that characterizes the washerwomen's language. Evening is falling, the cold is coming, and the river is dispersing into the sea. Jones may well have felt in this passage the chill of a Spenglerian winter. The scene is meant to depict the end of one historical cycle and the beginning of a new cycle in Joyce's mythic scheme.

> Wring out the clothes! Wring in the dew! Godavari, vert the showers! And grant thaya grace! Aman. Will we spread them here now? Ay, we will. Flip! Spread on your bank and I'll spread mine on mine. Flep! It's what I'm doing. Spread! It's churning chill. Der went is rising. I'll lay a few stones on the hostel sheets. . . . Wharnow are alle her childer, say? In kingdome gone or power to come or gloria be to them farther? Allalivial, allaluvial! (*FW,* 213)

Jones seems to have followed Joyce in the "Lady of the Pool" section of *The Anathemata*, especially in his use of a working-class local character whose words become vehicles for the enunciation of more universal themes than the speaker can intend. The puns in this brief passage from Joyce are already too numerous to catalog. The twisting of Tennyson's lines "Ring out the old, ring in the new" to serve the washerwomen's situation repeats the theme of renewal that pervades this chapter. "Der went"—a pun on the French word *vent* for wind—is also the name of an English river, while the "allalivial, allaluvial" connects Anna Livia to the "alluvial" river as it carries the silt of history out to sea. Jones pays homage to this passage at the end of "The Lady of the Pool," when Elen Monica, referring to the ancient kings and lords who lie buried under the city and the pool of London, remarks:

> here all's alluvial, cap'n, and as unstable as these old annals that do gravel us all. For, captain:
>
>   even immolated kings
> be scarce a match for the deep fluvial doings of the mother.
>
>   (164)

The inspiration of Joyce's "Anna Livia Plurabelle" section in *Finnegans Wake*, with its remarkable female speakers, is inescapable in Elen Monica, whose long monologue occupies the center of *The Anathemata*. Both Anna Livia—the spirit of the river Liffey—and Elen Monica—the Lady of the Pool of London—embody to some degree the "deep fluvial doings of the mother," and by portraying them also as sexually active women, Joyce and Jones bestow particularity on their versions of the cosmic feminine principle. Both figures celebrate an exuberance of bodily life that at once enhances and undermines the predominantly masculine political and technological concerns of Spengler's world history. Some of the details in Joyce may have suggested to Jones the scheme for "The Lady of the Pool," though the tone and feeling of the two texts are finally quite different. Elen speaks to a sea captain who is one manifestation of the shifting "him" of the poem's voyage sequence, associated with the early Phoenicians who explored the land of Britain and, archetypally, with Christ, who appears in "Keel, Ram and Stauros" as captain of the ship of the Church. Early in chapter 8 of the *Wake*, the washerwomen allude to a "gran Phenician rover" who similarly encountered Anna Livia during a voyage of exploration associated with human history (197). The washerwomen's hauntingly sensual recollection of a passionate union "one venersderg in juno-july, oso sweet and so cool and so limber she looked" (203) may lie behind Elen's account of her first meeting with her mason lover by the light of Venus "on a showery night's fall in the thunder nones of hot July" (*A*, 130).

Finally, though, the female voices in the two texts are quite different. The washerwomen speak about Anna Livia and her love affairs. Elen recounts her own amorous history, which belongs to a much more specific place and time than Anna Livia's cosmic lovemaking. In contrast to the washerwomen's gossip, Elen's account of her own experiences points beyond itself to the redemptive role of the feminine principle in history. Like Joyce's washerwomen, Elen is only one of many voices in the work that speak for the feminine principle. But in Jones's work these multiple female voices lead back to a silent feminine archetype who is at once mother earth and Mary, the human mother of the Incarnate God, much as the activities of priest, poet, and "man-the-artist" all lead to the silent person of Christ. The ultimate masculine and feminine presences in Jones are more numinous and are presented with more reverence than their counterparts in Joyce. Joyce's concern is ultimately with the consequences of human folly. Jones's focus is on the alliance between human action and a divine purpose.

Although "Anna Livia Plurabelle" appears to be the only part of *Finnegan's Wake* that Jones knew well while he was working on *The Anathemata*, he read and annotated other portions later in his life.[4] Blissett recalls a conversation of January 1959.

> His experience is the same as mine: there are bits and islands in *Finnegans Wake* that he keeps going back to, venturing a little further from them every time. He has never been right through it but intends to make the effort soon with the help of the *Skeleton Key*, which he finds useful, modest, and therefore admirable. (1981, 13; see also Jones, *LF*, 29–32)

Jones's markings suggest that the parts of *Finnegans Wake* most interesting to him were those dealing with the battle between the brothers Shem and Shaun (169–382) and with the reconciling role of the all-mother figure, Anna Livia Plurabelle.[5] He may have found Joyce's myth of Shem and Shaun particularly illuminating as a response to Spengler's myth. Shem and Shaun are the sons of Anna Livia and the cosmic father Humphrey Chimpden Earwicker, and their quarrels correspond roughly to the conflict Spengler discerned between "fact-men" and "truth-men" in history. Shaun is the father's favorite son, the analytic and politically oriented man. A puritanical moralist, he scorns the creative impulse in humanity, personified by his brother Shem. Shem the penman, alter ego of Joyce, is the mother's pet. Campbell and Robinson stress this connection between the poet and the mother in their introduction to "Shem the Penman": "The poet does not invent his verses but discovers their materials in those deep layers of the psyche where lurk the infantile, buried reminiscences of the mother. She is the Muse; the poet her favorite child" (1944, 123).

Shem's poetic talent, concretely reflected in the text of the *Wake*, is intimately associated with the body and is thus an offense to the abstract thinker Shaun. The role of the poet—at once subversive and sacramental—is evident in a self-reflexive passage from the *Wake* that Jones marks on the flyleaf of Campbell and Robinson: "110 nature of the wake." The commentators' note to this passage identifies it as "a statement of the nature and aim of the art of *Finnegans Wake*" (1944, 110). The passage in Joyce reads in part:

> Then, pious Eneas . . . the first till last alshemist wrote over every square inch of the only foolscap available, his own body, till by its corrosive sublimation one continuous present tense integument slowly unfolded all marryvoising moodmoulded cyclewheeling history (thereby, he said, reflecting from his own individual person life unlivable, transaccidentated through the slow fires of consciousness into a dividual chaos, perilous, potent, common to allflesh, human only, mortal). (185–86)

The emphasis on Shem's mortal body as the material of the *Wake*'s poetic art—chaotic, "perilous, potent, human only, mortal"—is in harmony with Jones's belief in the embodied character of poetic art. Joyce stresses the contrast between this incarnational view of the poetic text and the abstract legalism of Shaun, the policeman and scornful judge. The battle between the brothers suggests, as Campbell and Robinson put it,

> that each of the brother opposites has developed only one half of his man's nature. Shem, acutely aware of his need for assistance from the other half, has begged for help, but Shaun, unable to admit his need for the other, yet compelled to protest very elaborately his independence, has refused to collaborate. . . . The female power

clearly supports Shem's belief that neither of the male powers is
adequate by himself. (112)

Jones marks this last sentence and a reference a few paragraphs later to
"the all-dissolving, all-refreshing, all-recreating theme of the mother" that
shapes the washerwomen's dialogue in "The Washers at the Ford."

Perhaps the most subtle example of Jones's effort to create a poetic
language that will convey "how then became now" occurs in the brief
section of *The Anathemata* entitled "Angle-Land." Here Jones traces the
return of Britain to the control of native Celtic and newer Germanic
influences as Roman imperial influence receded. He uses the Latin
derivations of Welsh words and especially the etymologies of common
given names to show the cultural roots and transformations of post-
Roman Britain. Listening to the languages being spoken on the island of
Britain, the poet asks what has happened to this culture.

> Crowland-*diawliaidd*
> *Wealisc*-man lingo speaking?
> > or Britto-Romani gone *diaboli?*
> or Romanity gone *Wealisc?*
> Is Marianus wild Meirion?
> is Sylvánus
> > Urbigéna's son?
> has toga'd Rhufon
> > (gone Acta'eon)
> come away to the Wake
> > in the bittern's low aery?
>
> (112)

The allusion to a wake suggests the Joycean inspiration for this linguistic
demonstration of cultural shifts.

The homage to Joyce continues on page 114 of the poem, toward the
end of "Angle-Land." Jones cites the many British rivers that flow into "the
fathering river," recalling the convocation and outflowing of rivers in
"Anna Livia Plurabelle." The British rivers mingle with numerous German
rivers that have become a part of the Rhine—"Rhenus-flow"—all flowing
out together and mingling in "*Cronos*-meer." This image recalls the "river-
run" of time in Joyce's *Wake*, especially the widening and dispersing of the
waters at the mouth of the Liffey at the end of "Anna Livia Plurabelle." As
Joyce's chapter ends with a reference forward to the next chapter's "tale

told of Shaun or Shem" (*FW,* 215), so Jones's "Angle-Land" ends with a contemplation of the brother-battles that dominate his own "late phase" of civilization, in a pointed allusion to Spengler and to the war with Germany, which was going on during the composition of *The Anathemata.* The close of "Angle-Land" moves smoothly from a Joycean evocation of cosmic continuity in the rivers' flow into Cronos-*meer* to a cold, Spenglerian view of contemporary history and a poetic lament for the times.

> I speak of before the whale-roads or the keel-paths were from Orcades to the
> fiord-havens, or the greyed green wastes that they strictly grid
> quadrate and number on the sea-green *Quadratkarte*
> one eight six one G
> for the fratricides
> of the latter-day, from east-shore of Iceland
> *bis Norwegen*
> (O Balin O Balan!
> how blood you both
> the *Brudersee*
> toward the last pháse
> of our dear West.)
>
> (*A,* 115)

By juxtaposing the cosmic continuity stressed by Joyce's "riverrun" with the Spenglerian rigidity that the sea map evokes here, the poem manages at once to convey the deep pathos of the Spenglerian world order in the poet's time and to suggest other possibilities of renewal that belonged to cultural phases before our own and that the poem offers some hope of reengaging. It reflects indirectly the imagined dialogue between Joyce and Spengler that informs so much of Jones's mythic thinking.

Although I have been pointing out affinities and influences that connect Jones's work to that of Joyce, the Joycean influence on Jones can easily be exaggerated. The feeling and tone of Jones's poetry is utterly different from that of Joyce's writing. Jones's use of linguistic texture and etymology to demonstrate "how then became now" is much more overt and self-conscious than is Joyce's playful and often outrageous and deliberately obscure punning. Perhaps most striking is the difference in tone between the two poets' work. Joyce's vision is comic, often obscene, and always parodic and inventive. Jones appreciated the humor in Joyce but emulated it only rarely. His work is much more earnest in its tone, much more eager than Joyce's to be understood. This eagerness is obvious from the copious notes that Jones provides to his work. Joyce's multi-leveled language complements his sense of the cycles of history as an eternal recurrence, what Joyce's washerwoman calls "the seim anew" (*FW*, 215). Cycles that have passed will recur, in identical form, in the future, and the echoes that his language holds of previous cultural phases reinforce this sense of recurrence. Jones's use of etymology and multilingual verbal textures more usually serves his teleological and typological vision, showing one historical moment as the fulfillment of another. *The Anathemata* does not dwell on images of apocalypse, but the decline of civilizations and emergence of cultures, the building up and tearing down of mountains, and the departure and return of the archetypal voyager are types of redemption, and all ultimately foreshadow a "new heaven and new earth" at the end of time (21 Revelation). Joyce's recurring cycles offer a comic and ultimately absurdist view of humankind's fate. Redemption may come, in his vision, but human folly will always return, and a new fall will lead to a new redemption, in the endless cycle of repetitions reflected in the "riverrun" of history.

The teleological vision implied through Jones's use of Christian typology is at odds with the comic eternal recurrence of Joyce and with the determinism of Spengler, because it awaits a redemptive end to the cycles of human folly and presents "man-the-artist" as the ally of this ultimate redemption. In Spengler, Jones finds a clear vision of the need for redemption in a late civilization, and he appreciates Joyce's portrayal of the poet, the feminine principle, and poetic language as the agents of this redemption, however impermanent redemption may be in *Finnegans Wake*. The originality of Jones's mythic vision in *The Anathemata* is most evident in his use of a female speaker to articulate and reinterpret for his time the Catholic doctrine that celebrates the Virgin Mary, the type of assenting humanity, for making human salvation possible in history.

Chapter 7

"Her Fiat Is Our Fortune": Feminine Presences in *The Anathemata*

The Anathemata owes much of its power to the female figures who preside over its history of "man-the-artist." Like *In Parenthesis,* this poem relies on a complex of myths drawn from pre-Christian wasteland legends and fertility traditions, exploiting the typological parallels between the hero of the ancient fertility rites and the crucified Christ—the dying God on the tree of the cross. But *The Anathemata* enriches this complex of myths through its affirmation of woman's indispensable role in the process of incarnation and redemption and through its celebration of humanity's bodily nature. The power inherent in woman is embodied in Elen Monica, the speaker in "The Lady of the Pool." Her commentary is further elaborated by the mothers, lovers, goddesses, mermaids, witches, and queens who appear throughout *The Anathemata* to oppose, abet, and occasionally ridicule the masculine adventures of world history. Together these figures make possible and participate in the process of redemption celebrated in the anathemata of "man-the-sign-maker."

The Anathemata's account of the feminine influence on history responds to cruder oppositions between masculine and feminine sensibilities that Jones encountered in *The Decline of the West,* especially in Spengler's extension of the dichotomy between "Culture" and "Civilization" to an opposition between feminine and masculine cultural principles. In his letter to Grisewood, Jones writes that part of his discomfort with *The Decline of the West* rests on "the Jackson Knight thing. He has liquidated *Juno.* It is a male thought-world altogether" (*DGC,* 117). He alludes here to W. F. Jackson Knight's *Cumaean Gates,* which focuses on the role of female powers, notably the Cumaean sibyl and the many versions of the earth mother goddess, in the rise of Western culture and religion. For Jackson Knight, Juno exemplifies the way in which the goddesses of classical Greek culture were abandoned or transformed under imperial Rome, as the "feminine" values of art, storytelling, hearth, and religion gave way to the propaganda of conquest. He characterizes Juno as a "fiercely feminine" goddess whose legendary cruelty and hostility stemmed from her relative unimportance in the Roman pantheon. As Knight writes, "Rome worshipped male gods first; Rome began, because Juno acknowledged defeat" (1967, 170).

Spengler begins his chapter on "The State" with a distinction between "feminine" and "male" cultural principles that could be cited as a classic summary of patriarchal thinking in the West. Jones marks this passage with lines in the margins.

> The feminine stands closer to the Cosmic. It is rooted deeper in the earth and it is immediately involved in the grand cyclic rhythms of Nature. The masculine is freer, more animal, more mobile—as to sensation and understanding as well as otherwise—more awake and more tense.
>
> The male livingly experiences Destiny, and he *comprehends* causality, the causal logic of the Become. The female, on the contrary, is *herself* Destiny and Time and the organic logic of the Becoming, and for that very reason, the principle of Causality is forever alien to her. Wherever Man has tried to give destiny any tangible form, he has felt it as of feminine form, and has called it Moirai, Parcai, Norns. (1926, 2:327)

Jones seems to be in harmony with Spengler in his use of female figures to reflect the natural order and the cycles of birth and death in *In Parenthesis*. I have already shown how the absence of this order intensifies the bleakness of *The Book of Balaam's Ass*. But while Jones, like Spengler, uses woman as a symbol for all that opposes the male-dominated world of "high history," she is much more integral to his view of human history than the abstract and objectified "destiny" that thwarts masculine ambition in Spengler.

The Anathemata, even more than *In Parenthesis*, uses female figures to celebrate the fundamental creatureliness of all human life, the basic sacramental principle that the masculine forces of civilization and empire cannot control, though they try continually to suppress, violate, and dominate it. In a sense, Jones's portrayal of woman as the advocate of bodily life reverses a traditionally misogynistic strain in Christianity that sees woman as the temptress, enticing men away from God toward the pleasures of the flesh. Jones reinterprets this tradition by celebrating the life of the flesh as a divine gift. Invoking the teaching of Thomas Aquinas, he writes in "Art and Sacrament," "The body is not an infirmity but a unique benefit and splendour; a thing denied to angels and unconscious in animals. We are committed to body and by the same token we are committed to Ars, so to sign and sacrament" (*EA*, 165).

This association between womankind and incarnate experience is evident in a late letter to Grisewood where Jones tries to explain his lifelong inability to appreciate Dante. He complains about the lifelessness of Dante's Beatrice, which for him seems to deny the particularity and vitality of "this flesh."

> Oh! how much I agree with what you say touching the *Divina Commedia*. . . . Beatrix, as you say, is not a compelling girl of total pulchritude in all her members, impossible to resist because of the radiance of flesh and blood, not a "smasher" as the pre-Raphaelites would say [Editor's note: "stunner," surely?]. Not in any sense Helen of Troy—but a disembodied creature of some sort. Dante appears to have forgotten (in spite of his work being based on the Schoolmen) that Aquinas says that though we are *in order of "Being"* a little lower than the purer Intelligence of the angelic creatures, yet we have this advantage of having bodies and so senses that are necessarily denied the incorporeal hosts.
>
> . . . I was greatly consoled to hear that you find Dante fails to convey "this flesh" or the whole desire for feminine thing embodied in this flesh. His Beatrix seems to me a "have on," a kind of convenient "figure" necessary to his worked out scheme. (*DGC*, 239–41)

Whatever the reader may think of his critique of Dante,[1] the complaint that Beatrice is not sufficiently of "this flesh" does much to illuminate the purpose of Jones's female figures, who function as mediators of redemption, but who do so as members of humanity, embodying and celebrating our nature as incarnate beings.

Jones supplies what is lacking in Beatrice in his elaborate description of Queen Gwenhwyfar at Mass in "Mabinog's Liturgy." For him, this queen is the "stunner" that Beatrice is not. His language identifies her human beauty with the archetypal power and attractiveness of the earth, especially of the island of Britain.[2] Yet her beauty belongs to human mortality—

her fine bleached linen garment is compared to the "cere-cloth of thirty-fold" that shall be her pall. The poem connects her humanity to that of Christ Himself in the description of the crucifix that she is wearing: "the defeasible and defected image of him who alone imagined and ornated us, made fast of flesh her favours, braced bright, sternal and vertibral, to the graced bones bound" (*A*, 196).[3] The same theme is sounded again at the end of the sequence, when the queen's ornate handmade garments are juxtaposed to the luxurious altar-cloths and the ornaments surrounding this celebration of the Eucharist.

The end of the sequence comes perilously close to equating the "fleshly pulchritude" of the queen with the radiance of the Sacrament itself, as she is described from the perspective of the Welsh gentlemen, the "innate bonediggion of Britain" (see 205n), who are attending the Mass with her.

> It was fortunate for the innate *boneddegion* of Britain that when at the prayer *Qui pridie* she was bound as they to raise her face, she as they, faced the one way, or else when the lifted Signa shone they had mistaken the object of their Latria. (205)

This passage is rather daring in its acknowledgement that the men's confusion of the queen's beauty with that of the "lifted Signa" would border on idolatry, but its point is to emphasize the common ground between the Eucharistic Sacrament and the bodily and sensory experience of humanity. The danger of "mistak[ing] the object of their Latria" is one of which Jones, like the men in this passage, remains aware—this is evident in the repeated qualifications throughout his work that he "speaks by analogy only" in his discussions of the sacramental character of all human making (e.g., *EA*, 175). Yet the men at Mass avoid this mistake because the ritual obliges them to join with Gwenhwyfahr in a common and typically human gesture of worship: "She was bound *as they* to raise her face, she, *as they*, faced the one way" (my emphasis). For all her typic significance and numinous feminine beauty, she remains, like her admirers, a member of humanity.

At the end of this long digression in praise of Gwenhwyfahr and the whole "feminine thing" as manifest in the material world, we are left with a vision of men and woman together before the altar, facing the "lifted Signa" and preparing to participate in a sacramental celebration that is a defining mark of their shared humanity. This quiet portrayal of humanity as male and female together is remarkable in a male poet of Jones's generation, and it is essential to the originality of his mythic reimagining of history. Beginning with *The Anathemata,* his later poetry explores and develops the implications of a view of culture and history rooted in bodily experience and hence responsive to the feminine principle as an integral force in human affairs. The female figures in Jones's work reflect this unusually androgynous poetic sensibility. Womankind throughout his work represents less an incomprehensible other than a familiar and inescapable aspect of our human experience as "creatures with bodies" (see Blissett 1981, 39n).

This is why Jones is particularly impatient with Spengler's "male thought-world." His impatience with the "masculine" emphasis in culture extends to other writers. In his copy of John Pick's *A Hopkins Reader,* Jones marks an excerpt from the diary of Gerard Manley Hopkins criticizing the work of Frederick Walker. Hopkins writes, "Now this is the artist's most essential quality, masterly execution. It is a kind of male gift and especially marks off men from women, the begetting of one's thought on paper, on verse, on whatever the matter is" (Pick 1953, 209). In the margin next to this letter, Jones writes, "What balls." Feminists may take particular satisfaction in this annotation, because the Hopkins passage to which Jones objects expresses the same sentiment as the letter to William Dixon that Sandra Gilbert and Susan Gubar attack at the beginning of *The Madwoman in the Attic* as a classic example of "patriarchal" poetics (1979, 4–5). I do not claim that Jones gives any particular evidence, in his personal life or his writing, of supporting feminine power as a political program or even of eschewing the basic social stereotypes of women that prevailed in his day. I would not call him a feminist writer in any sense. But the originality of his vision is obvious if the female speakers in *The Anathemata* are compared to some of the better-known female figures in the works of Jones's modernist contemporaries.

Among other modernist portrayals of the feminine, Ezra Pound's goddesses in the *Cantos* and Eliot's "lady of silences" in "Ash Wednesday" can be cited as figures of woman as other—embodying a mysterious world of order and redemption beyond the male poet's grasp or comprehension. Jones's Queen of the Woods belongs to this conventional evocation of the feminine. We see her primarily as a symbol of memory and poetry, a disembodied mythic presence, rather than as anything approaching a person in her own right. She has no voice of her own. Joyce's Molly Bloom is perhaps the most vivid counterexample of a woman who speaks for herself in modernist literature, but she does so primarily as a realistic

character. Her typic dimension is considerably less important in her fa-
mous monologue than is her realistic experience. Anna Livia Plurabelle,
who partly inspired the character of Jones's Elen Monica, is developed in
greater typological depth and breadth. She is a woman with love affairs,
jealousies, and desires, and at the same time, she embodies a cosmic
feminine principle of renewal and reconciliation. But even Anna Livia
does not speak for herself in the famous Joyce fragment, though we do
hear her elsewhere in the *Wake*. She is *spoken of* by the washerwomen at the
river's edge.

A closer parallel to the use Jones makes of female speakers can be
found in some of H. D.'s female mythic figures, among them Demeter,
Eurydice, and Helen of Troy, who speak out forcefully to expose and often
to protest against the callousness of cultural myths constructed by men.[4]
Jones did not know H. D.'s work, and the thick and rambling texture of his
poetry contrasts utterly with her disciplined lucidity. Her classical masks
are far less individual than Jones's female speakers, and their monologues
are more concerned with expressing depths of personal and subjective
feeling than Jones's more culturally and historically oriented poetry.
Nonetheless, the autonomy that he bestows on his female speakers is in
sympathy with H. D.'s effort and points to an unusual sympathy in Jones
with what the Western tradition has identified as a "feminine" perspective
on history. He goes beyond his male modernist contemporaries in creat-
ing female poetic speakers whose autonomous personalities comment
lucidly on the abuses of "masculine" political and social orders through-
out Western history.

In *The Anathemata*, Jones's feminine principle speaks for herself in
multiple voices, taking on the characters of Ilia, mother of the Roman
people; Elen Monica, a fifteenth-century London lavender vendor; and
the Welsh witches of "Mabinog's Liturgy." These speakers deal frankly
with the limitations and joys of bodily life, especially of sexual experience,
often expressing a disdain for male self-importance that echoes
Chaucer's Wife of Bath. The poem also speaks to and about other female
figures who have no voice of their own, as when the sailors in "Middle Sea
and Lear Sea" pray to various tutelary goddesses for protection, or in the
Gwenhywfar sequence, which celebrates the feminine principle as experi-
enced in the British tradition. The other voiceless feminine presence in
the poem is Mary, whose assent to the angel's message made human
redemption possible. "Fiat mihi secundum verbum tuum," she says, in the
vulgate version: "Be it unto me according to thy word" (Luke 1:38). An

important theme in *The Anathemata* is the influence of this one woman's free choice on the course of history. The poem makes fruitful use of the Catholic teaching that the Incarnation could not have taken place without Mary's voluntary consent. The entire plan of human salvation—fulfilled in Christ's Passion and recalled in the Mass—rests on Mary's willingness to be the bearer of Incarnate God. As Elen Monica puts it, "Her fiat is our fortune" (*A*, 128).

The Anathemata introduces this aspect of feminine power by contrast, through its first female speaker, Ilia. According to myth, Ilia was raped by the god Mars and, as a result of this union, gave birth to the Roman people. In keeping with his commitment to a hidden history, Jones presents this union as a mechanical and brutal violation, and he lets us hear of it from Ilia herself, Mars's victim, who conveys a cosmic feminine perspective on the abuses of empire. The encounter takes place in ominous surroundings—"it was dark, a very stormy night" (87)—recalling the "tempest of soldier-emperors" that accompanies cyclic changes in Spengler (1926, 1:435). Mars appears as a Spenglerian "man of destiny," using the techniques of surveying, the technology that enabled the Romans to build their world-cities, in his approach to this intimate encounter (88 n. 3). Ilia's account of their union stresses above all the god's impersonal, coercive, and military manner.

> West-star, hers and all!
>   brighting the hooped turn of his scapular-plates enough to show his pelvic sway and the hunch on his robber's shoulders. Though he was of the Clarissimi his aquila over me was robbery.
> 'T's a great robbery
>   —is empire.
>
> (87–88)

Ilia's tale may have been inspired by a brief passage from "Anna Livia Plurabelle," where the washerwomen recall Anna Livia's first sexual encounter with HCE. HCE appears here as a rough warrior, indifferent to her innocence. Speaking of the young river-spirit Anna Livia, the washerwomen recall:

> She was just a young thin pale soft shy slim slip of a thing then, sauntering, by silvamoonlake and he was a heavy trudging lurching lieabroad of a Curraghman, making his hay for the sun to shine on. . . . She thought she's sankh neathe the ground with nymphant shame when he gave her the tigris eye! O happy fault! (*FW*, 202)

Both encounters stress the overpowering of the feminine principle by a strong male figure, and both mark turning points in history: Ilia and Mars brought forth the Roman people; Anna Livia and the "lurching lieabroad of a Curraghman" precipitated the Fall, suggested in the washerwomen's allusion to the phrase *felix culpa* ("happy fault"), which refers to the Fall of humankind. Ilia's language is less musical than the washerwomen's, however, and there is no suggestion of love or sexual pleasure in her monologue, as there is in Joyce. She is reporting an act of forcible rape. As she watches the armed "robber" leave her, by the light of Venus (the "Weststar"), Ilia expresses not awe but disdain for her rapist. Even though she acknowledges "how his glory filled the whole place where we were together" (87), she has a voice to protest, and through her Jones gives expression to St. Augustine's equation of empire with "robbery" (cf. *DGC*, 150; Blissett 1981, 78–79).

If the transition from classical culture to Roman imperial civilization came about through a violation of the feminine principle, the next civilizational turn, from the Roman to the Christian era, was possible only through the cooperation of a woman. "Mabinog's Liturgy" implicitly associates the Annunciation to Mary with the classical motif of divine love for a mortal woman by comparing Mary to Leda. The Annunciation takes place in the early spring of the year—and of Christian culture—and the poem's account of it stresses the theme of fertility rather than that of violation.

> Thirty-four years and twenty-one days
> since that germinal March
> and terminal day
> > (no drought that year)
> since his Leda
> > said to his messenger
> > > (his bright *talaria* on)
> *fiat mihi.*
>
> > > > (188–89)

We never hear Mary speak in her own voice during the poem. Like the figure of Christ, she is described indirectly, as a fulfillment of all the types we meet in the poem. But Mary's *fiat*, and the importance of the creaturely body and of feminine influence in human affairs, are celebrated and recalled with great vitality by Elen Monica, the speaker in "The Lady of the Pool."

Elen's voice is a composite of female voices that Jones has heard and appreciated. Soon after the publication of *The Anathemata,* Jones writes to his friend Desmond Chute that much of "The Lady of the Pool" was inspired by the conversation of "ordinary people," including some of his aunts (*IN,* 71). In a late letter to René Hague he explains that many of the stories Elen tells or refers to come from his mother, Alice Bradshaw, who was raised in the area around the pool of London at a period when British mercantile power was at its height (*DG,* 21–22). Her father, Eb Bradshaw, a mast-and-block maker at Redriff, is the speaker in "Redriff."

Elen belongs to the end of the Middle Ages, the period of Chaucer's Wife of Bath. Her frankness and exuberant sense of humor, especially when she speaks about her lovers, echo some of the qualities of Chaucer's character. Elen's name evokes the role of woman both as beloved (Elen-Helen) and as mother (Monica, mother of St. Augustine). Like the speech of Joyce's washerwomen, Elen's conversation is full of learned allusions that seem to clash with the simplicity of her character and class; she does not speak like a "real" woman. Yet Jones manages to bestow on this universal type an individuality belonging to a particular time and place in history and to a perspective on history that is plausibly feminine. Elen is a tutelary spirit of Britain and an exuberant and unapologetic embodiment of "this flesh." No "disembodied" virgin, Elen has received willingly a number of lovers who together have educated her in the history of Britain and London: "Yet dealing much / in the peregrinations of Venus," she says, "much have I learned of them" (135). In keeping with her connection to the poem's theme of incarnation, she insists on her roots in her own particular time and place. She tells her mason lover that she is "unversed . . . a simple person sponsored at Papeys-in-Wall, but reared up by Redriff mast-pond" (135). Her tale reflects her roots in the time and place she inhabits—that is, in Catholic Christian London, in a nautical environment.

The love affairs Elen recalls have obviously taken place in the past, though some of her remarks to the captain are sexually suggestive and even flirtatious ("good to sweeten y'r poop-bower, capt'n" [125]; "don't eye *me,* captain" [146]). It does not follow, however, that her recollections of love identify her as a pathetic character—what Dilworth calls "a bride without a groom." Emphasizing the echo of Wyatt's "They Flee from Me," Dilworth reads Elen's account of her tryst with the mason as a nostalgic account of "past happiness, which emphasizes subsequent loss." He comments that the refrain "they come, and they go, captain," which follows two of her recollections of love-trysts (129), is "at once sexually suggestive and pathetic in its understatement. . . . The suffering of her muted passion can be heard in her street-cry, 'come buy, good for between the sheets'" (Dilworth 1988, 222). It seems to me that the poem invites a different reading of Elen that recognizes her elemental, bodily vitality. Her memories are of a life of love, and she gives no clear evidence of regretting that she has not found a husband. There may even be a ribald suggestiveness in "they come and they go" (160) Dilworth also introduces Elen as "late middle-aged and corpulent" (1988, 215), an accurate enough description, but her own reference to her girth, "I'ld make a whale of a mere-maid, captain, had I scales to m'belly" (166), conveys not the regret of the aging spinster who has lost her looks—as Dilworth's reading implies—but a Rabelaisian vitality, an affirmation of the flesh that is central to both the typic and the "realistic" dimensions of her character. When we meet her, Elen is a woman of middle age, a more mature and matronly figure than she was during her amorous adventures, but one who speaks from the wisdom of experience about human nature and human affairs. She is also a prophet of sorts, foretelling the abuse of the feminine principle that will accompany the rise of the Tudor empire, with its ensign Britannia, at the next stage of British history.

Within the Spenglerian framework of *The Anathemata*, the setting and time of "The Lady of the Pool" suggest a particular cultural moment in the history of the West. It is early September, just before the feast of the Exaltation of the Cross—Holy Cross Day or "Crouchmass" (September 14)—and the lavender-seller's cry alludes to the dying of summer and the onset of the winter "chill" (125n). The setting is late fifteenth-century London. In Spengler's historical scheme, this puts it in the late summer of Faustian culture, which had reached the full flowering of its spring by 1300. Elen speaks just before the turn from the high culture of medieval England to the emerging civilization that would begin the British empire under the Tudors in the next century. Her monologue begins with a catalog of London churches sacred to Mary, where "Crouchmass" will soon be sung. This list reveals implicitly the symbolic connection between the speaker and the Virgin Mary, and between both of them and the "chthonic *matres* under the croft," the female fertility spirits whose cult is still remembered in some of the rituals of Crouchmass (127). The names of churches are given in popular form. St. Mary Whitechapel is called "Two sticks and a'Apple," in evident allusion to a folk rhyme, and St. Bride's Fleet Street and the Bridewell is called "Bride o'shandies well"

(127). Thus, the more universal significance of Elen as embodiment of the feminine principle is disguised under the particularity of her dialect.

Elen concludes her catalog by insisting on the decisive role of Mary's will in history, connecting her to earlier types of feminine influence in Iphigenia and Helen.

> In all the memorials
> Of her buxom will
>   (what brought us ransom, captain!)
> as do renown our city.
> She's as she of Aulis, master:
> not a puff of wind without her!
> her fiat is our fortune sir: like Helen's face
> 'twas that as launched the ship.
>
>   (128)

Helen's "face that launched a thousand ships" is here transformed into Mary's fiat, which launched the "ship" of Christianity. Jones's important note to this passage stresses the role of what he calls Mary's "pliant" or "compliant" will in redemption. Quoting the twelfth-century English saint Aelred of Rievaulx, Jones writes that Mary was

> "doubtless blessed in receiving the Son of God bodily into her womb, but she was much more blessed for first receiving him in her mind and heart." He [Aelred] goes on to say that but for Mary's acceptance the gospel could never have been preached. Which Irenaeus, in second-century Gaul, had expressed when he said "She was constituted the cause of our salvation." (128 n. 5)

Elen goes beyond this doctrine when she talks of Mary's "buxom will," suggesting a more wholehearted, fleshly compliance than is traditionally attributed to the Virgin. Elen's own response to her lovers, especially to the mason lover whom she recalls in some detail, suggests that the "buxom will" that Elen praises in Mary implies not only compliancy with divine love but eager agreement, a responding desire. Because of this, I would qualify Dilworth's suggestion that Elen's "unchaste sexuality is a metaphysical inconsistency which emphasizes that it is 'compliancy of. . . will,' not virginity, that makes Mary (and Elen) typic of co-redemptive humanity" (1988, 226). Elen embodies not only compliancy but an active and responding sexuality, which is in turn a metaphor for the intercourse between God and humankind. Dilworth may be acknowledging this else-where in his discussion, when he recalls Jones's statement that "there is, after all, but one tale to tell: *Dilectus meus mihi, et ego illi* as *The Canticle of Canticles* puts it" (206–7). The "one tale" of the connection of humankind to God is a love story ("My beloved is mine, and I am his"—to translate the *Song of Songs*, 2:16). Accordingly, the women in Jones's imaginative scheme often embody the desire of humanity responding to the love of God.

Much of Elen's monologue recalls her own "buxom" compliance to lovers she has received on this island. These include a university man—"a dunce of a maudlin inceptor" (128)—who tells her of the theological principle that "mother is requisite to son" (129) and a freemason whose use of Latin phrases irritates Elen because they seem to distract him from their lovemaking. In describing her affair with the freemason, Elen insists repeatedly on the fleshly character of their union, but she also reveals, in spite of herself, her own connection with more universal types of the feminine principle, including not only the freemason's Roman god-desses, Flora Dea and Bona Dea, but also the British St. Helen and the Virgin Mary.[5]

Elen claims to be oblivious to her own symbolic significance, and she even recalls with some impatience the mason's tendency to transform her into an allegory and to identify their physical union with momentous events and places in history. The first of his outbursts takes place after a tryst, as the lovers are resting in the clear moonlight following an evening thunderstorm.

An' in this transfiguring after-clarity he seemed to call me his . . . Fl - ora . . . *Flora Dea* he says . . . whether to me or into the darks of the old ragstone courses?

> . . . how are you for conundrums, captain?

> And again, once in especial,

at a swelt'rin' close August day's close. . . .

Between the heats and the cool, at day's ebb and night-flow, the lode already over the fen of Islington, pressed we was to the same cranny of the wall to right of the same 'brassure of the same right gate-jamb—so Janus save me, but bodies will. The whitest of the Wanderers, what was Julius Caesar's mother, white over Bride's Well, and this her fish day—and again he says it, but this time it's *Bona Dea* he cries. . . Hills o' the Mother he says, an' y'r lavender, the purple, he says, an' then he says, but more slow:

> Roma aurea Roma

Roma . . . amor, amor . . . Roma. Roma, wot's in the feminine gender, he
says.
What rogue's cant is this? I said. Whereas, inly, I for love languished.

(131–32)

In a number of its details, this meeting contrasts directly with the rape
of Ilia by Mars in "Middle Sea and Lear Sea." Ilia's narrative begins, "It was
dark, a very stormy night." Elen and her mason meet not during but after a
thunderstorm, and in early, luminous evening, rather than in the dark of
night. Like Ilia and Mars, Elen and the mason meet by the light of Venus,
and like Ilia, Elen comments on the event by giving her own twist to a line
from the *Song of Songs*. Ilia's quotation from that book was a bitter transfor-
mation of "his banner over me was love" to "his aquila over me was
robbery" (88). Elen adapts the vulgate biblical phrase *quia amore
langueo*—usually translated "I am sick with (or of) love"—to her own
sense of frustration with her lover, who appears to be talking not to her but
to the air. Though the mason relates her to the mystical figures of Bona
Dea and Roma, Elen's voice contains more immediacy and practicality
than a reader would expect in a universal type. She describes frankly the
intimate position in which she and her freemason found themselves, and
even her apology for this—"so Janus save me, but bodies will"—affirms
the bodiliness that her whole character so clearly exalts.

The mason becomes increasingly abstracted as he embraces Elen, and
she tells how he looks about him at the walls of London, by Ludgate and
the Fleet River, associating them with his memories of his military service
in France. Elen comments wryly that she listened "not carping nor cross-
ing him—best let him rehearse his tale awhile seeing as it touched his
service overseas—they all be apt at their rehearsals, captain, what was
upon a time and long since within far sound of a bombard, captain"
(134). But instead of telling her a tale, the mason has a vision of St. Helen
of Britain welcoming the conquering emperor Constantius Chloris to the
gates of London in 296 A.D. Contemplating the historic significance of his
surroundings and the symbolic significance of his mistress, who is a tute-
lary spirit of London, the mason cries out a Latin phrase that Elen does
not understand. She recalls for the listening captain how she interrupted
her lover's reverie in exasperation:

These, captain, were his precisive words—what sentiments I can't
construe—but at which, captain, I cried: Enough!

> Let's to terrestrial flesh, or
> bid good-night, I thought.
>
> (134)

By thus rebuking her mason for his tendency to objectify her as an abstract being, Elen is taking a sacramentalist's position, insisting on the primary importance of "terrestrial flesh" as a means to knowledge of transcendence. She continues her rebuke over the next twenty-five pages, as she recounts to the mason, and to the listening sea captain, the tale of the voyage of the *Mary* that she has heard from her sailors. In the pages that follow, she gradually emerges as a guardian of the oral tradition by which Christianity first came to the island and by which its culture was preserved in the early years of the modern era.

In her account of the *Mary*, the ship of the Christian church, Elen stresses the perils and temptations that the ship encounters and the damage it receives. The most dangerous of the temptations the *Mary* encounters are a group of "genuine rock-sirens" (142), mermaids who try to tempt the ship off course. These sirens, as Dilworth suggests, embody "the spiritual danger to mankind of imperialism, especially when in league with institutional religion" (1988, 246). The lust for power, identified here with the sexual lust aroused by the sirens, leads men astray from the right course, often by manipulating the symbols of fertility and regeneration that other myths associate with the earth mother and the benevolent aspects of womankind. The sirens strew flowers, associated elsewhere in the poem with Flora Dea, and in *In Parenthesis* with the benevolent Queen of the Woods, and they sing haunting songs.

As Elen insists, the belief in mermaids is an important part of the genuine tradition of "this Matriarch's isle" (186). But she shows what can happen to such native traditions when she transforms herself, for a moment, into a parodic personification of Britain's most influential mermaid, the siren Britannia. As she takes on Britannia's distinctive trappings—the looking glass, the tower lion, the nautical rope, and the ivory comb—Elen's charade implicitly warns of the abuses of the coming Tudor empire.[6]

> Here is our regnant hand:
> this ring you see upon it were gave us long since by a' ancient fisher; 'tis indulgenced till there be no more sea: kiss it.
> No, no, on y'r marrow-bones—though you hooked behemoth, you shall kneel!

                                                This bollard here
where keels tie, come from all quarters of a boisterous world, hand us to it to
sit upon.
                                                          (145)

The siren Britannia's insistence that her listener kiss the ring prophesies
the coming of the Reformation to England and thus the end of the
Catholic tradition, which for Jones is Britain's true heritage and its link to
the culture of Europe. Her bossiness and her primping are playful and
parodic, but her message is serious. She is showing how the native tradi-
tion of "this Matriarch's isle"—which includes the belief in water-maids—
will be distorted by imperialists in a coming age, to serve their lust for
conquest and assimilation.

Though the English generally look back on the Tudor era as Britain's
prime, Jones's Welsh heritage, together with his Catholicism, made him
deeply critical of this enthusiasm. For him, the flowering of English cul-
ture in the Tudor period also brought about the subjugation of Wales and
the beginning of the end of native Welsh culture, as the rulers imposed
both the English language and the Church of England on a Catholic
Britain. The vision of Britannia that Elen offers warns of the tendency of
empire to try to co-opt the feminine principle as a symbol for the mas-
culine forces of conquest and domination. Like the sirens who threaten
the typic voyage of the *Mary*, the figure of Britannia will lure the men of
the next century away from Elen's culturally unified late medieval world
into the robbery of empire. In this way, her personification of Britannia as
a water-maid anticipates dramatically a grimmer prophecy that closes
"The Tutelar of the Place," in which "the technicians manipulate the dead
limbs of our culture as though they yet had life" (*SL*, 64).

The Lady of the Pool goes on to quote Shakespeare, the poet of the
Tudors, who would speak prophetically to the century after her own:
"don't eye *me*, 'tis but a try-out and very much betimes: / For we live before
her time" (*A*, 146). This passage echoes the speech of the fool in *King
Lear*, who speaks to the Tudor audience out of the pre-Arthurian past of
early Britain, in a prophecy that seems to describe their own time: "then
shalle the realm of Albion / come to great confusion. . . . This prophecye
Merlin shalle make, for I live before his time" (3.2. 85–86, 94). Jones also
uses this last sentence from Lear's fool as an epigraph to *The Anathemata*,
and it reflects well the poem's perspective, speaking as it does out of the
distant past and prophesying to a modern world that finds itself in "great

confusion." Elen's impersonation of Britannia is only a "try-out," a mockery of all that will falsify the cultural vitality that she embodies and protects. In her prophetic commentary on empire, Elen suggests the resilience of the feminine principle in history—her confidence, as she puts it elsewhere in the monologue, that "what's under works up" (164).

The feminine principle also appears in *The Anathemata*, as she does throughout Jones's work, as a mediating figure to whom men pray in desperate situations. The soldiers of *In Parenthesis* pray to mother earth for protection and shelter in battle. Those in *The Book of Balaam's Ass* cry out in despair, praying "according to what breasts had fed them" (*SL*, 110). In "Middle Sea and Lear Sea," the suppliants are a crew of Phocaean and Phoenician soldiers serving on a Greek tin-mining ship. Their ship encounters rocks and shoals just after they have sighted the British land that is their destination. In a parody of sea chantey form, the men lament their apparent doom as victims of the thalassocracy, or sea empire, that they serve, and their chantey gives way to a prayer for protection to the maiden of the sea, who is their tutelary goddess. They seek refuge from their oppression by calling out the names of their "sweethearts," as Jones's note calls them: Themis, Phoebe, Telphousa, and Petra Agelastos. The names are chosen to reflect "various aspects of femaleness: . . . the moon, so the tides, the huntress, the mother. Telphousa in particular has affinities with Delphi and so with Petra Agelastos" (*A*, 104n). Petra Agelastos, the "laughless rock" of another passage in *The Anathemata* (56) and a goddess identified with Delphi, also shares the name of Eric Gill's daughter Petra, to whom Jones was engaged for a time during the 1920s.

The sailors sum up their prayers by asking "you many that are tutelar / regard our anathemata" (105). By presenting their invocation of feminine presences explicitly as an offering of anathemata, Jones underscores the androgynous character of the sacred order that his poem evokes. The sailors' prayer invokes the "vestals of Latium"—protectors of pre-Christian Rome, and therefore "not yet taught of the fisherman," St. Peter (106). It conflates these local priestesses of Rome with their typological fulfillment in the Virgin Mary—"stella maris," or star of the sea, "whose lode is the sea-star" (106)—and with the celebration of Mass, which is the poem's setting. The Phoenician sailors ask the vestals of Latium to pray for them, as the priests at Mass in a future Roman Catholic church will pray for all argonauts in the argosy of the Redeemer.[7] In this way, the prayer to the local feminine figures is subtly identified with the prayers of the priests. All these prayers reflect a rejection of the power of empire in any age, be it the technocracy of the moderns or the thalassocracy of the ancients. Although all the representatives of "man-the-sign-maker"—priest, poet, and Christ himself—are male, their world is presided over by feminine genii who protect particular places and cultures, and the poem repeatedly recognizes female figures as empowering all argosies, including the historic voyages of the early Phoenician and Greek thalassocrats and the argosy of the Redeemer that is remembered in the Mass and recalled allegorically in Elen's account of the *Mary*.

The Welsh witches who appear in "Mabinog's Liturgy" offer yet another view of the role of the feminine principle in history. Like the Lady of the Pool, these witches speak for themselves. But in an interesting contrast to Elen, who gains her knowledge of the world mainly from the men she has known, the witches present themselves as learned, self-educated women. The tone of this part of "Mabinog's Liturgy" is lighthearted, even comic, a kind of playful parody of learned theological discourse. The witches speak out of an insistently, even exaggeratedly "feminine" mode of perception that favors the details of human life over the abstracted jargon of theology and philosophy, and that discovers everywhere the presence of feminine figures in an overwhelmingly patriarchal tradition. As the witch Marged says, "There's always a Mari in it, I warrant you" (213).

This part of "Mabinog's Liturgy" is marred by several long passages of pedantic theologizing, apparently intended to underscore the witches' status as learned female speakers, but often becoming excessively discursive. However, there is great vitality in the voice of Marged, the bluestocking witch who is the chief speaker here and a delightful parodist of theological discourse. Rebuking her sisters for their jealousy, Marged appeals to their solidarity with Mary as women, at the same time parodying some of the theological phrases that traditionally describe the Virgin (in this passage, "chosen and forechosen").

> Sisters, not so jealous! *Someone* must be chosen and forechosen—it stands to reason. After all there should be solidarity in woman. No great thing but what there's a woman behind it, sisters. Begetters of all huge endeavor we are. The Lord God may well do all without the aid of man, but even in the things of god a woman is medial—it stands to reason. (213–14)

Marged's theologizing reflects the revisions and reinterpretations that are a dominant mode of this part of "Mabinog's Liturgy." When praising

Mary a bit further on, she appeals to women's experience of motherhood and of the details of daily life: "After all, sisters, he was her *baban*. / Who did him wash / and did his swaddlings wring? Who did and mended for him? . . . Of whom was his mother-wit?" (214–15). In a passage like this, one can almost imagine the kitchen-table conversation of the aunts whom Jones once cited as sources for the voice of Elen Monica (*IN*, 71).

Like Elen Monica, the witches present themselves as guardians of an oral tradition that has a local language and a long cultural history. They retell the Christmas story in a predominantly Welsh idiom, calling it "his *mabinogi*" (his story of infancy), and mixing Welsh titles—"son of Mair," "Atheling to the heaven-king"—with Latin Christmas carols that identify this story as an integral part of the Western oral tradition (207–8). They also look forward—again parodically—from the Incarnation to the Apocalypse, "when she, our West-light falls from her track-way. . . . when Clio has no more to muse about" (208). The witches' version of the story, though filled with echoes of the *Dies Irae* and the Roman liturgy, begins from the female figures of Venus ("our West-light") and Clio, the muse of history. It ends with Polymnia and Euterpe, muses of music and lyric poetry, who remain at the Apocalypse to play the "spondulaium," the hymn to the Lamb. The outrageous punning in "when Clio has no more to muse about" (208) also typifies the playful, comic tone of this part of Jones's poem.

The feeling of this sequence shares the comic incongruity of some of the early passages from the manuscript of *The Book of Balaam's Ass*, and the witches embody the kind of reversal, the transformation of curse into blessing, that was a dominant theme of those pages. Because it is Mary's night, they "tell their *aves* unreversed" (207), implicitly rejecting the traditional identification of evil with "eva," or Eve, the type of woman as temptress.[8] In praying their "un-witched aves," they also join with "all our sisters," and Marged coaxes them, in decidedly comic language, to kneel in company with all the dumb beasts who celebrate the nativity—perhaps even including Balaam's ass, who may be echoed here: "Kneel sisters! Graymalkin! Kneel. . . . For in the Schools, they say: /if he but take the posture / the old grey ass may bray a *Gloria*" (215). Piety is barely plausible in this passage, which mixes irreverence with good-natured parody, but the voice that Marged and her sisters contribute to the liturgy of tales of Christ's infancy is distinctly feminine. It revises and reimagines the tradition to suggest further ways in which "rite follows matriarchate" in Jones's mythological scheme.

The voice of the feminine principle, heard most fully in "The Lady of the Pool" and "Mabinog's Liturgy," is also associated very closely in Jones's mind with the particular tradition of "these isles"—or what The Lady of the Pool calls "this Matriarch's isle" of Britain. Elen Monica, Gwenhwyfar, and even the witches are local tutelary figures, embodying the influence of a sacramental tradition in the particular history of the British Isles. All the male figures united in the "He" who presides over the end of the poem—the priest, the poet, and Christ—are revealed to be intimately dependent for their power on female figures who tell and retell tales, who make signs and recall origins; as the witch Marged says, "No great thing but what there's a woman behind it." This is not exactly a "feminist" vision, because it still portrays women as mediators and enablers, rather than as independent agents in history. Nonetheless, through the interdependence between feminine figures and masculine sign makers, and especially through the voice of Elen Monica, *The Anathemata* clearly associates the "feminine" principle with the sign-making impulse that is its central theme. In so doing, Jones implies that the idea of humankind as a sacramentalist species includes both male and female sign-makers. By the end of *The Anathemata,* the more sinister masculine orders of Spengler's "failing numina" and of imperial Rome have been overcome by the vitality of the sign-making gesture, whose continuity the poem celebrates and demonstrates.

But the threat that the masculine order of conquest, empire, and civilization poses to the feminine principle—and to the humane values that she embodies and nourishes—is not forgotten in Jones's poetry. The deep gloom of Spengler's declining civilization returns more pervasively to the world of his last volume, *The Sleeping Lord and Other Fragments,* where it threatens to crush the feminine order of particularity, place, and continuing tradition that Jones chooses to embody in the land and legends of Celtic Wales.

Chapter 8

Open Questions: *The Sleeping Lord*

The more subtle character of the feminine influence in *The Sleeping Lord and Other Fragments* is anticipated in "The Myth of Arthur"—an essay dating from 1942, the period of Jones's immersion in Spengler. Here he expresses the hope that the "masculine emphasis" of his time may somehow be "tempered by the saving scepticism of the female mind." Returning to Jackson Knight's Juno as an emblem of both Roman and modern civilizational discord, he continues: "There is a danger of Juno being put into a concentration camp, of her being liquidated. There is danger that the deprivation of the Romans may be ours also" (*EA*, 240–41). In the world of *The Sleeping Lord,* Juno has not yet been liquidated, but her presence is by no means as influential as it is in *The Anathemata* or as reassuring as in the final section of *In Parenthesis.* There are moments when she is invoked as a palpable absence, particularly in the desolate prayer at the end of "The Tribune's Visitation." In the poems of this volume, the feminine presences that Jones embodied in the Queen of the Woods, in Elen Monica, and in Gwenhwyfar have gone underground, where they are fused with the figure of Arthur, asleep under the desolated landscape of Wales. The vision of hidden redemption in these poems—a vision at once self-consciously "Celtic" and subtly androgynous—is repeatedly set against the grim determinism of the Spenglerian and "masculine" world order.

What I call the *Sleeping Lord* sequence—the series of poems that begins with "The Wall" and ends with the title poem of the volume[1]—derives its poetic authority from its exploration of an open and finally unresolved dialectic between Spengler's deterministic and "masculine" view of history—associated here with the Romans—and a naturally sacramental mode of life that Jones associates with feminine Celtic spirits of place and with the sleeping Arthur. At issue in this open dialectic is not the victory of one or the other principle but the survival of what Jones sees as a fundamental humanity that partakes of both. For him, Spengler's blindness to the "inevitable and proper rebellion of human nature against the mon-strous regiment of the power-age" (*DG,* 159) is one of the chief weak-nesses in the German philosopher's argument. In Spengler's world, he writes, "it is indeed 'human nature' that is rebelling—it is man-as-artist that is in rebellion, and it is men-as-artists who are casualties in the strug-gle" (*DG,* 159). But the struggle is not a simple confrontation between absolute good and evil, civilization and culture, or even masculine and feminine. Writing to Aneirin Talfan Davies about an early radio presenta-tion of "The Wall" and "The Tutelar of the Place," Jones remarks that these poems present "the abiding situation of the good and bad things of an *imperium* face to face with the local and diverse and loved things—which also have goodness and badness." He goes on to reflect that most of his work has been preoccupied with this dilemma "because it is something which seems to me insoluble" (*LF,* 34).[2]

The interdependent dualities at work in *The Sleeping Lord* confront one another most directly in "The Tribune's Visitation" and "The Tutelar of the Place," companion poems that mark the structural center of the volume. The dialogue established here between Tribune and Tutelar and between Roman and Celtic worlds reflects nicely the ongoing dialogue between Spengler and Joyce that shapes so much of Jones's thinking. Both poems recognize that even the late phases of civilization harbor somewhere what "The Tutelar of the Place" calls the "secret seed" of culture, but they offer this insight from conflicting points of view. "The Tribune's Visitation" features as its primary speaker a "fact man" devoted to the empire of Rome. Its companion poem looks at the world from the perspective of a waning culture, mostly through the consciousness of a Celtic soldier in the service of Rome, who reflects nostalgically on the rooted and "feminine" world of his homeland.

More than any of the Romans in *The Sleeping Lord,* Jones's Tribune embodies the Spenglerian man of late imperialistic civilization. He refers to his men as a "mixed bunch," emphasizing the Celtic, Teutonic, and native Italian tribal heritages of the soldiers. Yet he sees it as his duty to flatten and assimilate their particular heritages in the service of empire—

> to discipline the world-floor
> to a common level
> till everything presuming difference
> and all the sweet remembered demarcations
> wither

to the touch of us
        and know the fact of empire.

                   (*SL*, 50–51)

The speaker dismisses patronizingly the "bumpkin sacraments" that are the native heritage of his men, though his reference to the "sweet remembered demarcations" suggests a touch of wistfulness at their passing. His attitude reflects what Spengler called the "Caesarism" of late civilization, which disguises its fundamental alienation from culture "under antique forms whose spirit is dead" (1926, 2:431).

In keeping with this account of Caesarism, Jones's Tribune presides over a ritual whose origins in early culture are evident, yet which has become the central rite of Caesarist civilization: the soldier's *sacramentum,* or oath of loyalty, to the emperor. The ratifying words of this oath were "*Idem in me*"—"the same goes for me."[3] When celebrating this ritual, the Tribune adopts the traditional role of the *paterfamilias* for himself, addressing the men under him as a family gathered for a communal meal, and substituting the military standards of the empire for the *penates,* or household gods. But these "signa" are admittedly "mutilated"—shorn, like the *penates,* of their former influence, and revived only to serve the interests of empire (57). Moreover, the language the Tribune uses in celebrating this debased Caesarist ritual looks ahead of his historical moment to a civilizational phase that will displace Rome. Jones's presentation of the ritual of empire shows how inevitably the imperial perspective is undone by the fundamental human impulses that it tries to exploit for its own purposes.

> See! I break this barrack bread, I drink with you, this issue cup, I salute, with you, these mutilated signa, I with you have cried with all of us the ratifying formula: *Idem in me.*
>
> . . . .
>
> Let the gnosis of necessity infuse our hearts, for we have
> purged out the leaven of illusion.
> If then we are dead to nature
>   yet we live
>   to Caesar
>   from Caesar's womb we issue
> by a second birth.
>
>   (58)

The "gnosis of necessity" recalls Spengler's assertion that twentieth-century man has the freedom only "to do the necessary or to do nothing"

(1926, 2:504). Yet the words and forms used here to enunciate this deterministic credo undercut its avowed pragmatism.

In addition to enjoying the obvious Christian resonance of the word *sacramentum*, Jones has his Tribune parody passages from St. Paul, whose writings nourished the springtime of the Christian-Faustian cultural phase, the successor to Rome. The Tribune tells his men that "all are members of the Strider's body," called "if not to one hope, then to one necessity" (58), a unity validated by their loyalty to the Strider Mars, the Roman god of war. St. Paul described the early church as one spiritual "body," trusting in "one Lord, one faith, one baptism," in a passage that also exalts the diversity of particular gifts within that body (Ephesians 4: 4–12). Similarly, the Tribune's allusion to a "second birth" doubles a passage from St. Paul's epistle to the Romans, a document historically contemporaneous with Jones's Tribune.

> For in that He died, he died unto sin once, but in that He liveth, He liveth unto God. Likewise reckon ye also yourselves to be dead indeed unto sin, but alive unto God through Jesus Christ our Lord. (Romans 6:10–11)

These Pauline echoes suggest that while the Tribune may be alert to the immediate historical necessity of Caesarism, he cannot see the larger pattern of history, which decrees that the inevitable "withering" of culture at the hands of empire can never be permanent. By embedding the scriptures of the coming culture-phase in the discourse of a man who believes himself to be wiping out all cultures, Jones reveals the limitations of Spenglerian determinism as applied to the military state. The doubleness of the Tribune's speech reveals, even within a late civilizational phase, a persistently imaginative mode of thought, natural to humanity, which must always reemerge after the final waning of a civilization. The "antique forms" that the Tribune thinks he is manipulating as "empty vessels" for the promotion of Caesarism are thus revealed as having a life of their own, a life that will reemerge in the cultural phase that is about to succeed the Roman world.

The bankruptcy of the *signa* in the Tribune's historical moment is underscored by his unconvincing attempts to adapt traditionally feminine symbols to the service of empire. For example, he compares the fire to a paternal hearth, and the fatigue men stirring it to "our sisters, busy with the pots" (57). Later, the Tribune incongruously pictures the new men of necessity issuing from the "womb" of the masculine Caesar (58).[4] This appropriation of feminine imagery for the propaganda of empire reflects again the symptomatic disorder that Jones objected to in Spengler—his presentation of a "male thought-world" that "has liqui-dated Juno" (*DGC*, 115). For Jones, imperialism is not only a violation of the feminine principle but a cruel deception of all that is positive in the masculine characters or in the fully integrated, androgynous human sen-sibility that is hinted at in parts of *The Sleeping Lord,* especially in "The Tutelar of the Place" and in the title poem. This dehumanizing effect is partly reflected in an irrepressible longing for feminine presences, even in a world that has deliberately and systematically excluded them. The Tribune reflects this at the end of the poem, when he follows the debased ritual of the *sacramentum* with a desperate prayer to Juno. He uses her other name, Lucina, which identifies her as "light-bringer, the goddess of birth" (*A*, 188 n. 5).

> Ah! Lucina!
> > what irradiance
> can you bring
> > to this parturition?
> What light brights this deliverance?
> From darkness
> > to a greater dark
> the issue is.
>
> > > > (58)

If the Tribune's world is one in which Juno has already acknowledged defeat, "The Tutelar of the Place" reflects and invokes a perspective sym-pathetic to what Jones earlier called the "saving sceticism of the female mind" (*EA*, 240). This poem responds obliquely to the Tribune's despair-ing prayer by bringing to life a typical culture that is on the verge of being assimilated by an encroaching civilization. Jones writes to Aneirin Talfan Davies that the "soliloquist" of this poem is "a Celt serving in the Roman army who is thinking of his homeland" (*LF*, 37). But the poem also incorporates other historical moments and other echoing voices, both male and female. It opposes to the Tribune's "forthright Roman" world the Celtic world of particular named place, where a feminine tutelary spirit presides over the natural cycles of fertility, birth, and death.

Dilworth has criticized "The Tutelar of the Place" as the weakest poem in this volume, largely because the psychology of its persona does not lend itself to the kind of psychological reading that Dilworth offers in his discussion of the Tribune. I argue, however, that "The Tutelar of the Place" succeeds as a more Joycean poem. It begins with a recognizable persona, perhaps, but it quickly becomes a kind of echoing collage of voices, of which the protagonist is only one—the gammer is another. By the end of the poem, the voice is more like the inclusive and impersonal voice that we hear through much of *The Anathemata* than it is like the voices we have been hearing in the Roman poems, especially in *The Tribune's Visitation*. This is true for all the Celtic poems in the volume, so the movement from specific persona to more omniscient speaker in "The Tutelar" leads into the Celtic poems that follow.

The feminine presences in "The Tutelar of the Place" may have been inspired in part by Joyce's *Finnegans Wake*, which Jones was reading sporadically during the period of the poem's composition, with the help of Campbell and Robinson's *Skeleton Key* (*LF,* 26–32; Blissett 1981, 13). Joyce's mythic mother, who completes the inadequacies of both "fact men" and "truth men," and who reconciles without resolving the brother-battles between Shem and Shaun, is echoed in the childhood scenes of "The Tutelar of the Place." In Jones, however, the children of the waning culture are not two brothers but brother and sister, experimenting with roles and imitating conflicts that will become deeply divisive in the ages to come (*SL,* 59–60). As if in ironic contrast to the "womb of Caesar" invoked by the Tribune's propaganda, the deliberate blurring of masculine and feminine roles in "man-travail and woman-war" (*SL,* 59) appears as a sign of cultural youth, before the great conflicts that led to the emergence of imperialist civilization. The androgynous character of early culture implied here suggests that just as "fact man" and "truth man" can be embodied in the same person, so masculine and feminine impulses together define our "human nature." The splitting apart of these coinherent principles is one symptom of the civilizational decline that Jones laments.

Most of the poem is an invocation to the local tutelary goddess—"she that loves place, time, demarcation, hearth, kin, enclosure, site, differentiated cult, though she is but one mother of us all" (59). Although the speaker is male, he acknowledges that the source of his prayer is a female consciousness when he refers to it as "our gammer's prayer" (61) and when he recalls the nurturing figure of the gammer leading the children's prayers at bedtime. The situation of a maternal figure ("our gammer") putting the children to bed late in the historical cycle echoes the section of *Finnegans Wake* that Campbell and Robinson label "The Children's Hour," a passage Jones annotated in several places in his copy of the *Skeleton Key*.

Using typically outrageous wordplay, the passage in *Finnegans Wake* connects the voice of a nurse calling the children home with the darkening of the historical world, as another thunderclap, marking the beginning of a new cycle, approaches. Despite the darkening scene, the tone here is primarily comic.

> Chickchilds, comeho to roo. Comehome to roo, wee chickchilds doo, when the wild-worewolf's abroad. Ah, let's away and let's gay and let's stay chez where the log foyer's burning!
>
> It darkles, (tinct, tint) all this our funnaminal world. Yon marsh-pond by ruodmark verge is visited by the tide. Alvemarea! We are circumveiloped by obscuritads. . . . What era's o'ering? Lang gong late. . . . Say long, scielo! . . . Now continicinium. As Lord the Laohun is sheutseyes. The time of lying together will come and the wildering of the nicht till cockeedoodle aubens Aurore. (*FW*, 244; cf. Campbell and Robinson 1944, 153–54)

The foreboding that pervades Jones's "The Tutelar of the Place" contrasts with Joyce's light, singsong, occasionally bawdy treatment of the passage of time and the waning and dawning of new cycles, but the cultural moment is the same in both texts. Calling the children home, Jones's gammer echoes the voice of the nursemaids in the opening poems of Blake's *Songs of Innocence and Experience* and the rather sinister nursery rhyme "Oranges and Lemons," which Jones recalls learning from one of his aunts (*A*, 42).

> Now come on now little
> children, come on now it's past the hour. Sun's to roost, brood's in pent,
> dusk-star tops mound, lupa sniffs the lode-damps for stragglers late to
> byre.
>
> . . . . .
>
> here's a rush to light you to bed
> here's a fleece to cover your head
> against the world-storm
>
>   (60)

The voice of the gammer here echoes in the speaker's memory, evoking an all-knowing female perspective that can foresee the coming "world-storm" threatening the "children" of culture entrusted to her. In this sense, the gammer, like Anna Livia, embodies the qualities of the feminine tutelary spirit whom she invokes.

These Joycean echoes in "The Tutelar of the Place" answer the Spenglerian gloom that pervades "The Tribune's Visitation," and the contrasting moods of the two poems again reflect the kinds of polarities that the volume as a whole sets against each other in its dialogical unfolding. In the first part of the gammer's prayer, narrator, gammer, and children pray together. Later, with the children safely asleep, the speaker goes on in a more universal mode. Still speaking as a nurturer, he continues, "Now sleep on, little children, sleep on now, while I tell out the greater suffrages, not yet for young heads to understand" (62). In contrast to the Tribune, who embraces Spengler's "gnosis of necessity" blindly (*SL*, 58), as the only possible course for the "men of now" (51), the gammer—together with the soldier who recalls her prayer—takes courage from her knowledge that although her local tutelary goddess's cult may pass, it is rooted in a more enduring order. This confidence in a persistent, though hidden, cultural vitality beneath the surface of world civilization recalls Elen Monica's affirmation that "what's under works up" (*A*, 164). Like Elen Monica's monologue, the gammer's prayer uses many different names to invoke the saving power of the feminine principle. The speaker calls simultaneously on "Sweet Jill of our tump," the "Queen of the differentiated sites," and the Virgin Mary, asking for protection "in all times of *Gleichschaltung*" (62–63).

The end of the prayer responds to the final scene of "The Tribune's Visitation," by echoing in more confident tones the Tribune's desolate invocation of Lucina.

> When the technicians manipulate the dead limbs of our culture as though it yet had life, have mercy on us. Open unto us, let us enter a second time within your stola-folds in those days—ventricle and refuge both, *hendref* for world-winter, asylum from world storm. Womb of the Lamb the spoiler of the Ram. (64)

When the Tribune alluded to a "second birth" of the soldiers from the womb of Caesar, and when he appropriated the "mutilated signa" for the ritual of the *sacramentum* (58), he was manipulating the dead limbs of a culture as though they yet had life. But he was also unconsciously foreshadowing the Christian era that would succeed his civilizational phase. In contrast to the Tribune's monologue, the gammer's prayer consciously prophesies the coming civilizational phase. The "Womb of the Lamb" is

Mary, bearer of the "Lamb," Christ, who through her took on flesh and entered history. By envisioning the Lamb as the "spoiler of the Ram," the gammer's prayer insists on the ultimate survival of the "secret seed" of culture (64), which is inherent in the creaturely world of natural cycles, and which is celebrated in human sign making.

The worlds of Tribune and Tutelar are opposed to one another at the center of *The Sleeping Lord,* but Jones makes it clear that the contrast between the two worlds is by no means absolute or dualistic.[5] Rather, the sequence shows clearly how "fact man" and "truth man," masculine and feminine principles, frequently occupy the same consciousness and the same mythic space. All the Roman poems of *The Sleeping Lord*—"The Wall," "The Dream of Private Clitus," "The Fatigue," and "The Tribune's Visitation"—present men who blend the qualities of Spengler's "fact men" and "truth men." Serving in Caesar's army in first-century Jerusalem, these speakers function, willingly or not, as the instruments of empire, and Roman civilization is their heritage. In this way, for Jones, they share the condition of modern man living under a late Western civilization.

The speakers in "The Wall" and "The Fatigue," in particular, demonstrate that the common soldiers of Rome have not attained the complete surrender of "human nature" that Spengler calls for in the "men of the age" (1926, 2:504). They have minds of their own, and they question what they see. The speaker in "The Wall" remarks, "You see a thing or two, you think a thing or two, in our walk of life, walking for twenty years, by day, by night, doing the rounds on the walls that maintain the world" (*SL,* 10). In contrast to the Roman leaders whom he obeys, this soldier still allows himself to remember Rome's origins as an agricultural state, and he knows how the earlier myths have been transformed into rallying cries for the growing empire. With justified cynicism, the end of "The Wall" recognizes that the "fact men" have transformed the native Roman myths into propaganda for their empire. At first these myths justified the urge for conquest—"They used to say we marched for Dea Roma behind the wolf sign to eat up the world"—but now, in the late phase of empire, within "the robber walls of the world city, trapesing the macrocosmic night," the myths have been changed. This soldier recognizes that he is being used in the service of a decadent empire's lust for riches.

> but now they say the Quirinal Mars
> turns out to be no god of war but of armed peace. Now they say we march for

kind Irene, who crooks her rounded elbow for little Plutus, the gold-getter,
and they say that sacred brat has a future. . .

> now all can face the dying god
> the dying Gaul
> without regret.

(14)

The "dying god" of this passage conflates the old fertility rites of pre-Christian cults and the death of Christ, who was crucified at the hands of the Roman empire. For Jones, the dying Gaul of suppressed Celtic culture is closely linked to the dying God of the Christian and pre-Christian West, because both promise a kind of triumph in defeat (*DG*, 50–59). But the skepticism about the claims of empire that pervades "The Wall" reminds us how difficult it is to see the redemptive side of the historical cycle from within a triumphant late civilization. In this regard, "The Wall" comes closer than any other poem in the *Sleeping Lord* sequence to reflecting Jones's historical situation.

All the Roman poems in *The Sleeping Lord* acknowledge that the mixture of "goodness" and "badness" accompanying any historical moment sometimes appears to be inherent in the myths that guide the people of that moment, particularly in an age where an imperial civilization uses the *signa* of conquered peoples in an effort to secure their loyalty. The resulting confusion is particularly striking in the multiple roles of the Roman mother goddess as she is described in "The Dream of Private Clitus." This dream vision, which Private Clitus narrates to his fellow Roman Oenomaus in rambling storyteller's prose, pursues in a new way the conflict that *In Parenthesis* first presented between the masculine domain of warfare and the feminine domain of home and hearth, to which the men on the line still feel a deep attachment. The dream of Private Clitus blurs these polarities by depicting from the common man's point of view a mother goddess whose function is simultaneously sacred and political.

The dream begins by recalling the Ara Pacis Augustae in Clitus's native Rome, a work of art that has now become an emblem of Rome as empire. In his dream, the figure of Terra Mater, illuminated by moonlight, seems to reach out from her place in the frieze, leaning toward the dreamer and his companion, a Gaul named Lugo. In this phase of the dream, she is a nurturing figure, offering protection within the folds of her *stola* (19). As Clitus and Lugo are "caught up into that peace," the Celtic soldier calls out to the Terra Mater figure in recognition, using the Welsh name for the earth mother, "Modron." In a significant parenthesis, Clitus recalls that the same invocation to the mother was Lugo's dying prayer.

And now (in my dream-now that is), from his side our gestatorial marble, Lugo cried out a name: Modron! he cries, and then—but very low-voiced though: Porth-Annwfyn. Some numinous, arcane agnomen, but which to my dream-cognition was lucid as moonshine and did plainly signify: Gate of Elysium.

Now I knew no word of Lugo's lingo, and it was, after all, *my* dream, not his. Well, Oenomaus, what do you make of that one? But I'll tell you further: when they got him I was next by him in the traverse—and that was no dream—and he cried loud the same cult-name, but not the last bit, for he was done before he could utter it. (20)

Clitus sees the Terra Mater figure as "Matrona," a specifically Roman tutelary goddess, enshrined in "our gestatorial marble," who rewards her sons for keeping the watch and preserving the empire. Yet his dream recognizes that she belongs to Lugo's mythology as well. The irony here is pointed, for Lugo belongs to one of the peoples whose culture is threatened by the expanding Roman empire. Though he and Clitus respond to the same basic myth of the mother goddess, Lugo is, historically and individually, a "dying Gaul," doomed by the forces who take the Roman goddess of the Ara Pacis as their protector.[6]

Clitus here speaks for the humane impulses that Jones associates with "the natural and proper rebellion of all men, of man," against imperial civilization. His overall gesture, in telling his dream-vision, is one of accommodation and inclusion. Though he mourns Lugo as his friend and soul mate, his imaginative world also finds a place for "old Brasso." He tells Brasso's story and, in so doing, reveals how even the controlling myths of imperial propaganda are manifestations, albeit perverted and distorted, of a persistent human impulse to tell tales and make signs. As Brasso's voice shook Private Clitus from his dream, so Clitus insists that "fact-men" like Brasso are an inevitable part of life under the empire, which breaks up and dissipates the dream worlds of culture from which the men have emerged: "He always will be with us, while there's any us to make memento of. . . . There's always a Brasso to shout the odds, a fact-man to knock sideways and fragmentate these dreamed unities and blessed conjugations" (21). Yet if Brasso's role is to "fragmentate" the cultural world that has nurtured men like Clitus, he is also a typic figure in the controlling myth of the empire. Without Brasso and the ruling "fact men" that he represents, "Roma," beloved of Clitus and of his fellow Roman soldiers, could not exist.

Clitus acknowledges this irony through the two alternate accounts of

Brasso's origins that he offers toward the end of the poem. First he recalls, "Some say he was born shouting the odds, in full parade kit, with a pacing stick under his cherubic little arm." But the second version of Brasso's story sets him up more obviously as the representative of imperial man, whose beginnings are still commemorated in military ritual. Here he is the son of an imperial mother, her body "ventricled of bronze" with "ubera of iron," who fed him "by numbers"—an allusion to a method of army drill (22).[7] Brasso's mother stands in marked contrast to the soothing and nurturing figure of Terra Mater in the dream vision. Yet like Lugo's Modron, who is also Clitus's Dea Roma, Brasso's mother represents another aspect of the same mythic principle, and Clitus's dream has revealed how inadequate the imperial myth is to her full power and significance. The irrepressibility of the feminine principle suggested here was already implied in *The Anathemata,* when Elen Monica transformed herself for a moment to mimic the figure of Britannia. Elen's impersonation at once demonstrated how persuasive the imperial co-opting of feminine imagery can be and showed that the feminine principle herself, as genuine guardian of humane values, remains unconvinced and unchanged even when her power and presence seem weakened by the "mutilated signa" of propaganda. Private Clitus's account of Dea Roma instinctively acknowledges this persistent presence of a nurturing feminine principle, but it also exemplifies the general confusion that reigns in a late civilization over the signs and stories that embody and carry forward her influence.

The competing visions of a Dea Roma who is the goddess of empire and the receding tutelary goddess of the Roman soldiers' home-places reflect the complexity that Jones discerns in Spengler's opposition between "fact-men" and "truth men." Clitus and Lugo, at once native sons of their particular home-places and servants of empire, mingle both perspectives. Clitus, devoted to Terra Mater and the earlier Roman culture she represents for him, knows that when the "fact men" decline, the entire cultural complex that he knows will fall with them: "Dea Roma, Flora Dea / meretrix or world nutricula / without Brasso. / There are some things / that can't be managed / even in these dreams" (23). Lugo, whose dying prayer is addressed to Modron, dies in the service of the empire that will destroy his native culture. This seems to be Jones's way of acknowledging a historical necessity in the emergence of imperial world civilizations, even as he deplores the inhumanity and "robbery" of empire. In a similar vein, in *The Anathemata,* he laments his own culture, the "failing / (finished?) West" (*A,* 231), now only fragmentarily surviving in the technocratic civilization that is its last phase.

This sense of a historical necessity that can be resisted only by a kind of subterranean imagination also pervades "The Fatigue." Dilworth has argued that among the poems of *The Sleeping Lord*, "The Fatigue" represents the most direct and fully realized expression of Jones's Christian belief, and he shows how the form of this poem presents what he calls "the Christian synthesis" as an alternative to the bleakness of life under a world-empire (1988, 287). He argues suggestively that this poem presents in poetic form the traditional visual topoi of a Crucifixion scene. It is a triptych, with the crucified Christ in the center—corresponding to the long excursus on the victim who hangs on the "Dreaming Tree" (*SL*, 31–38)—and the good and bad thieves on either side of him. To his right, at the beginning of the poem, is the "good thief"—common man as represented by the soldier-speaker and his friends, who are the unwitting instruments of the Crucifixion, and who rebel in their minds against the oppressive orders they must follow. To his left, at the end, is the "bad thief" of imperial bureaucracy, represented in a meandering series of phrases beginning "From where" (38), which together trace the bureaucratic labyrinth in which the order for the Crucifixion originates (Dilworth 1988, 291). For Dilworth, this threefold structure of the poem traces "the reciprocal relationship each to the other of ordinary man, Jesus, and the world." More specifically, he argues that the relationship of Christ to the world-city is "dialectical, with the world as thesis, Christ as antithesis, and the implied transformation of the former by the latter as synthesis" (284, 287). What Dilworth calls the "Christian synthesis" draws together all the Roman poems and "centres" them on the Passion of Christ—much as *The Anathemata* is centered—by positing some hope of deliverance from the evil that is allowed to dominate human experience in a late civilization (294).

Dilworth's reading of the poem is tempting for its elegance, but it does not square with Jones's repeated refusals of summaries that choose one polarity over another. Nor does it explain the sense of disruption and displacement that the reader necessarily experiences in following the dramatic form of this poem. "The Fatigue" begins and ends as a psychologically convincing interior monologue by a common soldier. Yet it breaks out of this into an extended meditation on the Crucifixion, which ultimately exceeds what the meditating consciousness of that soldier could plausibly imagine or prophesy. Parts of this central meditation are reminiscent, both in form and in typology, of *The Anathemata,* and the poetic persona here sounds more like the omniscient and shifting voice of that poem than like the more individualized soldier whose monologue frames this long digression. The soldier who speaks here can derive no solace from the Christian synthesis that his meditation reveals, because it looks beyond his historical moment. Unlike the Tribune, he is a completely sympathetic character, so there is no sense of irony in the poem's evocation of a coming synthesis that he cannot see. By expanding the poem's meditative range beyond the immediate historical situation of the speaker, the central section of "The Fatigue" breaks out of the dramatic situation to foreground the poet's activity of sign making. Its form implies once again that redemption continues, in and through the darkest times, in the poetic process itself, which defines our humanity. Within this framework, the central elaboration on the tree of the cross, which wanders far from the historical situation of the meditating soldier, then returns, becomes a conscious demonstration of an associative poetic imagination that belongs both to the speaker and to the poet who is imagining this poem in the twentieth century.

The manuscripts of the poem reveal that, as with some of the most elaborate and evocative parts of *The Anathemata*, the meditation on the cross here arose as a late addition, splitting the original two parts of the poem at what are now pages 31 and 40 (see Dilworth 1988, 294) and growing out of the center. This digressive elaboration opens up the poem from the center, gesturing toward and celebrating a source of hope that the rest of the poem, rooted as it is in its historical moment, cannot fully embrace. In this respect, the poem typifies the open character of many of the poems in *The Sleeping Lord* and in the volume as a whole. It foregrounds creative process over synthesis, and it gestures toward a possibility of wholeness even as it refuses to come to rest in any final or encompassing statement. In this way, the form of the poem reflects Jones's recognition of the continuing conflict between the hope for wholeness, synthesis, and creative freedom and a historical reality that appears to deny and undermine these hopes. It is a strikingly original formal expression of what Jones elsewhere called the "'optimism' of the saints," the fundamental affirmativeness implied by any human act of making (*DG*, 159).

The muted protests of the soldiers in the Roman poems demonstrate how a "late" civilization tends to drive underground and to distort the imaginative life and the necessary rebellion that Jones defines as natural to humanity as a sign-making species. In "The Hunt" and "The Sleeping Lord," the Celtic poems that close the *Sleeping Lord* sequence, Jones uses the land and legends of Wales to embody a hidden cultural vitality, suppressed and weakened by the course of world history, but always harboring potential renewal. In these two poems, Jones's imagination draws on the material and oral culture of medieval Wales to create a particular place in time that becomes a natural home for the poet and hence an appropriate setting for his own act of recalling in a bleak historical moment.

Jones draws his Arthurian material from Malory and from the earliest, fragmentary tales found in the Welsh cycle *The Mabinogion*. In one essay, he notes that Malory wrote his "Morte d'Arthur" on the eve of the modern era ushered in by the Tudors. Thus, he was writing very late in his historical cycle, "just in time" to avoid a complete severing of connection with the ancient tales. Jones identifies his own enterprise with Malory's in this respect (*EA*, 244). Like Malory, he himself is writing late in a civilizational phase—almost too late, perhaps, because he draws on material that represents a very ancient layer in the deposits of his native culture. What Jones calls the "subterranean" tradition of Arthur and of early Wales (*EA*, 221) is associated in his mind with the impressive and prosperous material culture recorded in Old Welsh sagas, of which little has survived into the present. The lack of "tangible relics to evoke the past" symbolizes for Jones the sense of loss and exile that he feels as a modern poet seeking his "homeland." "Truly native and truly informative archaeological finds from the Age of the Princes are very, very few indeed," he writes; "The empty stone coffin of Llywelyn the Great is, alas, symbolic of what I am trying to say, and, in a sense, this loss of evidence or relic or image or figuration ties up well with the tradition of a vanished Arthur" (*EA*, 228).

The verbal texture of "The Hunt" and "The Sleeping Lord" represents Jones's most successful attempt to evoke, even to create, an embodied tradition in verbal form. As in *The Anathemata*, the carefully worked language of these poems draws attention to the poetic maker at work. Even more than the Roman poems of the sequence, the Celtic poems present themselves, in language and form, as "tangible relics," fashioned out of a language whose very texture evokes and recalls an older cultural complex whose subterranean vitality persists into our time.

Among the few fragments of "evidence or relic or image or figuration" of the vanished Arthur, for Jones, are the Arthurian tales collected in the Welsh *Mabinogion*. These tales, which Jones describes as "outcroppings of the oldest strata" of the matter of Britain, originated in the prehistoric oral tradition of the Celts and appeared in written form in the eleventh or twelfth centuries A.D. (Gantz 1976, 21–25). "The Hunt" and "The Sleeping Lord" imitate some of the native verbal techniques of the tale of

"Culhwch and Olwen" in *The Mabinogion*. This fragmentary and somewhat rambling narrative tells how Culhwch, a cousin of King Arthur, undertook a series of adventures to win Olwen, the daughter of the giant Ysbaddaden Pencawr. Archetypally, the story belongs to the tradition of fertility myths that require the death of an aging father figure before a younger generation can succeed. The giant in the tale imposes a series of apparently impossible tasks on his daughter's suitor, for he knows that the marriage of his daughter will mean his own death. One of these tasks is the hunting of the giant boar Twrch Trwyth, who has torn up and ravaged three-quarters of Ireland and Wales. The defeat of the boar, undertaken with the help of Arthur and his men, fulfills the mythic pattern of the restoration of the land after its destruction by evil natural forces. The tale ends with the death of the giant and the marriage of Culhwch and Olwen.

The tale of Culhwch shapes "The Hunt" and "The Sleeping Lord" not only through its central story of the boar hunt but through its style, which derives from an oral tradition that revels in ornament, lists, and detail. Early in the tale, for example, we encounter a list of the lords in whose names Culhwch demands Olwen. The list has the quality of an incantation summing up and recalling the major people and events of a now-lost culture. In Lady Guest's translation, this list takes up five pages of the tale. Though many of the names here are unfamiliar, the verbal technique of this list, with its repetitions, epithets, and long descriptive parentheses, represented for Jones an authentic and somehow material outcropping from a lost Welsh oral culture.

> This boon I likewise seek at the hands of thy warriors. I seek it from Kai, and Bedwyr, and Greidawl Galldonyd, and Gwythyr the son of Greidawl, and . . . Gwiawn Llygad Cath (who could cut a haw from the eye of the gnat without hurting him). Ol the son of Olwydd (seven years before he was born his father's swine were carried off, and when he grew up a man he tracked the swine, and brought them back in seven herds). Bedwinin the Bishop (who blessed Arthur's meat and drink). . . . And all these did Culhwch son of Kilydd adjure to obtain his boon. (Guest 1913, 223–29)

As he invokes Arthur's attendant lords, Culhwch tells their histories. In the course of this retelling, he offers a kind of verbal anamnesis of the customs and traditions of his whole culture. Stylistically, this use of a list of names, relished for their sound and cultural associations, also belongs to the Celticity that Jones admired in Joyce's style. We see it, for example, in the list of people who received gifts from Anna Livia Plurabelle (*FW*, 210–13).

"The Hunt" uses the style of the ornamented list to suggest a link between Jones's contemporary text and the older tradition that it recalls. Although Jones's list gives far fewer names than that of Culhwch, his incantatory and rhythmic repetitions echo the music of *The Mabinogion*.

> . . . the men of proud spirit and the men of mean spirit, the named and the unnamed of the Island and the name-bearing steeds of the Island and the dogs of the Island and the silent lords and the lords of loud mouth, the leaders of familiar visage from the dear known-sites and the adjuvant stranger lords with aid for the hog-hunt from over the Sleeve. (65)

In the "Culhwch and Olwen" narrative, the boar hunt is but one of several quests undertaken by the hero, and the figure of Arthur remains in the background, a shadowy, but benevolent and supernaturally powerful, supporter of his cousin's undertaking, whose efforts lead to the defeat of the boar and the restoration of the land. In "The Hunt," however, Arthur becomes at once the "diademed leader" of the men of Britain and an embodiment of the stricken land, a suffering fertility god (69). In this poem, the victory of the men of the island is not so clear, and the hope of a resurrection implicit in the comparison of Arthur to Christ is dim. The identity between the hog and the civilizational and technical forces that have "helped a lot of Gauls and gods to die" (14) becomes explicit in "The Sleeping Lord." In this poem, the hope of redemption comes from the shape of the text, rather than from the cultural situation it depicts, which is bleak indeed. Here the legend of the hog hunt and the technique of listing borrowed from "Culhwch and Olwen" enable the poet to give tangible shape to the things that have been lost and to hint—albeit obliquely—at the ultimate persistence of the "secret seed" (69) of the sacramental world, despite the triumph in his time of the forces of destruction that the hog represents.

The account of the Boar Trwyth given in the climactic section of this poem epitomizes the difference in feeling between "The Hunt" and "The Sleeping Lord" (*SL*, 89–90). In the first poem, the hog was an adversary to be hunted "life for life" (69) but Arthur was still awake to take the wounds and to resist the destructive power that the Boar represented. In "The

Sleeping Lord," however, the results of the hog's destructive power persist unopposed. The postmedieval destruction of Welsh culture has prevailed, and Arthur has gone underground, leaving no outward resistance to the hog. The hog's power corresponds much more explicitly to the unbridled destruction of loved things and places that industrial civilization brings about. The things that his tusk has destroyed included the white-wattled huts and the hearthstone that "The Tutelar of the Place" identified with the roots of a culture. More ominously still, he has destroyed the Queen of the Woods and "stamped out the seeds of fire" (89–90), striking at the tutelary goddess herself. Both the land and the men, beloved of of the "diademed leader" of "The Hunt," fall across the Boar's path and are mown down, suggesting again the alliance between the hog and the progress of modern civilization. Other parts of the poem underscore this alliance—for example, the mingling of Arthur's tears with the slag of the coalfields at the beginning of the poem (71) and the North Sea oil slick in which the "dying gull" suffers toward the end (93). Yet this passage also describes the Boar, insistently, in the Welsh language and the Celtic style of the older culture. The Welsh words with which it is studded and the bardic repetitions of its style mark the text as a kind of material survival. By pointing to its status as a verbal artifact in this tradition, the poem insists on a kind of continuity despite the current devastation.

The landscape of "The Sleeping Lord" is utterly bleak. What hope it holds lies hidden deep beneath its surface, and the poem offers no concrete promise of deliverance—although the flickering of the candlebearer's flame and the sound of the wind over the contours of the hills, which the guards at a Tudor fortress mistake for the sounds of a stirring rebellion (95), may be taken as signs of hidden life. Nonetheless, there is a powerful affirmation in what this poem does with its materials, particularly in the rhetorical gestures to which it adapts the Celtic narrative techniques of naming and cumulative listing. The first of these gestures, essential to the *Sleeping Lord* sequence as a whole, is reflected in the prayer of the hall priest, which takes up almost one-third of the poem. The second is implicit in the decisive poetic act of asking the question with which "The Sleeping Lord" opens and closes.

In the poetic sequence formed by the Roman and Celtic poems of *The Sleeping Lord,* the prayer of the hall priest in the title poem is a decisive and redemptive verbal action that fulfills the prayers of the Tribune and the gammer together. It underscores the nature of the poet's activity in a late civilization, the curse transformed into blessing that underlies all David Jones's later work. Prayer is important throughout Jones's work as a verbal action characteristic of "man-as-sign-maker." We see this in Dai's prayer to "Blessed Bran" at the center of *In Parenthesis* and in the repeated refrain of *dona eis requiem* throughout *The Anathemata*. The act of prayer recurs with particular insistence throughout *The Sleeping Lord and Other Fragments;* it may be seen as the sequence's primary rhetorical gesture. The volume as a whole opens with the prayer of the poet in an alien situation, in the title's invocation, "A, a, a, DOMINE DEUS." It closes with the prayers of the men of Passchendaele, who invoke an invisible matriarchate in the fragment from *The Book of Balaam's Ass,* and with the saving prayers of Mrs. Austin for her son. Moreover, the invocations of Modron and Dea Roma in "The Dream of Private Clitus" and the complementary prayers of Tribune and gammer, which oppose one another at the center of the volume, reflect the complexity of human responses to civilizational crisis. In the devastated cultural and natural landscapes that *The Sleeping Lord* presents, the act of prayer appears as a performative utterance,[8] establishing the links between "man-the-sign-maker" and a sacred order. In this way, its function is continuous with the recurring acts of offering and anamnesis that testified to cultural continuity in *The Anathemata.*

In the longest section of "The Sleeping Lord," Arthur's hall priest, offering grace before his meal, prays for all the men and women of the island's heroic past and, ultimately, for all who belong to the culture of the West, a culture nourished by the ancient tales of early Britain and by Christianity. The list of names, punctuated with parenthetical explanations and glosses, recalls once again the list in "Culhwch and Olwen." Many readers may feel that the list in Jones is irritatingly obscure and excessively precious in its archaic style. Others may appreciate the characteristic texture of Jones's idiosyncratic style and recognize that the obscurity, however annoying, is part of the point of the act of anamnesis that Jones is making here. Even more than in "The Hunt," the list in "The Sleeping Lord" evokes not only the men and women named but the whole lost tradition to which this style of listing names and embedding tales belongs. The priest recalls, for example,

the Blessed Bran of whom the tale-tellers tell a most wondrous tale and then the names of men more prosaic but more credible to him: Paternus of the Red Pexa, Cunedda Wledig the Conditor and, far more recent and so more green in the memory, the Count Ambrosius Aurelianus that men call Emrys Wledig, associated, by some, with the eastern defences called the Maritime Tract and Aircol Hîr and his line, *protectores* of Demetia in the west . . . and many, many more whose names are, for whatever reason, on the diptycha of the Island; and vastly many more still, whether men or womenkind, of neither fame nor recorded *nomen*, whether bond or freed or innately free, of far back or of but recent decease, whose burial mounds are known or unknown or for whom no mound was ever raised or any mark set up of even the meanest sort to show the site of their interment. (84–85)

This list, which continues for one-third of the entire poem, resembles that in the Culhwch narrative in its allusions to tales and traditions largely lost. Like that list, it begins with the lords of the islands and then moves to the ladies. Echoing the richly embellished style of the *Mabinogion* and other medieval Welsh works, the hall priest's prayer presents itself as an artifact, an outcropping or survival from a lost culture. The poet's evident enjoyment of the sheer sound and music of the Welsh words and the strange names further identifies this lost world as a tangible, if increasingly indecipherable, reality.

The hall priest mumbles the prayer for the dead using the Latin of the Roman Mass—"saying less than half-audibly, *Requiem aeternam dona eis, Domine*"—and the candlebearer "sings out in a high, clear and distinct voice, the respond: ET LUX PERPETUA LUCEAT EIS" (86–87). At the time of writing this poem, shortly after the Second Vatican Council abolished the Latin Mass and many of its accompanying rituals, Jones was keenly aware that the priest's and candlebearer's Latin would soon be as opaque to a contemporary reader as their Welsh words. Yet the rhetoric of the "*requiem aeternam*" prayer (which translates, "Grant them, O Lord, eternal rest, and may light perpetual shine upon them") always implies hope, affirming continuity even as it acknowledges loss. Thus, both in language and in rhetorical force, this prayer, repeated here by the hall priest, epitomizes the blend of grief and defiant hope that lies at the heart of "The Sleeping Lord."

Jones's presentation of the hall priest's prayer as a kind of redemptive verbal action parallels another mode of action that is performed by the poet in Jones's scheme: the asking of the Grail hero's question. Like the "*requiem aeternam*" prayer, this question always implies hope for the wasteland. In the Grail story of Peredur, the hero's failure to "ask the question"

results in the continued suffering of the maimed king and the blighting of
the wasteland. The question he fails to ask is "why?"—why is the king
wounded, why does the spear drip? why is the land waste, and by implica-
tion, how can it be delivered? Like the prayer, the Grail question recurs
throughout Jones's work. Dai Greatcoat exhorts his listeners, "You ought
to ask: Why, / what is this, / what's the meaning of this. / Because you
don't ask, /although the spear-shaft / drips, /there's neither steading—
not a roof-tree" (*IP*, 84). In *The Anathemata*, Christ's redemption of the
world is equated with the asking of the Grail hero's question: "Unless he
ask the question / how shall the rivers run / or the suitors persuade their
loves / or the erosion of the land cease?" (*A*, 226).[9] At the beginning of
his essay "Art in Relation to War," Jones evokes the same myth to explain
the purpose of the essay. "Because the Land is Waste," he writes, ". . . [the
essay] seeks to do what the hero in the myth was rebuked for not doing,
i.e. it seeks to 'ask the Question.' " In contrast to the myth, Jones's essay
does not suppose "that in asking the question the land can be 'restored.'
Although if all the world asked the question," he adds, "perhaps there
might be some fructification—or some 'sea-change' " (*DG*, 123).

The questions at the beginning and end of "The Sleeping Lord" sim-
ilarly represent the poet's effort to ask the question that will heal the king
and restore the land. Although the answers to his questions remain ob-
scure, the act of asking, like the act of offering anathemata and the act of
prayer, matters fundamentally. Hence the poem begins, "And is his bed
wide /is his bed deep on the folded strata / . . . where is his bed and /
where has he lain him?" (70), and the whole poem is cast in an interroga-
tive mode. It ends with two open questions whose potential answers sum
up the obscure and tenuous hope that pervades this volume.

> Does the land wait the sleeping lord?
> or is the wasted land
> that very lord who sleeps?
>
> (96)

If the land "wait the sleeping lord," renewal must come through an apoc-
alyptic change that would transform the sleeper into the bridegroom of
the land or into the hero of a new wasteland story, perhaps of a new
civilizational cycle. But if the wasted land *is* "that very lord who sleeps,"
renewal must come about through forces within the devastated
landscape—the cyclic rhythms implicit in Elen Monica's belief that
"what's under works up" (*A*, 164). Both questions remain open, allowing

two mythic possibilities to play against each other without proposing a solution to the cultural decline and loss that the poem depicts. But if the answers to the poet's questions remain indeterminate, the failure to ask them will always result in the wasteland. In this sense, the poet's persistence in asking the question, like the hall priest's prayer and the continuing sacramental offering of *The Anathemata,* can only be a gesture of hope, however obscure, in the face of contemporary cultural decline.

The four Roman poems and three Celtic poems of *The Sleeping Lord and Other Fragments* form together a relatively coherent poetic sequence in which Jones articulates his mythic understanding of Western history. In the volume as a whole, this sequence is framed by "A, a, a, DOMINE DEUS" at the beginning and "From *The Book of Balaam's Ass*" at the end, two fragments developed out of the *Balaam's Ass* manuscript—the work based on the late stages of the Great War, in which Jones was trying to show how the poet's curse is transmuted into a blessing, simply because he expresses that curse in a made thing. The relation of these two fragments to the volume's central sequence is important for understanding the significance of *The Sleeping Lord* as a whole. Dilworth sees an organic unity in the sequence and argues that it offers a "Christian synthesis," which he finds in "The Fatigue" and elsewhere, as a resolution to the dialectic between imperialism and culture, between Roman and Celtic worlds, that organizes these poems. Accordingly, he argues that the opening and closing poems of the volume unify the sequence by bringing the dialectic represented by the Roman and Celtic worlds into the twentieth century. For Dilworth, the dialectic is resolved in *The Book of Balaam's Ass,* which in his view gestures beyond the present suffering that the poem describes toward a salvation beyond this life, discovered primarily in the meditating consciousness of the soldier who observes the dying soldiers and hears their litany. In this sense, he argues, "From *The Book of Balaam's Ass*" is "a Catholic's Protestant poem," appealing primarily to a hope of transcendence beyond this life (1988, 355).

To me, this kind of reading seems too tidy. It reaches for a synthesis that Jones's poetry resists at every moment, though its language takes every opportunity to gesture toward a divine presence and to reveal a consistent human response to that presence even in the worst of times. Even in the despair of Passchendaele, in *The Book of Balaam's Ass,* Jones refuses to leave behind the historical world and its genuine suffering and losses. His honesty in this regard, reflected in the form of the poetry, and particularly eloquent in the starkness of the concluding poem, is part of the unique strength of *The Sleeping Lord and Other Fragments* as a poetic response to utterly dehumanizing times.

The volume begins with the poet's question "I said, what shall I write?" and ends with a bleak line from *The Book of Balaam's Ass:* "But for all the rest there was no help on that open plain" (111). These two fragments together summarize well the balance between blessing and curse that *The Book of Balaam's Ass* sought to convey—from the poet's desperate *"Eia, Domine Deus"* to the dying soldiers' invocation of an invisible "matriarchate" in the desolate mud-fields of Passchendaele. But because they have no other obvious thematic relationship to the Roman and Celtic sequences at the center of the volume, these two fragments work against whatever sense of thematic coherence the reader might wish to find in the poems from "The Wall" through "The Sleeping Lord." By including these two fragments, Jones opens his sequence, dispelling any sense of mythic coherence or totalizing statement that might have been implied if *The Sleeping Lord* had consisted only of the Roman-Celtic sequence, and reminding us that the poet is offering no answer to the question posed by his persistent opposition of Roman and Celtic worldviews. Jones insisted to friends in correspondence regarding *The Sleeping Lord* that the voices we hear in this volume do not enunciate any program for the salvation of the world. His point is rather to let these voices be heard.[10] The muted protests of "truth-men" against "fact-men" in the Roman poems, Lugo's dying invocation of Modron, the Tribune's whispered invocation of Juno, the prayers of gammer and priest, and finally the poet's questions in the introductory poem and the title poem record the ways in which human nature, in Jones's view, rebels against the inhumanities of cultural and historical circumstances—circumstances that are also, paradoxically, the product of human decisions and actions.

Taken as a whole, then, *The Sleeping Lord* reflects little of the serene confidence implicit in the affirmation of "what is done in many places" at the end of *The Anathemata*. By the late 1960s, when "The Sleeping Lord" was written, even the continuity implicit in the Mass seemed threatened by the real events of the poet's time—especially by the loss of contact with the past that the Second Vatican Council represented to Jones. Instead of offering any explicit affirmation, *The Sleeping Lord* attempts to strike a balance, however precarious and tenuous, between the real losses of the age and the continuing memory of the poet. Thus, if Jones is resigned, with Spengler, to the decline of culture in his time, he nonetheless continues to portray the poet's role as an affirmative one, parallel to that of the speaker in "The Tutelar of the Place," though also sharing the ambivalent allegiances and historical perceptions of Private Clitus and the Tribune. As the gammer looks for signs of the nurturing Tutelar's presence "in all times of *Gleichschaltung*" (*SL*, 63), so *The Sleeping Lord* as a whole offers glimmering evidence that a humane culture and even a hope of redemption persist through the darkest times. As in all of Jones's work, the remnants of this subterranean order of value find their fullest expression in the actions of the poet, who continues to make signs, to pray, and to question, even in the most barren cultural landscape.

Conclusion: "Before His Time?":
The Jones Legacy

There is only one tale to tell even though the telling is patient of endless development and ingenuity and can take on a million variant forms. I imagine something of this sort to be implicit in what Picasso is reported as saying: 'I do not seek, I find.'

—Preface to *The Anathemata*

. . . Lie down
in the word-hoard, burrow
the coil and gleam
of your furrowed brain.

. . . .

Keep your eye clear
as the bleb of the icicle,
trust the feel of what nubbed treasure
your hands have known.

—Seamus Heaney

I am making a mappemunde. It is to include my being.

—Charles Olson

As a poetic theorist and as a self-conscious maker, drawing on and transforming the mythic-historical insights of Joyce and Spengler, David Jones responds in unique ways to the sense of cultural lateness that preoccupied so many writers of his generation. Yet to read him simply as a minor modernist or a lesser Joyce would be to slight the profound originality and the remarkable timeliness of his poetics. I have suggested throughout this discussion that Jones's most original contribution has been his presentation of poetry as a mode of verbal action. This work has important implications for ongoing theoretical debates in our time regarding the character of poetry after modernism and the nature and possibility of an epic poetry in the twentieth century.

Critics writing on twentieth-century poetry have tended to use the distinction between "open" form and "closed" or "spatial" form as the basis for definitions of modernist and postmodernist poetic styles (see Altieri 1973 and 1979). Charles Olson's 1950 essay "Projective Verse" is commonly used as the basic critical text for this distinction, though as Marjorie Perloff (1973) has acutely pointed out, the terms *postmodern* and *modern* become problematic here, because many of the formulations in Olson's essay derive from the writings of Pound, Williams, and other poets whose work Olson claims to be surpassing and displacing. In his essay, whose style is informal and antiformal, Olson insists on "the *kinetics* of the thing." Rejecting the "closed" forms favored by Eliot and what Olson calls the "classical-abstract" tradition of English poetry, he insists that poets should work not with line, stanza, and the drive toward internal coherence suggested by "over-all form" but with what he calls "open-field composition," an associative technique where "ONE PERCEPTION MUST IMMEDIATELY AND DIRECTLY LEAD TO A FURTHER PER-CEPTION" (1950, 17). Olson admits that his notion of poetry tends toward the public forms of drama and epic rather than toward the lyric forms that tended to attract his modernist predecessors (15, 20). He is insistent in calling for verse forms that will be closer to communal speech patterns and oral modes of communication, that will work in, rather than apart from, the temporal and experiential world. He shows some important affinities with Jones, who similarly takes the oral poet as the model for his enterprise. Jones's more conservative point of departure is implicit in his view of the poet as the custodian of a tradition, and his work shows none of the radical subjectivity that we find in much of Olson's poetry. Nonetheless, he anticipates Olson's declaration, echoing Robert Creeley, that "THE FORM IS NEVER MORE THAN AN EXTENSION OF THE CONTENT" (1950, 16).

All three of Jones's major poetic works proceed by "opening" or improvising on more traditional formal structures that make for an underlying organic coherence. *The Sleeping Lord* organizes a sequence of poems around the dichotomies suggested by Roman and Celtic worlds, "fact-man" and "truth-man." Yet the individual voices in the poems, the questions that open and close the title poem, and the inclusion of "A,a,a, DOMINE DEUS" and "From *The Book of Balaam's Ass*" at the beginning and end of the published volume work against the effect of schematic or dialectical organization suggested by the confrontation between Tribune and Tutelar at the center of the sequence. *In Parenthesis* is primarily a narrative organized around a linear sequence of events. Yet what I have called the lyric digressions or set pieces of *In Parenthesis* repeatedly break out of the linear narrative of the poem to expose deeper symbolic and mythic connections and, perhaps more important, to display the poetic imagination at work. Such interludes as the "rat of no-man's land" meditation at the end of part 3 (54), the meditation on groves in part 4 (66), Dai's boast (79–84), and the "Queen of the Woods" sequence in part 7 (185–86) look forward to the more pervasive digressive technique that becomes fundamental to the evolving structure of *The Anathemata*.

The Anathemata remains the fullest and most successful realization of Jones's formal technique, which is in turn a major contribution to the poetics of the long poem or modern verse epic in the twentieth century. What makes *The Anathemata* unusual among longer modern poems is its blend of formal closure—a shape that returns to its beginning—with an improvisatory openness that has much in common with Charles Olson's sense of poetry as an ongoing process, enacted in the shape of the text, and with the more radical modes of poetic invention advocated by William Carlos Williams.

Readers of *The Anathemata* have tended to stress either the poem's "openness" or its ultimate coherence. Advocates have defended the poem by pointing to patterns of coherence beneath the appearance of randomness and allusive opacity (Alexander 1967; Blamires 1972, 113–50; Hooker 1975; Hague 1967). Thomas Dilworth has argued that the poem unfolds as a series of concentric circles, always returning to an ultimate focus on the Mass, the Passion, and anamnesis (1988, 111–13). Neil Corcoran, however, recalls David Jones's insistence on "the essentially open nature of his writing." "The *Anathemata*, more than most long poems perhaps," writes Corcoran, "manifests form as process, as discovery, as 'invention' " (1982, 25, 43). Vincent Sherry has argued that the poem's thematic coherence identifies it as part of an essentially British modernist tradition that favors "formal and thematic completeness" over the often radically subjective and associative openness of American modernist and postmodernist long poems. "All in all," writes Sherry, "*The Anathemata* transcends the elliptical, discontinuous and fragmented state of its surface—its typically modernist qualities—and achieves the larger arch of formal and thematic closure" (1985, 243).[1] The coexistence of formal closure and improvisatory openness—what Jones in one letter calls "a *prose method* breaking out, where the tension demands it, into a *quasi-verse method*" (*IN*, 48)—is a key to *The Anathemata*'s significance as a contribution to poetic practice on both sides of the Atlantic. George Steiner appears to see this when he suggests that *The Anathemata* may be "among prologomena to future forms" (1967, 309).

Seen in the context of the poetics of open form, Jones stands as a pivotal figure between modernism and whatever comes after it.[2] A contemporary and friend of Eliot, he shared the modernist view of a poem as a well wrought, internally coherent form in which fragmentary and lyric materials are unified by methods analogous to those of the visual arts. But Jones was also attracted by techniques of composition that resemble in significant ways the oral and associative patterns favored by Olson and Williams, whose work he did not know. Jones—who like Olson preferred the thick and highly syllabic language of late medieval poetry to the more lyrical and formally coherent English poetry of Spenser and Milton[3]—was most attracted by the verbal texture of poetry written to imitate speech patterns, especially the patterns of middle English and of Welsh. He was particularly inspired by the originally oral and improvisatory forms of medieval Welsh poetry. He makes a significant contribution to the poetics of the modern long poem in his adaptation of the techniques of this rooted oral tradition to the needs of the twentieth-century bard.

Gwyn Williams describes the typical form of works from the Welsh oral tradition in the introduction to his book *The Burning Tree*, which Jones read and reviewed with admiration. The poetry that Williams describes and translates is characterized by such oral techniques as "echoing, running parenthesis, the purposeful reiteration which has been given the ugly name of incremental repetition, the identity of end and beginning." Through these devices, Williams says, the early Welsh poet achieves a "collateral rather than consecutive presentation of his experience" (1956, 16). The end result is a decentered poetic form, analogous in its effects to the intricacies of early Celtic manuscripts or of stone crosses, "where what happens in a corner is as important as what happens at the centre, because there often is no centre" (15). Gwyn Williams includes Jones and Dylan Thomas as modern examples of this compositional tradition, comparing the interweaving pattern of *In Parenthesis* and *The Anathemata* to old Welsh epic, and Jones's painting *Merlin Land*, reproduced opposite page 185 of *The Anathemata*, to the centerless character of Celtic art. The decentered, meandering effect of *The Anathemata*'s form shares some aspects of the more conscious efforts of Olson and others to construct open and projective forms, even though it has older and firmer cultural roots.

The digressive shape of *The Anathemata* is akin in its effects to the method of poetic invention that William Carlos Williams advocates in his preface to *Kora in Hell* and in book 2 of *Paterson*. Invention in Williams's sense is a mode of imaginative insight that reinterprets the poet's materials by discovering new connections and patterns in the language and form of poetry itself.[4] Thomas Whitaker summarizes its implications well when he writes of Williams: "Becoming aware of the immediacy of his own contact, he invents. Opening himself so that nature may work in and through him, he both finds and makes" (1969, 17). If one substituted a term like *history* or *deposits* for "nature" in Whitaker's summary, this definition could apply equally well to Jones's poetic procedures. Although Jones never uses the word *invention* in precisely this sense, his preface to *The Anathemata* suggests that he too views the poet's activity as a process of discovery or finding, in the etymological sense of the Latin *invenire*. This sense of poetic composition as a process of discovery or invention is already established in the self-reflexivity of *The Anathemata*'s opening lines: "We already and first of all discern him making this thing other. His groping syntax, if we attend, already shapes" (*A*, 49). The poem, like the Mass that "we" attend on the opening pages, originates in an act of sign making, and this act will be its principle subject. By repeating and embellishing these acts of sign making and tale-telling, the poem gradually discovers an identity for its "we"[5] and new contexts and implications for its central tale. In this sense, *The Anathemata*, like *Paterson* and *Maximus*, is a poem in and about process. The structure of *The Anathemata*, as reflected in the published text and as it emerges in the manuscripts of the poem, reveals Jones as a poet working at the edge of modernist poetics, blending a modern traditionalist's effort to "make it cohere" (Pound 1975, 796) with a digressive imagination and an improvisatory technique that harmonize remarkably with the postmodern poetics of open form.

An examination of the manuscripts of *The Anathemata* suggests that the poem did grow, as the traditional epics of Gwyn Williams's accounts grew in the hands of successful bards, out of a few basic and interconnected themes or motifs—the Mass, the Passion, and the voyage—into the multiplicity of digressive and illuminating inventions that direct the experience of the reader. The first five pages introduce virtually all the thematic motifs to which the poem will return repeatedly as it unfolds, connecting them disarmingly through the associative and rambling imagination that is Jones's hallmark. These motifs include the celebration of Mass among the "failing numina" and "house treasures" of a late civilization, the Last Supper, the Passion, and the typic voyage. The earliest surviving manuscript, which consists of only twenty-four folio sheets, moved directly from this opening sequence on pages 49–53 to what is now the end of the poem, pages 241–43. As arranged and collated by Phillip Davies and Daniel Huws of the National Library of Wales the remaining manuscripts show how the poem developed as a series of long elaborations and digressions within digressions. The first of these digressions begins from the reference to "this hill" (53) to spin out the history of "oreogenesis," the making of hills, which makes up much of "Rite and Fore-Time." Later, Jones expanded this new digression into a further series of reflections on the emergence of "man-master-of-plastic" (59). Similarly, the voyage sequence began from a very brief core narrative about the voyage of a Phoenician captain to the shores of Britain and expanded into the four sections and multiple voices of the finished poem. Each of these digressions, though it wanders far from the multiple thematic centers of the poem, achieves its own kind of decentered coherence through the repetition of a series of verbal motifs analogous in their function to the repeated motifs used by oral traditional poets.

Although all the digressions ultimately circle back to at least one of the poem's core themes of Mass, Passion, and sign making, the process of free association that the poem follows in spinning them out displays the poet's imagination at work in a manner that is consistent with the theory of open field composition. The poem leads its reader through a series of discoveries, uncovering new connections between then and now, ritual and history, paganism and Christianity, and modern and ancient worlds. This process of discovery as creation is the subject of one of the poem's most self-reflexive passages, which depicts evolution as a liturgical dance conducted by the Creator as "Master of Harlequinade, himself not made, maker of sequence and permutation in all things made," who calls forth the human race in the "*Vorzeit*-masque" (63). This passage focuses attention on the process of invention in the cosmic scene being described and in the text itself. Thus, when "the mimes deploy / anthropoid / anthropoi," the wordplay that transforms *anthropoid* (manlike) to *anthropoi* (man) reflects in a single change in spelling the miraculous subtlety of the evolutionary shift from human forebears to the first human makers. The evolution of humankind is compared to a dance in which evolution is a series of gratuitous variations in form engineered by the Creator as "Master of Harlequinade," and in turn to a series of permutations in musical harmony, which correspond to major climatic changes in the evolution of the earth—"If tonic and final are fire / the dominant is ice / if fifth the fire / the cadence ice" (*A*, 63). Throughout this sequence, the connections between drama, music, and ritual as gratuitous forms are reinforced by the use of liturgical patterns, especially the antiphonal response form and the use of epithets. Moreover, the rhythm of these lines seems calculated to display the formal richness of language itself—especially in a line like "Unmeasured, irregular in stress and interval, of interior rhythm, modal," which demonstrates metrically the form it describes. There is also a marvelous self-reflexivity in "himself not *made, maker* of sequence and permutation in all things *made,*" which offers a series of permutations on the verb "to make"—the key verb for this passage. The whole passage blends erudition and whimsy to emphasize the vast disproportion between the cosmic liturgy and its repetitions in human making, but it insists on an essential analogy between the two kinds of gratuitous activities.

In a letter to his friend Father Desmond Chute, written shortly after the publication of *The Anathemata*, Jones attempts to explain the unusual combination of linguistic artisanry and free-associating improvisation that led to the poem's structure. "As far as I am *consciously aware*," he writes, "the *form* of *The Anathemata* was determined by the inner necessities of the thing itself." Disavowing any desire to "experiment" with poetic form, Jones insists, "I merely tried, as hard as I know how, to say with precision what I wanted to say and to lose as little as possible of the overtones & undertones evoked by the words used" (*IN*, 24). Yet he also acknowledges that this search for unity and precision has led to unorthodox forms. In distinguishing his poetry from that of poets working in "recognized forms of versification," he implies that his work was in some ways improvisatory, "catch-as-catch-can" in its method of composition.

It looks as if blokes like me when they write tend to employ scansions and/or accentuations of a recognizable and traditional nature "by accident" but that the "accidents" are directed by the changing moods and meanings of the "poem." . . . A work made to recognizable and known "laws" of metre, scansion, accent, etc. has this great advantage of being read in the way intended by the writer. . . . Whereas the eclectic or patch-work or catch-as-catch-can method such as I employ (Or as some will say "Irish-stew" method—though I

think it would be an unfair description, for the bits of carrot, old
bones, gobbets of meat, peelings of onions, etc. are not, as in a stew,
floating about, but are placed with precision in the pot of the poem)
leaves a wide no-man's land for debate as to exactly *how* a given line
or passage should be read in order to get the full intention of the
writer. (27 January 1953; *IN*, 39)

This passage is mainly concerned with answering Chute's questions about
Jones's use of meter and its relation to the poet's thematic intentions. But
in the course of its apologia for *The Anathemata*'s oddities of form, the
passage also summarizes rather colorfully the aspects of Jones's approach
to poetry that ally him with poets who have described themselves more
assertively as practitioners of open forms.

In pursuing the "inner necessities" of the poem, Jones sees himself as
responding to the formal demands imposed by his peculiar choice of
poetic content. His "eclectic or patch-work or catch-as-catch-can" meth-
od, which leads to a paradoxically ordered "Irish Stew," summarizes nicely
the unique blend of open and closed formal procedures in *The Anath-
emata*. In this sense, for Jones, the form is an extension of the content in
much the way that Olson demands in his self-conscious promotion of a
projective or open poetics. His unique blend of the oral bard's improvisa-
tory genius with the poetic maker's devotion to a completed shape gives
Jones an important place among twentieth-century writers of long poems,
especially among those who have sought appropriate forms for an epic
poetry in the twentieth century.

In an early and frequently quoted review, W. H. Auden hailed *The
Anathemata* as "a contemporary epic" (1954). Yet Jones and many of his
readers have been understandably hesitant about using the term *epic* in
any traditional sense to describe his work (see, for example, Corcoran
1982, 109–10). John H. Johnston (1964) was the first to argue that *In
Parenthesis* might be the best example in the twentieth century of a mod-
ern epic, both because it uses the fundamental war-narrative typical of
traditional heroic and epic poetry and because it employs in innovative
ways many of the traditional motifs of epic, notably the descent to the
dead, paralleled by Dai's boast at the center of the poem, and the focus on
a decisive battle that changed the history of the people and the culture to
whom the tale belongs. Bernard Bergonzi, on the other hand, takes issue
with Johnston's account of *In Parenthesis* as epic on the grounds that Jones
does not "reach out beyond the personal to appeal to a system of public

and communal values which are ultimately collective, national and even cosmic." Nonetheless, Bergonzi concedes that *In Parenthesis* remains "the nearest equivalent to an epic that the Great War produced in English" (1965, 202).

Thomas Dilworth's reading of Jones accepts *In Parenthesis* as an example of what might be called "modern epic." But his somewhat limited definition of the term leads him to argue that *The Anathemata* cannot be considered an epic because it is not a narrative. He later classifies the poem tentatively with *The Cantos* as an example of "displaced epic" (1988, 152), but by concentrating on the form of the poem rather than on its motivating intention, he fails to give adequate emphasis to the broader communal and cultural statement that *The Anathemata* makes in both its form and its content.

Dilworth's understandable caution about applying the term *epic* to *The Anathemata* suggests to me that we need a better critical definition of modern epic, as distinguished from traditional epic, so we can talk about the kinds of qualities that *The Anathemata* shares with such works as Ezra Pound's *The Cantos*, William Carlos Williams's *Paterson*, Charles Olson's *Maximus*, Basil Bunting's *Briggflatts*, and other longer poems of this century. A better understanding of the claims and implications of *The Anathemata*, with all its formal idiosyncracies, may be of some help in the overall critical effort to understand why poets continue to write long poems of apparently epic pretensions in an age that seems to have lost the communal cohesiveness and recognized formal conventions that defined traditional epic poetry.[6]

Michel André Bernstein mentions *In Parenthesis* and *The Anathemata* in passing as important examples of what he calls the "modern verse epic" (1980, 192). In so doing, he focuses on what may be the most interesting connection between Jones's work and that of other modern poets who have experimented with longer poetic forms in the effort to make some kind of encompassing cultural statement. *The Anathemata*, like *The Cantos*, *Paterson*, and *Maximus*—the poems that Bernstein includes in his account of this important contemporary genre—abandons narrative in favor of more lyric and dramatic modes, and like these poems, it claims to tell what Pound called "the tale of the tribe." Jones also joins Pound and Olson in recognizing and lamenting the lack of the kind of shared culture that once united the bard and his readers. Yet in the process of its unfolding, *The Anathemata* attempts to reconstitute that tradition under new forms, to educate a readership, to create a "polis," a community, a sense of tradition, however provisional, out of the admittedly fragmented and receding remnants of a shared past.

In his discussion of Olson, Bernstein equates "a will towards 'epic'" with "a necessarily stubborn resolve to find (or create) a readership with whom a renewed community can be planned" (1980, 231). The poet in Olson's *Maximus* shares in common with Jones the effort to be for his own historical moment "the custodian, rememberer, embodier and voice of the mythus, etc., of some contained group of families, or of a tribe, nation, people, cult" (*A*, 21), despite the conflict between this vocation and the surrounding culture. As in Olson and Williams, Jones's sense of the poet as part of a "we" rather than as the isolated "I" of Pound's *Cantos*, who stands apart from and laments a vanishing cultural totality, suggests another way in which Jones's work anticipates the problems that have occupied self-consciously post-Poundian American poets. David Jones shares with the poets in Bernstein's account this urgent concern to "find (or create) a readership." The effort to define a "we" in imaginative terms, central to Jones's poetic enterprise, may also be a defining characteristic of the epic impulse among poets of this century. Fuller understanding of *The Anathemata* as a modern verse epic in Bernstein's sense must await a more coherent and comprehensive understanding of the nature and significance of this trend in recent poetry. Nonetheless, Jones's work contributes significantly to the poetics of the long poem in this century through its emulation of the techniques of a rooted oral traditional poetry and through its consequent development of an improvisatory poetic form that seeks to respond to the cultural rootlessness and disorder of the poet's civilizational moment.

As a writer who responds to his time by seeking to make signs that name and preserve "the inward continuities / of the site, of place" (*A*, 90), Jones speaks in a unique and original way to the needs of the later twentieth century. He has gone unread partly because of the density and strangeness of his poetic style and partly because of the apparent unfamiliarity, for many potential readers, of his cultural frame of reference. Yet I believe that another important reason for the neglect of his work has been the difficulty of classifying him or assimilating him to the mainstream of Anglo-American modernism, where critics have wanted to place him. The very effort to classify his work as modernist or postmodernist exposes the ambiguities and inadequacies of those labels, yet Jones's work addresses important concerns of both these major twentieth-century trends.

I have discussed his work in connection with Eliot, Pound, Joyce, and Spengler, but Jones himself was keenly aware of affinities between his historical position and that of Gerard Manley Hopkins, whom he admired profoundly as a "modern" poet. An unpublished and still fragmentary manuscript essay on Hopkins dating from about 1968 suggests a subtle analogy between the critical reception of Hopkins's poetry and what Jones hoped might yet be the fate of his own work. In a section of the essay that he drafted and redrafted many times, Jones argues that Robert Bridges did Hopkins a service by withholding publication of the poetry until 1918, a historical moment that proved more receptive to Hopkins's unique insights than the Victorian world of 1890 would have been. Recalling conversations from the years immediately following the Great War, Jones remarks that although Hopkins was "a Victorian—and *how* Victorian," "we discussed him as though he were a contemporary." Of Hopkins's achievement, he writes:

> The particular nature of his contribution (the poems, diaries letters, etc.) is of that sort which prompts, goads, alerts. To borrow from an important motif in the medieval romance-tale of Peredur (Perceval), Hopkins requires us to "ask the question"—or rather a complex of questions. Should we fail in this, no amount of appreciation of the beauty of this or that poem will suffice against the danger of our taking him for granted.
>
> Hopkins chanced to be one of those sorts of "makaris" whose making has the quality to condition in a certain way the works of those who come after them.
>
> This, in itself, is no unfamiliar thing, such artists crop up from time to time in any medium you like to name. But few men of this sort can have experienced more isolation and less recognition during their life days than Hopkins, to be recognized a few decades after their deaths as not only of singular genius but as harbingers whose work would have a special relevance for the poets, artists, makers, call them what you will, of a few decades later.[7]

Jones's sense of affinity with Hopkins is evident in his allusion to the Grail hero's question, an emblem throughout his work for his own vocation as a poet working in a late phase of civilization. His account of Hopkins's importance and of his isolation during his lifetime summarizes well the kind of subtle influence that Jones's work has begun to have on a later generation of British poets. We are far from the peril of "taking for granted" the work of David Jones, and it remains to be seen whether he will ever attain widespread recognition as a poet whose originality approaches that of Hopkins and Joyce—especially the Joyce of *Finnegans Wake*. But like these highly original and idiosyncratic poets, David Jones anticipated poetic issues and problems that would be more important to later generations of poets and readers than they were to his own. Perhaps in this sense, Jones, like the Shakespearian fool quoted in his epigraph to *The Anathemata*, "lives before his time" (*King Lear* 3:2. 94).

Jones writes in the preface to *The Anathemata*, "It may be that the kind of thing I am trying to make is no longer makeable in the kind of way in which I have tried to make it" (*A*, 15), and to some extent, he may be right. His work draws on an abiding religious faith and a sense of Western rootedness that is shared by few poets in this age. Although Jones does not insist that his reader share his beliefs, his appeal to a numinous dimension gives shape, authority, and an obscure hopefulness to his work, and these qualities shape the form and tone of his poetry in ways that cannot be influenced or emulated. Though his ultimate thematic focus is always transcendental, Jones insistently roots his work in the actual, in the temporal, and in the historical and material world. His most important legacy to the poetics of our time remains this acknowledgment that the act of sign making—the process of discovering and re-presenting connections and continuities—has an abiding value in itself, even in a civilization that has lost track of deeper links between culture and culture, past and present, and human and divine. Though idiosyncratic, difficult, and rooted in a religious tradition that has been abandoned by most writers in this century, Jones's work shows how one man, speaking with rigorous objectivity from within "the limits of his love" (*A*, 24), can discover links between himself and other makers, between his time and other times. The poets who inherit the Jones legacy will continue to recognize the need to rediscover the places, things, and events that have made them, to make connections between "one's own *res*" and a contemporary community of poet and listeners, and thus to persevere in the effort "to make a shape out of the very things of which one is oneself made."[8]

Notes

Chapter 1

1. As a practical matter, I have retained Jones's term "man-the-artist" because alternative language seems distracting and inappropriate to the political consciousness level of Jones and his generation. Jones's imagination was formed in a tradition that is fundamentally patriarchal and that therefore implicitly excludes women in much of its language. Within the limitations imposed by this tradition, however, Jones's vision of *homo faber/ homo sapiens* as a species (see *EA,* 185) could be seen as unusually inclusive for a man of his time. One of the most important friendships of his life was with Prudence Pelham, a stonecutter whom he recognized and respected as a fellow maker. I discuss Prudence Pelham and the important role of femaleness in Jones's vision in part 2.

2. See Matthias 1989, 25–28.

3. See Dilworth's rebuttal of Fussell in 1988, 95, 106–7. See also Sherry 1982a, 375–80; Ward 1983,103–6, 110.

4. Geoffrey Hartman dismisses Jones as a nostalgic modern poet (1980, 89). Frank Kermode criticizes his "atavism," his tendency to think only in "primitivistic" terms (1962, 30). M. L. Rosenthal and Sally Gall imply a similar judgment when they classify him as a "neo-regionalist" British poet (1983, 298–99).

5. Dilworth (1988, 382–83 n. 56) also takes issue with Ward's view of Jones as protofascist. For an extended and cogent refutation of Ward's overall approach to Jones, see Whitaker 1989, 472–85.

6. Eric Gill's political ideas are expounded in his collections of essays, especially *Beauty Looks After Herself* (1966) and *In a Strange Land* (1947). See also Speaight 1966; Attwater 1969.

7. On the origins and purpose of the Guild of St. Joseph and St. Dominic at Ditchling, see Attwater 1969, 58–60. Although Ward makes much of what she views as the protofascist sympathies of Dawson and his circle (1983, 54–60), Dawson envisioned a European Christendom led by a nonviolent ruler, a new Augustus who would bring not violent military revolution but peaceful consolidation (1929, 215–16). This position hardly identifies Dawson as a fascist sympathizer, even though he presents it unapologetically as a corrective to contemporary liberalism. For more about Dawson's ideas and their influence on Jones, see chapter 6.

8. On Jones at Ditchling, see Speaight 1966, 111–12. On the conflicts that led to the dissolution of the community at Ditchling, see Speaight 1966, 138–49; Attwater 1969, 85–89.

9. Ward argues that Jones's myth turns on "an ambiguity: the potentially subversive effect of genuine reaction" (1983, 6). For her this ambiguity is so pronounced that it justifiably alienates Jones both from conservative thinkers who sympathize with his ideology but dislike his experimental style and from modernists "who appreciate his originality but object to the ideological implications of his poetry" (6). She also notes that what she calls Jones's "nostalgia" leads to "a subversive, if not revolutionary attitude towards contemporary civilisation" (223). Although I cannot agree with Ward's overall argument, it seems to me that her identification of the "subversive" implications of Jones's myth in relation to the modern world points to one of his most original insights rather than to an unresolvable contradiction in his thought. Hence I adopt her useful term without assenting to her argument. Neil Corcoran (1989, 220) uses the same term in a similar way in his essay "Spilled Bitterness: *In Parenthesis* in History," which also explores provocatively the conservative political implications of *In Parenthesis*.

10. Corcoran (1989, 213–16) is critical of the more sympathetic portrayal of Jones's relationship to fascism found in Dilworth 1989.

11. Frederic Jameson indirectly illuminates the historical context of the period in his study of Wyndham Lewis subtitled *The Modernist as Fascist* (1979). He analyzes probingly the widespread protofascism that prevailed among many intellectuals before the Second World War and that led to a surprisingly sympathetic reception of Hitler's ideas among some intellectuals, including Lewis. The ideology that Jameson describes defined itself as a critique of capitalism and Marxism and as a reaction against "the various hegemonic and legitimizing ideologies of the middle-class state" (15). In discussing some of Lewis's early writings about Hitler, however, Jameson distinguishes carefully between the roots of this protofascism as a response to the perceived injustices of the time and the anti-Semitic bigotry that fueled Hitler's rise to power (179–83). Jameson's analysis suggests that Jones was not alone in feeling that Hitler's work, despite its fanaticism and propagandistic rhetoric, was responding to genuine evils in postwar Europe.

12. This is a slip on Jones's part. *Pange lingua*, the Good Friday hymn from which these words were taken, is not by St. Thomas but by Venantius Fortunatus. My thanks to William Blissett for pointing this out.

13. The classic treatment of the tradition of typological or figural interpretation and its implications for literature is found in Erich Auerbach 1959. For a more recent account of biblical typology and its relevance to the interpretation of Western literature, see Frye 1982.

Chapter 2

1. Representative accounts of this critical debate can be found in Bruns 1974; Harari 1979; Barthes 1979; Genette 1979.

2. See, for example, Lentricchia 1980; Jameson 1971.

3. On the connection between visual and verbal art in Jones, see Dilworth 1988, 8–25.

4. For a fuller discussion of the philosophical and linguistic basis of Altieri's theory of action and its implications for literary interpretation, see Altieri 1981, 96–159.

5. See, for example, Derrida 1972, 1974.

6. It was first published in Pakenham 1955.

7. Jones's reading of Maurice de la Taille makes René Hague characteristically uneasy with what he seems to see as a deviation from orthodox Catholic doctrine (see Hague 1977, 6–7). On this tendency in Hague's reading of Jones, see Whitaker 1989, 469–71.

Chapter 3

1. Chapters on *In Parenthesis* appear, for example, in Johnston 1964; Bergonzi 1965; Fussell 1975. See also Blissett 1973.

2. On John Ball and his role in *In Parenthesis,* see Dilworth 1988, 47–48, 115; Hughes 1989.

3. Cf. Dilworth 1988, 48: "If there is a single figure in the poem whose sensibility corresponds to that informing *In Parenthesis* it is Aneirin Lewis. He is an associative, rather than a narrative, reflector. Even more than Dai Greatcoat, he perceives and meditates fully in the poem's allusive mode."

4. See Barnard 1979, 20. Dilworth argues that "it is in the context of the political wickedness of most wars that the poem's recurring references to Shakespeare's *Henry V* must be understood" (1988, 99). Though Dilworth notes most of the allusions that John Barnard discusses, he seems to miss the positive implications of the phrase "disciplines of the wars," both in Shakespeare's sympathetic portrayal of the common soldier and in the "good kind of peace" discovered among Jones's common soldiers.

5. My terms *synchronic* and *diachronic,* drawn from Roman Jakobson, correspond roughly to what Dilworth calls the "narrative" and "associative" modes that interact in the poem. Dilworth offers a much more complete analysis of the structure of *In Parenthesis* in his account of what he calls "dialogic tension" between "climactic movement" and "parenthetical structure" (summarized in 1988, 146–51). See also Blissett 1986. Since my focus is on the foregrounding of the acts of remembering and sign making, I am emphasizing the ways in which the text draws attention to itself as a kind of made memorial.

6. Cf. Blissett 1981, 107; Dilworth 1988, 43–53.

7. See Sherry 1982b. Dilworth suggests that Dai does reappear later in the poem, in an account of the death of a wounded man named Dai who is blown to bits during the assault on the wood: "He seems to be Dai Greatcoat. The poem's economy of characters suggests it and so does Dai Greatcoat's nickname. 'La Cote male taile,' which Malory translates 'The Evyll Shapyn Cote,' can be read as a bilingual pun on 'evil-shaped slope' (cote)" (1988, 115). Perhaps this is true, but the uncharacteristic tentativeness of Dilworth's "He seems to be" is justified here. It seems to me that Dai Greatcoat is an effective presence in the poem largely because, like the Queen of the Woods, he is more type than character, not individualized even as much as Aneirin Lewis or John Ball or Sergeant Watcyn. He does not die as an individual because, as he says, "Old soljers never die, they simply fade

away" (*IP*, 84). Dilworth brings us around to the same point when he acknowl-
edges that the shell-blast that kills Dai (*IP*, 176–77) leaves no corpse behind: "Dai
cannot be declared dead but only 'missing in action.' His death is an explosive
version of the fading away of old soldiers. . . . Because he is not certifiably dead, he
achieves imaginative permanence as an archetype" (115). I argue that the poem
sustains equally well a reading of the "Dai" who dies in the battle as a typic Welsh
soldier—a Dying Gaul figure, as Dilworth suggests, but not necessarily identical
with Dai Greatcoat.

    8. See Sherry 1982b, 126; Dilworth 1988, 108–9.

    9. "Cf. the Welsh Percivale story, *Peredur ap Evrawc:* 'Peredur, I greet thee not,
seeing that thou dost not merit it. Blind was fate in giving thee favour and fame.
When thou wast in the Court of the Lame King, and didst see the youth bearing
the streaming spear, from the points of which were drops of blood . . . thou didst
not enquire their meaning nor their cause. Hadst thou done so, the King would
have been restored to his health and his dominion in peace. Whereas from hence-
forth he will have to endure battles and conflicts and his knights will perish, and
wives will be widowed, and maidens will be left portionless, and all this is because of
thee.' See also Jessie Weston, *From Ritual to Romance,* chap. 11 [1920]" (Jones's
note, *IP* 210n).

    10. Cf., for example, Blissett 1981, 152–53; Whitaker 1989, 465.

    11. For more about the role of fertility myth in Jones, see chapter 5.

    12. Levi 1983, 189; Blissett 1981, 75–76; Dilworth 1988, 341.

Chapter 4

    1. Cf. Auden 1963; Dilworth 1988, 152.

    2. Patrick Deane (1989) offers the best analysis to date of what many critics
have recognized as the "material" or "thingy" quality of the text of *The Anathemata.*

    3. Cf. "I know that I hung on the windy tree
        For nine whole nights
        Wounded with the spear, dedicated to Odin,
        Myself to myself."
(From *The Havamal,* as translated by Frazer in *Adonis, Attis, Osiris.*) (Jones's note,
A, 225 n.1).

    4. On *The Anathemata* in the context of the Second World War, see Corcoran
1982, 32–34; *DGC,* 98–112.

    5. See Staudt 1986a for a fuller discussion of *The Anathemata* and *Four Quartets.*

    6. For the significance of burial mounds in Jones, see Blissett 1973.

    7. Blissett (1967, 265) makes a similar point, and Jones's response to this
reading further illuminates the difference between his sacramentalism and
Eliot's: "I thought what you say on page 265 about Tom Eliot (who I can hardly
believe is not still alive, I was deeply devoted to him) and the 'centre of the silent
Word' as contrasted to my sort of centre stated very truly something jolly difficult to
state at all. It is a real distinction. I have a sort of feeling that it may be to do with my
being first a visual artist & so terribly concerned with tangible, contactual
'things'—not 'concepts' really, except in so far as the concrete, creaturely mate-
rial 'thing' is a *signum* of the concept & that it must be that way now because we are

creatures with bodies" (from a letter of 15 May 1967, quoted in Blissett 1981, 39n).

Introduction to Part 2

1. Jones uses the words *myth, mythus,* and *mythoi* in the Aristotelian sense, to refer to the plots or stories that he uses as poetic material. Dilworth (1988, 62) points out that "'mythos' also denotes archetypal meaning, and it is in this sense that David Jones uses the word in his own prose, preferring it to 'myth' because 'mythos' lacks any connotation of falsehood." See also Hague 1977, 8–9.

2. I outlined my chief objections to Ward's argument in chapter 1 above and in Staudt 1986b. See also Whitaker 1989, 473–76, 485.

3. On Jones and Freud, see Dilworth 1988, 203–6.

4. Jones recalls that René Hague first read him "Anna Livia Plurabelle" "in about 1928" (*DGC*, 188).

5. Jones probably encountered Spengler much earlier, at Ditchling and in Catholic intellectual circles between the wars. Nonetheless, his annotations indicate that only during the 1940s did he begin the thorough immersion in Spengler with which I am concerned here.

Chapter 5

1. Other poets writing about the Great War frequently associated the men "sacrificed" in battle with the sacrifice of Christ. Jones was uncomfortable with this association because he saw a kind of blasphemy in equating these individual deaths with the redemptive death of the Son of God. Jones makes this point in a letter recording his admiration for Wilfred Owen's poetry, adding that "in writing *In Paren.* I had no intention whatever in presuming to compare the varied maims, death-strokes, miseries, acts of courage etc. of the two contending forces . . . with the Passion, self-Oblation and subsequent Immolation and death of the Cult-hero of our Xtian tradition. For that is a unique and profound Mystery of Faith" (*DGC*, 246).

2. Dilworth (1988, 372n) notes that the allusion to "sweet princes . . . maligned" also refers to the abdication of Edward IV.

3. Neil Corcoran (1989, 217–20) shows insightfully how this pointless killing of young men is connected to the motif of sexuality in *In Parenthesis,* which in turn furthers the poem's subversive comment on the experience of war.

4. Cf. Dilworth's discussion of sex and death (1988, 83–94).

5. Much has been written on this theme in recent years. The critique of this dualistic view of the feminine is a primary argument of de Beauvoir 1953. A good overview of some of its consequences can be found in Rich 1986, 84–109, and in the poetry of Susan Griffin's *Woman and Nature* (1978). See also Nina Auerbach 1982; Gilbert and Gubar 1979, 17–34.

6. "Sweet Sister Death" alludes to "Sister Bodily Death" in St. Francis of Assisi's "Canticle of the Sun." See Blissett 1973, 275. See also Dilworth 1988, 87, where Dilworth notes that "Sweet Sister Death" is an allusion to St. Francis of Assisi. "In this epic personification," he writes, "Francis of Assisi's 'Sister Bodily Death' has

lost her natural chastity. She lives up to ominous premonitions of a lewd, vampirish Geraldine in the poem's earlier allusions to Coleridge's 'Christabel.'"

7. On Dai and the Queen of the Woods, cf. Dilworth 1988, 141–49.

8. This manuscript is part of the David Jones Collection at Boston College.

9. Jones used the phrase "bloody lie" as a synonym for *myth* in a letter to René Hague (1977, 8), where he objects to the dictionary definition of *myth* as "a purely fictitious narrative."

10. Neil Corcoran (1989, 210) goes so far as to read this passage as "a savagely hostile criticism of the procedures of *In Parenthesis* composed by the author himself prior to the work's completion." Corcoran's provocative argument rests on the assumption that the use of myth in *In Parenthesis* supports a neo-heroic ruling-class ideology and that a deconstructive reading reveals the vulnerability of this poem to the kind of reading that Paul Fussell would later offer and to which Corcoran gives a qualified assent. I am not convinced that the myth in *In Parenthesis* even claims to provide the "assuaging and emollient reconciliations" that Corcoran sees. A deconstructive reading of a text as self-conscious as Jones's also raises theoretical problems because the philosophical bases of deconstruction and of Jones's poetics tend to make nonsense of each other. In any event, I do not read the Lavinia passage as repudiating—either overtly or deconstructively—the procedures of *In Parenthesis,* though I agree that they reflect Jones's understandable ambivalence about the possibility of making art out of the intolerable human conditions of Passchendaele.

11. On the significance of this litany, cf. Dilworth 1988, 351–54; Peck 1989, 381–84.

12. For further reflections on the relation of the life to the work, see John Matthias's introduction to *David Jones: Man and Poet* (1989, 21–26).

Chapter 6

1. Letters of David Jones to Harman Grisewood. Manuscripts. This quotation is from a marginal note to Jones's important letter on Spengler, portions of which appear in *DGC,* 115–17.

2. For a brief critical debate on the issue of Spengler's influence on Pound, see Bush 1976 and Surette 1977.

3. For a fuller discussion of these annotations, see Staudt 1989.

4. His copy of *Finnegans Wake* was a gift from Prudence Pelham, dated 27 May 1948. This volume contains only a few annotations, most of them recording Welsh material in the *Wake.* More annotations appear in his copy of Campbell and Robinson's *Skeleton Key to "Finnegans Wake",* which is inscribed "D Dec. 1954 from Eric D[rysdale]."

5. Jones made notes in the following chapters of Campbell and Robinson: book 1, chapter 7, "Shem the Penman"; book 1, chapter 8, "The Washers at the Ford" (the chapter that includes "Anna Livia Plurabelle"); book 2, chapter 1, "The Children's Hour"; book 2, chapter 2, "The Study Hour—Triv and Quad"; and book 2, chapter 3, "Tavernry in Feast." There is also one note in book 3, chapter 1, "Shem Before the People."

Chapter 7

1. Elsewhere in the same letter, Jones concedes that his failure to appreciate Dante may also stem from his inability to read him in the original. His letters report several unsuccessful attempts throughout his life to read translations of the *Commedia* and especially to share in his friend René Hague's appreciation for Dante.

2. See Dilworth's fuller explication of Gwenhwyfar (1988, 228–34). He comments that Jones is "careful to preserve the theological distinction" between Gwenhwyfar and the Sacrament "because, typologically, he does imply an equivalence" (233).

3. This line also echoes Hopkins's "The Wreck of the Deutschland" and exemplifies Jones's admiration for the music of Hopkins's alliterative language and sprung rhythms. Cf. Dilworth 1988, 233.

4. See Friedman 1981, especially 229–70; du Plessis 1979.

5. Jones's note points out that Elen is named for a British saint who appeals to the poet because of the "diversity of significance" associated with her in tradition. As St. Helen, mother of Constantine, she is associated with the finding of the Wood of the Cross, an association that helps to reinforce the hidden focus here on Holy Cross Day. In Welsh and British myth, Helen is a kind of repetition of Helen of Troy, as Jones puts it, "the beauty of Britain beguiling the emperor and directing the power-struggles." In short, she is "the fusion of typic figures of great splendour and depth, *imperatrix* plus numinous 'beauty' plus Holy Woman" (*A*, 131–32n).

6. On the siren Britannia, see Hague 1977, 176–78; Dilworth 1988, 247–251.

7. Jones writes in a note to this passage that "what is pleaded in the Mass is precisely the argosy or voyage of the Redeemer, consisting of his entire sufferings and his death, his conquest of hades, his resurrection and his return in triumph to heaven. It is this that is offered to the Trinity (Cf. 'Myself to myself' as in the *Havamal* is said of Odin) on behalf of us argonauts and of the whole argosy of mankind, and, in some sense, of all sentient being, and, perhaps, of insentient too, for, as Paul says, 'The whole of nature, as we know, groans in a common travail all the while' (Romans viii, 22. Knox translation)" (*A*, 106n).

8. Cf. the Latin refrain of a traditional English Christmas carol, "Noa, Noa, *ave* fit ex *eva*."

Chapter 8

1. I return in the conclusion to the question of the form and coherence of the volume as a whole.

2. This remark to Davies also explains why Jones rejected William Blissett's suggestion of Tertullian's phrase "Regnum Caesaris regnum diaboli" (The kingdom of Caesar [is] the kingdom of the devil) as an epigraph for *The Sleeping Lord* (Blissett 1981, 90).

3. Dilworth 1986, 113–14 gives more details on the origins of this ritual. Here and in 1988, 305, Dilworth shows the ironic correspondences in Jones between the Roman *sacramentum* ritual and the Easter Vigil Mass. My debt to Dilworth's

readings of *The Sleeping Lord* poems (1988, 258–359) will be obvious throughout this discussion.

4. Teresa Godwin Phelps, in "The Tribune and the Tutelar," writes that here "the Tribune suggests a perversion of the act of birth itself." Phelps uses this to illustrate her point that the Tribune is "the very antithesis of all that is feminine, finally even the fertile, life-giving aspect, whose exclusive province is birth" (1989, 340–41). To me, the presentation of the Tribune seems more ambiguous, the polarities less clear-cut, than Phelps's reading allows. In this passage, the Tribune is not perverting "the act of birth itself" as much as the mythology of feminine origins that his men cling to as their heritage. His prayer to Lucina at the end of the poem suggests that even this effort to manipulate the myth for propagandistic purposes is not wholly successful, because the longing for "a second birth" is so fundamental, even to the Tribune himself.

5. For a contrasting reading, see Ward (1983, 156–204), who criticizes this volume severely for "a schematisation of ideas inimical to real poetic spontaneity" (157). Dilworth discusses the "dialectical" and "dialogical" form of the sequence (1988, 260–61). As my argument suggests, however, even Dilworth seems to me to wander into an excessive dualism.

6. As Dilworth points out, the myth commemorated by the Ara Pacis is "a spurious myth . . . built to commemorate a political pretence that Lugo and the three legions die defending. (It is by a reversal of irony that the dream of Clitus redeems this sham, transforming it into an experience of the peace that passes understanding)" (281).

7. The phrase "by numbers" may also be an allusion to Spengler, for in his essay "Art in Relation to War," Jones misquotes Spengler as saying "only numbers matter" (*DG*, 159; cf. Spengler 1926, 2:504).

8. I use this term suggestively, but in a way that I believe is consonant with the theories outlined in J. L. Austin's *How to Do Things with Words* (1965) and M. L. Pratt's *Toward a Speech Act Theory of Literary Discourse* (1977). See also Altieri 1981, part 1.

9. John Terpstra (1982) was the first to point out the connection between the questions in "The Sleeping Lord" and the Grail hero's question; see especially pages 98–99. Dilworth also points out a connection between the Grail question and the poet's questions at the end of *The Anathemata* (see 1988, 255).

Dilworth carries the argument further in 1988, 339–40, where he writes: "To restore the king and his wasted land, Peredur must enquire the meaning of what he sees. We saw that at the end of Dai Greatcoat's boast in *In Parenthesis,* the reader is urged to ask the restorative questions. At the conclusion of *The Anathemata,* the poet himself asks them. He seems to be doing the same thing in the broken series of questions that largely comprise the 'Sleeping Lord' fragment. But although the poet asks questions, the land is not, as far as he can tell, renewing itself. . . . While the land lies waste, the artist—in this poem, the poet—has a special role, which seems to be the inspiring of questions."

What concerns me, extending the insights of Terpstra and Dilworth, is what might be called the foregrounding of the act of asking the question in the *Sleeping Lord* sequence as a whole and especially in the title poem. The poet's questions remain open; unlike those at the end of *The Anathemata*, they are not rhetorical, but real. Though there may be no visible renewal of the land, the act of asking the question goes on, which itself constitutes a kind of affirmation, however faint.

10. See, for example, *LF*, 37, where Jones denies "special pleading" in "The Tutelar of the Place."

Conclusion

1. Sherry's discussion is based on a definition of British modernism more deliberately limited than my Anglo-American model. In a later essay, "Contemporary British Modernism," Sherry writes that the best postwar modern British poetry "seems driven by an impulse to learn from the contradictory energies of Modernism, to balance its anarchic and constructive impulses" (1987, 614).

2. Dilworth touches on this point in his conclusion when he writes that "the poems of David Jones deserve a special place in modern literary history primarily because, while they are structurally whole, they remain 'open' in immediate and intermediate form. In other words, they mediate between the traditional prescription of formal unity and the discursive, organic 'open form' which originates in modernism and continues in postmodern literature" (1988, 362). See also Staudt 1990, 579.

3. He writes to Harman Grisewood in February 1957: "Dearest Harman, I don't feel I know the answer to *anything any more*, but I *do* know that you can't really see what's 'right' with Langland unless you can see what's 'wrong' with Milton" (*DGC*, 173).

4. See Bruns 1982 for an interesting theoretical extension of the idea of invention as practiced by Williams and others. On Williams and invention, see also Martz 1966, 149–51.

5. See Whitaker 1976.

6. The best definition of this genre, so far as it can be called a genre, remains the one developed by Roy Harvey Pearce in *The Continuity of American Poetry* (1961, especially 71–134). But Pearce's American, Whitmanian model is not entirely appropriate to the British tradition (cf. Sherry 1985). Rosenthal and Gall (1983) discuss the problem in their accounts of "Neo-Regionalism and Epic Memory" in MacDiarmid, Kinsella, Bunting, Jones, Hill, Montague, Crane, and Olson. But because their focus on the modern poetic sequence emphasizes poetry that aspires to lyric intensity rather than to the communal breadth of epic, they are dubious about the possibility of a modern epic poetry. They criticize most of the poems discussed in this context, including *The Anathemata*, as excessively "discursive" (271–349). A special issue of *Genre* on the long poem, edited and introduced by Joseph Riddell (1978), reflects Riddell's sense that the long poem is of its nature a self-deconstructing genre, always pointing to its own impossibility or unreadability. In a deviation from this special issue's generally Heideggerian and deconstructive critical orientation, Charles Altieri's "Motives in Metaphor" sorts out usefully the relation between "epic intention" and "lyric form" in the long poem (Altieri 1978, 653–65), defining the long poem provisionally as "a space constituted of multiple voices and perspectives in which the sceptical impulse to analytic lucidity can be fully explored and still absorbed into a lyrical vision" (657).

But on the whole, critics have stumbled in efforts to locate or define the nature of what I would call an "epic impulse" in the poetry of this century—the desire to make a poetic statement of epic historical and cultural scope, using the necessarily fragmentary forms and often idiosyncratic cultural materials that determine what Jones called the modern poet's own "*res*" or "thing."

7. Quoted from Jones's 1968 "Gerard Manley Hopkins," an unpublished manuscript in the Boston College collection.

8. (*A*, 10). The English poet Jeremy Hooker once echoed this remark of Jones's in a conversation with me about his own poetry. Hooker is one of a number of British and American poets who acknowledge, implicitly or explicitly, a debt to the "Jones legacy." Others who could be mentioned in this context include Geoffrey Hill, Basil Bunting, Seamus Heaney, John Montague, and the American poet John Matthias. See Corcoran 1982, 107–12.

Works Cited

Works by David Jones

The Anathemata: Fragments of an Attempted Writing. London: Faber and Faber, 1952. (*A*)

Dai Greatcoat: A Self-Portrait of David Jones in His Letters. Ed. René Hague. London: Faber and Faber, 1980. (*DGC*)

David Jones: Letters to a Friend. Ed. Aneirin Talfan Davies. Swansea: Triskele, 1980. (*LF*)

The Dying Gaul and Other Writings. Ed. Harman Grisewood. London: Faber and Faber, 1978. (*DG*)

Epoch and Artist: Selected Writings. Ed. Harman Grisewood. London: Faber and Faber, 1959. (*EA*)

"From *The Book of Balaam's Ass.*" Unpublished manuscript drafts. Burns Library, Boston College. (*BA* MS.)

"Gerard Manley Hopkins." Unpublished manuscript, 1968. Burns Library, Boston College.

"Hitler." Unpublished typescript essay, 1939. Burns Library, Boston College. ("*H*")

Inner Necessities: Letters of David Jones to Desmond Chute. Ed. Thomas Dilworth. Toronto: Hugh Anson-Cartwright, 1985. (*IN*)

In Parenthesis: Seinnyessit e gledyf ym penn mameu. London: Faber and Faber, 1937. (*IP*)

Letters of David Jones to Harman Grisewood. Manuscripts. Beinecke Library, Yale University. (*HJG*)

The Roman Quarry and Other Sequences. Ed. Harman Grisewood and René Hague. New York: Sheep Meadow, 1981. (*RQ*)

The Sleeping Lord and Other Fragments. London: Faber and Faber, 1974. (*SL*)

Other Works Cited

Alexander, Michael. "David Jones, Hierophant." In Cookson 1967, 116–23.

Allchin, A. M. "A Discovery of David Jones." In *The World Is a Wedding*, 157–87. New York: Oxford University Press, 1978.

Altieri, Charles. "From Symbolist Thought to Immanence: The Ground of Postmodern Poetics." *Boundary* 2, no. 1 (1973): 605–41.

———. "The Poem as Act: A Way to Reconcile Presentational and Mimetic Theories of Literature." *Iowa Review* 6 (1975): 103–24.

———. "Motives in Metaphor: Ashberry and the Modernist Long Poem." *Genre* 11 (1978): 653–87.

———. *Enlarging the Temple: American Poetry in the 1960's*. Lewisburg, Penn.: Bucknell University Press, 1979.

———. *Act and Quality: A Theory of Literary Meaning and Humanistic Understanding*. Amherst: University of Massachusetts Press, 1981.

Aquinas, Thomas. "Treatise on the Sacraments." In *The Summa Theologica of St. Thomas Aquinas*, trans. the Fathers of the English Dominican Province, part III, vol. 17, third number qq. LX–LXXXIII. London: Burns, Oates and Washbourne, 1914.

Attwater, Donald. *A Cell of Good Living: The Life, Work and Opinions of Eric Gill*. London: Geoffrey Chapman, 1969.

Auden, W. H. "A Contemporary Epic." *Encounter* 2, no. 2 (1954): 67–71.

———. "Adam as a Welshman." *New York Review of Books*, March 1963.

Auerbach, Erich. "Figura." In *Scenes from the Drama of Western European Literature*, 11–96. New York: Meridian Books, 1959.

Auerbach, Nina. *Woman and the Demon: The Life of a Victorian Myth*. Cambridge: Harvard University Press, 1982.

Austin, J. L. *How to Do Things with Words*. New York: Oxford University Press, 1965.

Barnard, John. "The Murder of Falstaff, David Jones and the 'Disciplines of War.'" In *Evidence in Literary Scholarship*, ed. René Wellek and Alvaro Ribeiro. Oxford: Clarendon, 1979.

Barthes, Roland. "From Work to Text." In Harari 1979, 73–81.

Bergonzi, Bernard. *Heroes' Twilight: A Study of the Literature of the Great War*. London: Constable; New York: Coward-McCann, 1965.

Bernstein, Michel André. *The Tale of the Tribe: Ezra Pound and the Modern Verse Epic*. Princeton: Princeton University Press, 1980.

Blamires, David. *David Jones: Artist and Writer*. 1971. Reprint. Toronto: University of Toronto Press, 1972.

Blissett, William. "David Jones: Himself at the Cave Mouth." *University of Toronto Quarterly* 36, no. 3 (1967): 259–73.

———. "*In Parenthesis* among the War Books." *University of Toronto Quarterly* 42 (1973): 258–88.

———. *The Long Conversation: A Memoir of David Jones*. Oxford: Oxford University Press, 1981.

———. "To Make a Shape in Words." *Renascence* 38, no. 2 (1986): 67–81.

Bonnerot, Louis. "James Joyce et David Jones." In *Ulysses 50 ans apres: Témoignages Franco-Anglaises sur le chef d'oeuvre de James Joyce*, 223–42. Paris: Librairie Marcel Didier, 1974.

Bruns, Gerald L. *Modern Poetry and the Idea of Language*. New Haven: Yale University Press, 1974.

———. *Inventions: Writing, Textuality and Understanding in Literary History*. New Haven: Yale University Press, 1982.

Bush, Ronald. "Pound & Spengler: Another Look." *Paideuma* 5 (1976): 63–66.

Campbell, Joseph, and Henry Morton Robinson. *A Skeleton Key to "Finnegans Wake."* New York: Harcourt, Brace and World, 1944.

Cookson, William, ed. *Agenda* 5, nos. 1–3 (1967), David Jones Special Issue.

———. *Agenda* 11, no. 4; 12, no. 1 (1973–74), David Jones Special Issue.

Cooper, John X. "The Writing of the Seen World: David Jones' *In Parenthesis.*" *University of Toronto Quarterly* 48, no. 4 (Summer 1979): 303–12.

Corcoran, Neil. *The Song of Deeds: A Study of "The Anathemata" of David Jones.* Cardiff: University of Wales Press, 1982.

———. "Spilled Bitterness: *In Parenthesis* in History." In Matthias 1989, 209–25.

Dawson, Christopher. *Age of the Gods.* London: J. Murray, 1928.

———. *Progress and Religion: An Historical Inquiry.* London: Sheed and Ward, 1929.

Deane, Patrick. "The Text as 'Valid Matter': Language and Style in *The Anathemata.*" In Matthias 1989, 307–29.

de Beauvoir, Simone. *The Second Sex.* New York: Alfred A. Knopf, 1953.

de la Taille, Maurice. *The Mystery of Faith and Human Understanding Contrasted and Defined.* London: Sheed and Ward, 1930.

de Man, Paul. "Lyric and Modernity." In *Blindness & Insight: Essays in the Rhetoric of Contemporary Criticism,* 142–86. New York: Oxford University Press, 1971.

Derrida, Jacques. "Structure, Sign and Play in the Discourse of the Human Sciences." In *The Structuralist Controversy,* ed. Richard Macksey and Eugenio Donato, 247–72. Baltimore: Johns Hopkins University Press, 1972.

———. "White Mythology: Metaphor in the Text of Philosophy." Trans. F. C. T. Moore. *New Literary History* 6, no. 1 (Autumn 1974): 6–74.

Dilworth, Thomas. "Wales and the Imagination of David Jones." *Anglo-Welsh Review* 69 (1981): 41–52.

———. "Form Versus Content in David Jones's 'The Tribune's Visitation.'" *Renascence* 38, no. 2 (1986): 103–16.

———. *The Shape of Meaning in the Poetry of David Jones.* Toronto: University of Toronto Press, 1988.

———. "David Jones and Fascism." In Matthias, 1989, 143–59.

Dix, Dom Gregory. *The Shape of the Liturgy.* 2d ed. 1945. Reprint. London: Dacre Press, 1975.

du Plessis, Rachel Blau. "Romantic Thralldom in H. D." *Contemporary Literature* 20 (1979): 178–203.

Eliot, T. S. "Ulysses, Order and Myth." *The Dial* 75 (1923): 483.

———. *Notes toward the Definition of Culture.* New York: Harcourt, Brace and World, 1949.

———. *Selected Essays.* New York: Harcourt, Brace and World, 1950.

———. "A Note on *In Parenthesis* and *The Anathemata.*" *Dock Leaves* 6, no. 16 (1955): 21–23.

———. *Complete Poems and Plays 1909–1959.* 21st printing. New York: Harcourt, Brace and World, 1971.

Frazer, Sir James G. *The Dying God.* 1912. Reprinted as volume 9 of *The Golden Bough: A Study in Magic and Religion.* London: Macmillan and Co., 1966.

———. *The New Golden Bough.* Abridged ed. Ed. Theodore H. Gaster. 1923. Reprint. New York: Criterion, 1959.

Friedman, Susan Stanford. *Psyche Reborn.* Bloomington: Indiana University Press, 1981.

Frye, Northrop. *Anatomy of Criticism*. Princeton: Princeton University Press, 1957.

———. "Spengler Revisited." In *Spiritus Mundi: Essays on Literature, Myth, and Society*, 179–98. Bloomington: Indiana University Press, 1976.

———. *The Great Code: The Bible and Literature*. New York: Harcourt, Brace, Jovanovich, 1982.

Fussell, Paul. *The Great War and Modern Memory*. Oxford: Oxford University Press, 1975.

Gantz, Jeffrey. Introduction to *The Mabinogion*, 9–41. Hammondsworth, Middlesex: Penguin, 1976.

Genette, Gerard. "Valéry and the Poetics of Language." In Harari 1979, 359–73.

Gilbert, Sandra M., and Susan Gubar. *The Madwoman in the Attic: The Woman Writer and the Nineteenth Century Imagination*. New Haven: Yale University Press, 1979.

Gill, Eric. *Beauty Looks After Herself*. 1933. Reprint. Freeport, N.Y.: Books for Libraries Press, 1966.

———. *Essays: Last Essays and In a Strange Land*. London: Jonathan Cape, 1947.

Griffin, Susan. *Woman and Nature: The Roaring Inside Her*. New York: Harper and Row, 1978.

Guest, Lady Charlotte, trans. *The Mabinogion*. London: J. M. Dent and Sons, 1913.

Hague, René, "David Jones: A Reconnaissance." *The Twentieth Century* 168, no. 1001 (July 1960). Reprinted in Cookson 1967, 27–45.

———. *David Jones*. Cardiff: University of Wales Press, 1975.

———. *A Commentary on "The Anathemata" of David Jones*. Toronto: University of Toronto Press, 1977.

Harari, Josue V., ed. *Textual Strategies: Perspectives in Post-Structuralist Criticism*. Ithaca: Cornell University Press, 1979.

Hartman, Geoffrey. *Criticism in the Wilderness*. New Haven: Yale University Press, 1980.

Heaney, Seamus. *Poems 1965–1975*. New York: Farrar, Strauss and Giroux, 1980.

Hills, Paul. "The Pierced Hermaphrodite." In Matthias 1989, 425–40.

Holloway, John. "A Perpetual Showing: The Poetry of David Jones." In *The Colours of Clarity: Essays on Contemporary Literature and Education*, 113–23. London: Routledge and Kegan Paul, 1964.

Hooker, Jeremy. *David Jones: An Exploratory Study of the Writings*. London: Enitharmon, 1975.

———. "In the Labyrinth: An Exploration of *The Anathemata*." In Matthias 1989, 263–84.

Hughes, Colin. "David Jones: The Man Who Was on the Field. *In Parenthesis* as Straight Reporting." In Matthias 1989, 163–92.

Huws, Daniel, and Phillip Davies. *A Catalogue of the Manuscripts of "The Anathemata."* Unpublished manuscript and typescript. David Jones Deposit. National Library of Wales, Aberystwyth.

Jameson, Frederic. *Marxism and Form*. Princeton: Princeton University Press, 1971.

———. *Fables of Aggression: Wyndham Lewis—The Modernist as Fascist*. Berkeley: University of California Press, 1979.

Johnston, John H. "David Jones: The Heroic Vision." *Review of Politics* 24, no. 1 (January 1962): 62–87. Reprinted in *English Poetry of the First World War,* 284–340. Princeton: Princeton University Press, 1964.

Jones, Huw C. *Catalogue of the David Jones Personal Library.* Unpublished typescript. David Jones Personal Library. National Library of Wales, Aberystwyth.

Joyce, James. *Finnegans Wake.* 1939. Reprint. Hammondsworth, Middlesex: Penguin, 1977.

Kenner, Hugh. *The Poetry of Ezra Pound.* Norfolk: New Directions, 1952.

———. *The Pound Era.* Berkeley: University of California Press, 1971.

Kermode, Frank. "On David Jones." In *Puzzles and Epiphanies: Essays and Reviews, 1958–1961,* 29–39. London: Routledge and Kegan Paul, 1962.

Knight, W. F. Jackson. *Cumaean Gates: A Reference of the Sixth Aeneid to the Initiation Pattern.* 1936. Reprinted in *Virgil: Epic and Anthropology.* Ed. John D. Christie. New York: Barnes and Noble, 1967.

Langbaum, Robert. *The Poetry of Experience: The Dramatic Monologue in Modern Literary Tradition.* New York: Norton, 1957.

Lentricchia, Frank. *After the New Criticism.* London: Athlone, 1980.

Levi, Peter. "Requiem Sermon for David Jones." 1974. Reprinted in *The Flutes of Autumn,* 187–91. London: Arena, 1983.

Levy, G. Rachel. *The Gate of Horn: A Study of the Religious Conceptions of the Stone Age and Their Influence upon European Thought.* London: Faber and Faber, 1948.

Maritain, Jacques. *Art & Scholasticism.* 1923. Reprint. Trans. Joseph W. Evans. New York: Charles Scribner's Sons, 1962.

Martz, Louis. *The Poem of the Mind.* Oxford: Oxford University Press, 1966.

Matthias, John, ed. *David Jones: Man and Poet.* Orono, Maine: National Poetry Foundation, 1989.

Mukařovsky, Jan. *The Word and Verbal Art.* Ed. and trans. John Burbank and Peter Steiner. New Haven; Yale University Press, 1977.

Olson, Charles. *Selected Writings.* Ed. Robert Creeley. New York: New Directions, 1950.

———. *The Maximus Poems.* Ed. George F. Butterick. Berkeley: University of California Press, 1983.

Pakenham, Elizabeth, ed. *Catholic Approaches to Modern Dilemmas and Eternal Truths.* London: Weidenfeld and Nicholson, 1955.

Pearce, Roy Harvey. *The Continuity of American Poetry.* Princeton: Princeton University Press, 1961.

Peck, John. "Poems for Britain, Poems for Sons." In Matthias 1989, 367–92.

Perloff, Marjorie. "Charles Olson and the 'Inferior Predecessors': 'Projective Verse' Revisited." *ELH* 40 (Summer 1973): 285–306.

Phelps, Teresa Godwin. "The Tribune and the Tutelar: The Tension of Opposites in *The Sleeping Lord.*" In Matthias 1989, 331–50.

Pick, John, ed. *A Hopkins Reader.* London: Oxford University Press, 1953.

Pound, Ezra. *A Guide to Kulchur.* Norfolk: New Directions, 1952.

———. *Selected Poems.* New York: New Directions, 1957.

———. *The Cantos.* 1970. Reprint. New York: New Directions, 1975.

Pratt, Mary Louise. *Toward a Speech Act Theory of Literary Discourse.* Bloomington: Indiana University Press, 1977.

Raine, Kathleen. "The Sign-Making of David Jones." *Iowa Review* 6 (1975): 96–101.

Rich, Adrienne. *Of Woman Born: Motherhood as Experience and Institution.* 1976. Tenth anniversary ed. New York: Norton, 1986.

Ricoeur, Paul. "Metaphor and the Main Problem of Hermeneutics." *New Literary History* 4 (1974): 95–110.

———. *The Rule of Metaphor: Multidisciplinary Studies of the Creation of Meaning.* Trans. Robert Czerny, with Kathleen McLaughlin and John Costello S. J. Toronto: University of Toronto Press, 1977.

Riddell, Joseph. "A Somewhat Polemical Introduction: The Elliptical Poem." *Genre* 11 (Winter 1978): 459–77.

Rosenberg, Harold. "Aesthetics of Crisis." *The New Yorker,* 22 August 1964, 114–22.

Rosenthal, M. L., and Sally Gall. *The Modern Poetic Sequence: The Genius of Modern Poetry.* New York: Oxford University Press, 1983.

Schneidau, Herbert. "Style and Sacrament in Modernist Writing." *Georgia Review* 32 (1979): 427–53.

Shakespeare, William. *The Riverside Shakespeare.* Ed. G. Blakemore Evans. Boston: Houghton Mifflin, 1974.

Sherry, Vincent B., Jr. "David Jones's *In Parenthesis:* New Measure." *Twentieth Century Literature* 28 (Winter 1982a): 375–80.

———. "A New Boast for *In Parenthesis:* The Dramatic Monologue of David Jones." *Notre Dame English Journal* 14 (1982b): 113–28.

———. "Current Critical Models of the Long Poem and David Jones's *Anathemata.*" *ELH* 52 (1985): 239–55.

———. "Contemporary British Modernism." *Georgia Review* 41 (1987): 612–27.

Spanos, William. *The Christian Tradition in Modern British Verse Drama.* New Brunswick: Rutgers University Press, 1967.

———. "Modern Literary Criticism and the Spatialization of Time: An Existential Critique." *Journal of Aesthetics and Art Criticism* 29 (1970): 87–104.

Speaight, Robert. *The Life of Eric Gill.* London: Methuen, 1966.

Spender, Stephen. *The Struggle of the Modern.* Berkeley: University of California Press, 1963.

Spengler, Oswald. *The Decline of the West.* Vols. 1 and 2. London: George Allen and Unwin, 1926.

Staudt, Kathleen Henderson. "The Language of T. S. Eliot's *Four Quartets* and David Jones's *Anathemata.*" *Renascence* 38 (1986a): 118–30.

———. "Recent Criticism on David Jones." *Contemporary Literature* 27, no. 3 (1986b): 409–22.

———. "The Decline of the West and the Optimism of the Saints: David Jones's Reading of Oswald Spengler." In Matthias 1989, 443–63.

———. "Anatomizing David Jones." *Contemporary Literature* 31, no. 4 (1990): 570–84.

Steiner, George. *Language and Silence: Essays on Language, Literature and the Inhuman*. New York: Atheneum, 1967.

Surette, Leon. "A Case for Occam's Razor: Pound and Spengler." *Paideuma* 6 (1977): 109–13

Terpstra, John. "'Bedad He Revives, See How He Raises!' An Introduction to David Jones's *The Sleeping Lord*." *University of Toronto Quarterly* 52 (Fall 1982): 94–105.

Ward, Elizabeth. *David Jones: Mythmaker*. Manchester: University of Manchester Press, 1983.

Weston, Jessie L. *From Ritual to Romance*. Cambridge: Cambridge University Press, 1920.

Whitaker, Thomas R. *William Carlos Williams*. New York: Twayne, 1969.

———. "Since We Have Been a Conversation . . . " *Clio* 6, no. 1 (1976): 43–69.

———. "*Homo Faber, Homo Sapiens*." In Matthias 1989, 465–87.

Wilborn, William Francis. *Sign and Form in the Poetry of David Jones: A Study in the Poetics of the Image*. Ph.D. diss., Cornell University, 1976.

Williams, Gwyn, ed. and trans. *The Burning Tree: Poems from the First Thousand Years of Welsh Verse*. London: Faber and Faber, 1956.

Williams, William Carlos. *Paterson*. 1946. Reprint. New York: New Directions, 1963.

———. *Selected Letters*. Ed. John C. Thirwall. New York: MacDowell, Oblensky, 1957.

Unpublished Manuscript Collections Consulted

David Jones Collection. Burns Library, Boston College.

David Jones Deposit (letters and manuscripts). National Library of Wales, Aberystwyth.

David Jones Letters to Harman Grisewood. Beinecke Library, Yale University.

David Jones Letters to René Hague. University of Toronto Library.

David Jones Manuscripts of *The Anathemata*. National Library of Wales, Aberystwyth.

David Jones Personal Library. National Library of Wales, Aberystwyth.

Index